KU-258-658

Pelican Books
Flights into Yesterday

Leo Deuel was born of Swiss parentage, but
has been an American citizen for many
years. He has lived in Europe, Australia,
Latin America and the Near East, and holds
a master's degree from Columbia University
and a Ph.D. in philosophy from the
University of Zurich. From 1948 to 1954 he
served on the editorial staff of the Columbia
University Press and the Encyclopedia
Americana. In 1955 he was a technical
assistant for the World Health Organization
in Geneva, and from 1958 to 1961 he was a
member of the History Department of New
York's City College.

Leo Deuel

Flights into Yesterday

The Story of Aerial Archaeology

Penguin Books

Penguin Books Ltd, Harmondsworth,
Middlesex, England
Penguin Books Australia Ltd, Ringwood,
Victoria, Australia

First published in the U.S.A. 1969
First published in Great Britain by Macdonald & Co. 1971
Published in Pelican Books 1973

Copyright © Leo Deuel, 1969

Made and printed in Great Britain by
Richard Clay (The Chaucer Press) Ltd, Bungay, Suffolk
Set in Linotype Pilgrim

For my brothers Herbert and Peter Deuel

Contents

List of Illustrations   9
Preface by Glyn Daniel   13
Author's Foreword   15

1. Archaeology in the Air   23
2. Ghosts of Wessex   38
3. Contours of Culture   55
4. That Marvellous Palimpsest   72
5. Roma Deserta   93
6. Italia Aeterna   121
7. Buried Etruria   141
8. Spina: Lost Pearl of the Adria   165
9. Lindbergh Searches for Maya Cities   186
10. Wings over Ancient America: I   210
11. Wings over Ancient America: II   228
12. Between Past and Future   252

Acknowledgements   285
Selected Bibliography   289
Sources of Quoted Passages   303
Index   310

List of Illustrations

Figures

1. Caricature by Daumier of Nadar's balloon exploits   31
2. Diagram of 'Celtic' and Saxon lynchets at Thornham Down, Wiltshire   44
3. Plan of Stonehenge   48
4. Sketch map of prehistoric monuments in the Stonehenge area   50
5. Probable transportation route of blue stones to Stonehenge   51
6. Schematic drawing of a shadow-site   60
7. Lynchets brought out by shadows and by highlights   61
8. Diagram showing the formation of soil-marks   64
9. Positive and negative crop-marks   66
10. Plan of prehistoric timber circles of Woodhenge   76
11. Street net with main buildings of Calleva Atrebatum (Silchester)   80
12. Ground plan of Ditchley 'villa'   84
13. Map of Roman Britain   89
14. Zone of Poidebard's aerial explorations of *limes* in Syria   99
15. Outline of centuriation pattern in Tunisia   113
16. The Roman frontier in northern Africa traced from the air by Colonel Baradez   119
17. Plan by Bradford of a Neolithic settlement near Foggia in Apulia   133
18. Prehistoric circular settlements superimposed by centuriated Roman roads near Lucera, Apulia   139
19. Diagram of an Etruscan tumulus   151
20. Plan of the Monte Abbatone necropolis outside Cerveteri (Caere)   155

21. Resistivity graph of two Etruscan tombs   160
22. Schematic drawing of periscope photography   163
23. Sketch map of Etruscan Italy   166
24. Geometric street and drainage systems of the Etruscan city of 'Marzabotto'   171
25. Location map of ancient Spina   183
26. Area covered by the Lindberghs on their pioneering aerial survey of the Pueblo region   190
27. Map of the Maya territory with routes of the Lindbergh-led Pan American Airways-Carnegie Institution archaeological flights   196
28. Maya causeways radiating from Cobá   211
29. Shippee-Johnson flights in Peru, 1931   224
30. Nazca desert drawings   236
31. Nazca ground figure   239
32. Principal effigy sites along and near the Colorado River   242
33. Sketch plan of Poverty Point site   245
34. Outline map of Colombia   250

Plates

1. Aerial view of Boston from a captive balloon, 1860/61
2–4. Megiddo, Palestine : photographing from a balloon and an extensible ladder
5. Low oblique photograph of Old Samarra, Iraq
6. 'Celtic' fields on Fyfield Down, Wiltshire, traced in shadow-marks
7. Section of the Stonehenge Avenue
8. Damp-marks in ploughed fields at Neufmoulin, Somme Valley
9. Crop-marks, Burcot pit near Dorchester
10–11. Site of Roman 'villa' of Ditchley, Oxfordshire, in November and June
12. Razed prehistoric barrows and 'cursus', Crowmarsh, Oxfordshire
13. Roman centre at Wroxeter, Shropshire
14. Deserted medieval village at Newbold Grounds, Northamptonshire

15. Hutton Moor circle near Ripon, Yorkshire
16. Roman field division (centuriation) in Tunisia
17. Low oblique photograph of 'Passo di Corvo', a Neolithic settlement near Foggia
18. Etruscan necropolis, Monte Abbatone (Cerveteri)
19. Frescoed wall of the 'Tomb of the Olympiad', Tarquinia
20. Probing an Etruscan tomb through 'periscope'
21. The Etrusco-Greek city of Spina
22. Maya causeways south of Cobá
23. Pre-Columbian ruins, Petén, northern Guatemala
24. Terraced 'bowls' at Maras Pampa, south-west of Cuzco
25. 'Great Wall' of Peru
26. Giant Indian pictograph above the Colorado River near Blythe, California
27. Nazca 'roads', central Peru
28. Earthworks at Poverty Point, Louisiana
29. Artificial ridges along San Jorge River, Colombia
30. Gallo-Roman estate, Somme Valley, frost-marks
31. Roman training camps near Xanten, West Germany

Preface

Williams-Freeman, a doctor and field archaeologist in southern England, once said, 'one ought to be a bird in order to be a field archaeologist'. Those words were spoken to O. G. S. Crawford, in the years before the 1914–18 war. The air camera and the aeroplane enabled the field archaeologist to become a bird, and among those who realized this opportunity, in the First World War and immediately afterwards, Crawford was the most distinguished pioneer. Half a century has passed since those pioneer days, during which air archaeology has developed enormously and the interpretation of air photographs and visual air reconnaissance has become one of the major instruments of archaeological research. Yet, until now, no one has given us a full account of the history and development of this fascinating technique. Now, Leo Deuel, who has already put the general reader and the practising archaeologist in his debt by works like *The Treasures of Time* and *Conquistadors Without Swords*, has written such a book.

Dr Deuel deals fairly and objectively with all the pioneers, British like Crawford and Beazeley, German like Wiegand, French like Rey and Poidebard. He describes the progress of air archaeology in the interwar years and brings to life the enormous advances made in the technique of air photography during the Second World War, when so many archaeologists, including the writer of these words, were interpreting air photographs as part of military intelligence. He is generous and accurate in his account of men like Allen, Bradford, and St Joseph in Britain, Agache, Chombart de Lauwe, Baradez, and Chevallier in France, Adamesteanu in Italy, and Irwin Scollar, whom he describes as 'an unusual American', in Germany. Much of what he says about the development of air archaeology in the Old World will be known, though perhaps not in detail, to professional archaeologists in Europe, but they may not be familiar with the story of air photography in American archaeology, which Deuel tells absorbingly from the pioneer flights of Lindbergh onwards.

If Dr Deuel's book occasionally seems a paean of praise, this is because he is writing the chronicle of an amazing series of incidents in the history of archaeology, and therefore of man. It is difficult not to be enthusiastic as one reads the moving story of how in the last fifty years the buried past of our ancestors has been revealed by the technical skill of the air camera and the expertise of observer and interpreter. But, of course, observer and interpreter must always remember that every curious mark they see is not necessarily evidence of the occupation of ancient man; and Deuel amusingly reminds us of the early troubles Crawford had with fairy rings and the circles made by tethered goats, of Major Allen's problems with frost cracks and natural pipes, and Irwin Scollar's difficulties with insecticide sprayed from a circling tractor. And I remember my excitement during the last war when I thought I had found off the coast of Brittany an ancient settlement hitherto unknown to French archaeology, and my chagrin when I discovered I was looking at modern oyster beds. Dr Deuel provides us with an excellent survey of the history, achievements, and pitfalls of air archaeology.

GLYN DANIEL

Author's Foreword

In as much as archaeology calls for the recovery of material evidence from the more or less remote human past, its sources as well as its methods have assumed an ever greater variety and refinement. Not unexpectedly, information on some of the advances in this quest remains largely confined to specialized texts. A perhaps inevitable time-lag has always existed between the recent developments in a field of knowledge and the popular concepts about its procedures and goals. The general literature on archaeology, so responsive to the subject's wide appeal, is no exception. No one will doubt the public's enthusiasm for archaeology; however, we have now almost reached a point where one is reminded of Bertrand Russell's caustic observation on philosophy: just when the people at large have been persuaded to believe in its validity, philosophers themselves have lost their belief. Archaeology, of course, like philosophy, is far from dead; and modern archaeologists have every reason to put considerable trust in its progress. But a great deal of traditional archaeology with which everybody is so much enamoured is hopelessly antiquated.

The present book reports on one bustling new frontier of the study of antiquities: aerial archaeology. Again and again in my previous researches I have come across its marvellous accomplishments and wondered about its still vaster promises. Yet, though scientific papers galore have been written on it, no work giving an overall non-technical survey has come to my attention. John Bradford's magisterial *Ancient Landscapes* (1957), an expensive and somewhat cumbersome tome out of print for several years, concentrates in the main on his own important investigations. A comparable volume by his French colleague Raymond Chevallier, *L'Avion à la découverte du passé* (1964), has not been translated. Bradford himself was puzzled by the lack of comprehensive treatment, noting that after the pioneering publication in 1928 of *Wessex from the Air* Britain had to wait twenty-four years for another book on the subject, a mostly photographic compilation entitled *Monastic Sites from the Air*. And this in the country that led the field for many decades!

Here then is one reason so few people outside the archaeological profession seem to be conversant with aerial archaeology. When I told friends about my absorption in the subject, they owned that they did not think there was 'a book in it'. In fact, they vaguely ranked archaeological exploration from flying planes as 'gimmickry' of negligible consequence. At best it evoked such incidents as the spotting, some years ago, of 'Noah's Ark' on an army survey photograph of Mount Ararat in north-eastern Turkey, and a few other entertaining oddities on which the illustrated papers occasionally feast.

That aerial archaeology is anything but a mere gimmick the reader will find out in the following pages. But why is there so little general literature on it? It is unlikely to be simply an oversight, a good opportunity missed by the industrious producers of popular non-fiction. Can it be that the subject is simply too 'technical'? Does its very nature reject a popular mould? Or is it too slight to warrant an extensive summing up?

Bradford probably hinted at the right answer when he commented: 'It is not altogether surprising that discoveries on so large a scale and so far-reaching in scope should be much more slowly assimilated.' It is the novelty and magnitude of the discoveries – their sheer size, quantity, depth in time, and variety – and the average audience's unpreparedness for them that have been a stumbling block. And this is where, maybe rashly, I saw my challenge.

The task I set myself was not so much to dissect a revolutionary technique or to furnish a manual; the theoretical and technical side of the subject is amply covered in a number of fine articles by seasoned practitioners listed in the bibliography. There is no scarcity of first-rate handbooks on all aspects of aerial photography, including photogrammetry, with which it would be absurd to try to compete. Though the basic principles will be discussed when and where necessary, my main purpose is to show that aerial archaeology is more than an ingenious method and implies a radical departure in the study of antiquities. Extending to the range of material covered as much as the objectives, it entails a new vision of the past, whch, though stimulated by the view from above, transcends mere photographic images of obliterated monuments.

Now, such a vision is itself a product of insight and growth, evidently more realized at some stages than at others. I aimed to let it materialize in terms of the discipline's own development, or rather in what seemed to me some of its principal phases and highlights.

Needless to say, my account does not claim to furnish an exhaustive catalogue of all the aerial surveys and discoveries made. Purposely I chose to describe it in the subtitle as 'story' rather than 'history'. Just the same, I made an effort to touch on as wide a variety of settings and problems as possible in order to show that aerial archaeology is truly ecumenical in its applications. Like archaeology in general, which is sometimes thought, quite erroneously, to make valid contributions only where written testimonies are in short supply or non-existent, aerial archaeology can meaningfully bear on all ages of man. Through air photographs the past can speak as eloquently as by means of written chronicles and manuscripts – and often more profoundly. Photographed landscapes thus amount to nothing less than historical records, and a book on aerial archaeology is, in the last analysis, also a book on historiography.

In the various chapters I have singled out some larger themes – selected case histories, in a way – relevant both to the unfolding 'story' of aerial archaeology and to the knowledge its explorations could shed on human history and prehistory. After a more sweeping introduction, we shall see how pioneering researches from the 1920s onwards illuminated England's yesterdays, particularly those of the pre-Roman and Roman eras. A brief discussion reviews basic rules first formulated in England. Roman military establishments at Britain's outposts form a link with the far-flung imperial defence systems in the arid wastes of Syria and North Africa. Then, once more, we cross the Mediterranean to wing over the Italian mother country. There we glimpse the Neolithic beginnings of Western Europe. Two further chapters chart the substantial contributions made to the study of the first masters of much of the peninsula, the Etruscans. Last, we shall roam the Western Hemisphere and probe from above its pre-Columbian limbos. A final chapter looks at aerial archaeology as resurrector of the past with a future, and, in the course, touches on scientific ramifications and potentials; auxiliary and supplementary methods; the post-war growth of the discipline, particularly in France, Italy, and Germany; and its extension to the underwater realm and to the sister science of anthropology.

How much my work has relied on the labours of others, notably such men as Crawford, Bradford, and St Joseph, and virtually all issues of the archaeological journal *Antiquity*, will become apparent to the reader at every turn.

Without apology I want to stress that mine is the book of a non-specialist for non-specialists. This is not to say that I did not do my homework to the best of my ability. I have personally visited many of the sites reviewed and followed up data in collections and museums. Yet a work dealing with a relatively novel subject, very much in flux, so wide in scope and so devoid of synthesis, is bound to exhibit limitations and errors. I find a little solace in the fact that even the specialist will lack first-hand knowledge once he ventures beyond his own research results. But naturally he deserves a leniency from his peers that the brash intruder cannot hope for.

One more word about the designation of this field. Various names have been coined and there is no real unanimity. Each one proposed lends itself to a futile semantic argument. However, I found 'aerial archaeology' (French *archéologie aérienne*) sufficiently descriptive, succinct and widely used to be serviceable. 'Archaeology from the air', 'aerial aid to archaeology', 'archaeological air surveying', 'air photography for archaeological purposes', 'aerial prospecting in archaeological research', 'air archaeology', and the like may be judged acceptable alternatives.

This being a 'general' work, I have, if somewhat reluctantly, chosen not to burden the reader with footnotes and other eyesores. However, an appendix furnishing precise references to quoted sources should satisfy the curious, beside abiding by the rules of common courtesy when picking other people's prose. For further guidance, the reader is directed to a selected bibliography in the back of the book.

Finally, I have the pleasant duty to acknowledge my debt to many. Mr Jeffrey Baker, a former editor of St Martin's Press, New York, offered encouragement from the beginning. I much profited from the advice of Dr Stephan F. Borhegyi of the Milwaukee Public Museum and his superb command of Old and New World archaeology. Dr Glyn Daniel of Cambridge University not only contributed a spirited preface but helped to rectify several misconceptions, particularly in reference to the English material – though, of course, I must take the blame for all the blunders that I unintentionally perpetrated. (Apologies are also due to the men who pioneered the new aerial frontier of archaeology if, despite my great admiration, I chance to have misinterpreted their achievements.)

For procuring essential, but out-of-the-way, research literature, my thanks go to learned institutions, and to friends and relatives everywhere, above all to Mr Jean Adra of New York, Mrs Gertrud Deuel of Zürich, and Mr Gunter Philipp of Johannesburg. Once again, Mrs Madeleine Edmondson and Mr Charles Blackwell were kind enough to plough through my manuscript and improve upon its editorial quality.

For a bird of the air shall carry the voice,
and that which hath wings shall tell the matter.

Ecclesiastes x.20

1. Archaeology in the Air

By nature and purpose – and almost by definition – archaeology belongs to the ground. Down on their knees, shovelling dirt, raising clouds of dust, burrowing into layers of soil, cutting trenches, tunnelling warrens through man-made mounds, opening tombs, and divesting the dead of their travel goods to the nether world – amateurs and professionals have toiled for generations to wrest buried relics from lost civilizations. The spade has become the very symbol of their exploits. Again and again pick-and-shovel teams have turned over the tells of Mesopotamia, sunk shafts into royal graves in Egypt and Mycenaean Greece. Battalions of diggers have roamed from the slopes of Mount Vesuvius, where volcanic eruption had abruptly cut off Roman town life, to Danish bogs in which rested the fully preserved bodies of men and women ritually executed by pagans of some two thousand years ago. From Inner Mongolia, Lebanon, and Peru, to France, the Aleutians, and the Orkneys searchers for the past have turned over the earth for age-old detritus and have thus added epochs and empires to the framework of human history.

Is it any wonder that in the popular mind, not to mention popular literature, archaeology has come to be equated with excavation? By now the stereotype has become fully enshrined. A recent survey of world archaeology pertly opens with the chapter heading 'Archaeology Only Begins with Digging', clearly mirroring this shop-worn view. In the same vein, a number of books aimed at a wide audience of laymen continue to dramatize colourful episodes of resurrecting the dimmed past by the spade.

But the dearly beloved and oft-told version of intrepid Victorian gentlemen ploughing through desert sands in inhospitable lands to come up with glittering treasures of dead

Pharaohs and Homeric heroes is only part of the story. Archaeology, as an adventure or as a science, is a growing field calling on many sophisticated methods and approaches. A host of problems beyond the ken of a Schliemann or even a Flinders Petrie are now being tackled by twentieth-century technology, and the subject is constantly enriched, if not redefined, by novel concepts.

Though digging will always have a prominent part in archaeology, it has ceased to be its alpha and omega. For one thing, the modern archaeologist no longer searches for beautiful isolated objects interred in the soil with which to fill glass museum cases, but rather for cultural units and defunct societies. Even when digging he ultimately wants to recapture a way of life, not merely aesthetically pleasing dead matter. His eye becomes attuned to a whole environment in which our remote ancestors moved: their physical setting, their villages and towns, their industries, their roads, their modes of worship, their farming and husbandry, their contacts with other people, and their part within a chain of human aspiration and achievement. The change in outlook is, of necessity, mirrored in archaeological methods, just as it parallels and benefits from developments in other areas of inquiry. A case could be made that it has a counterpart in the concepts of 'field' and 'Gestalt' in modern physics and psychology. In pursuing such goals, twentieth-century archaeology increasingly has come to depend on all the sciences: including genetics, biochemistry, astronomy, geophysics. It has borrowed stratigraphy from geology, pollen analysis from the botanists, and the sampling of blood groups from the physiologists. At times it finds the computer, the mine detector, the camera, and the aircraft – not to speak of a pair of sturdy walking shoes – more useful than the spade. And while the radiocarbon clock has given depth of time to our search for ancient vestiges, further, equally productive, dimensions have been added in space. The modern archaeologist, a contemporary of scuba divers and astronauts, has added water and air to his media.

That water bodies – inland seas, lakes, drowned shorelines and continental shelves, and the like – would yield archaeological relics of considerable value comes as no surprise. But diving for sunken galleons or cities, on the whole, has produced few types of evidence that differed basically from that obtained in land digs. The excitement of underwater exploration, so much enlarged in scope by the invention of the aqualung, is undeniable, yet neither results nor techniques can be said to have inaugurated a new phase. Competent practitioners of waterborne archaeology have rightly insisted that submarine archaeology is simply archaeology that happens to be carried out in water rather than on mountain-tops or in the jungle. Should the water retreat, shipwrecks would be cleared and cities uncovered by conventional methods. 'Corinth was a famous Greek city,' George Bass, the prominent archaeologist of the University of Pennsylvania, observed,

whose life archaeologists have been recreating by uncovering and recording its architectural remains, by cataloguing and publishing its pottery and sculpture and coins, and by interpreting its inscriptions. Port Royal was a lively city in Jamaica which suddenly disappeared beneath the waves during a virulent earthquake on 7 June 1692. In the study of its remains, walls and streets have been mapped, and objects of pottery, metal, and glass have been brought to the surface to be restored and preserved. Is there any difference between the two excavations except that in one case the excavator had to carry a supply of air strapped to his back?

Airborne archaeology, on the other hand, is not traditional archaeology that happens to be carried out in the air. It introduces more than the adaptation of established techniques to another sphere of operation. First and foremost, it has no part in excavation, though it often does and should precede, succeed, or accompany it. Its lofty medium defines its opportunities just as it dictates its methods, and implies a radically new approach which has given archaeologists one of their most effective instruments of research.

That archaeologists should take to the air is by itself perhaps not so extraordinary. Yet the consequences of the new perspective from space to the entire study of antiquities could not be foreseen and were only dimly realized by the first pioneers. The sky view, far from being a mere oddity or trick, has opened up vistas on the past that continue to elude the most perspicacious of ground observers. By the same token, in its highly sensitive manner of recording and interpreting, it relies on a whole set of principles that could only now be formulated.

Whether or not aerial archaeology deserves to be proclaimed an autonomous branch of archaeology is of little moment; what matters is that it revolutionized the science of antiquities perhaps even more than the discovery of radiocarbon dating. It has made, in fact, in the words of one of its founders, as vital a contribution to archaeological investigation as the invention of the telescope did to astronomy. What is more, no other technical advance in archaeology has come so close to fulfilling the goal of recovering intricate cultural contexts, of glimpsing whole prehistoric landscapes, and of capturing a fabric of human existence through the flux of time.

What is it that makes observation from the air unique? Without even direct physical contact with relics on and in the ground, how is it that the past may be revealed with an amazing clarity never beheld before? Why the paradox that distance rather than proximity can be a boon for students of buried yesterdays?

For all the 'Platonic' overtones there is nothing really mysterious in catching glimpses of the past in distant shadows and patterns. Magic properties of the camera play little or no part. The conjured-up sight is quite simply compounded from the advantages of a bird's-eye view.

Unlike his brother on the ground, the aerial archaeologist is not confined to any one limited area: his roving eye takes in a wide panorama at one glance. The earthbound worker searching for a site to dig may get lost in a wasteland dotted by hillocks, chunks of wall, and all kinds of dilapidated aggregations of soil and rubble. He is at a loss to pick the 'best' site, and the general scheme and meaning of the scattered ruins may well escape him. Sometimes the enormous extent of the remains prevents recognition. In short, he can't see the forest for the trees. He is trapped by the particulars, while our Platonist up in the sky perceives the universals, so to speak – an entire city criss-crossed by streets or canals and petering out into the desert with cemeteries, caravan roads, and forts. O. G. S. Crawford, who more than anybody else put aerial archaeology on its feet – or rather wings – drew an apt comparison between the view of an Oriental carpet as gained by a cat lounging on it and a man standing above it. The cat from its low position by the fireplace will only see a few nebulous flecks and stripes, while to the human observer all the coloured blotches melt into beautiful, orderly patterns and arabesques. In the same manner we may take a close look at the dotted screen of a half-tone illustration. Under a magnifying glass we see nothing but spots of varying degrees of black. We fail to notice the image until it is reassembled by a more distant view. The man up in the air does just that when organizing shapes into intelligible schemas which, because of their magnitude and fragmentation, did not coalesce at ground level. Since any more or less geometric arrangement almost invariably betrays a human builder, the airborne archaeologist has relatively little difficulty in identifying artificial structures, no matter how much their substance has been reduced.

Aerial archaeology thus offers stunning potentials for reconnaissance. Its ability to act as a kind of guide dog for the fieldworker down below is obvious. It has an honest part to play in the clarification and pinpointing of excavation sites. Once the dig is under way, it is particularly effective in keeping a record of the various phases of the operation. At a later stage it will provide vivid material for teaching and demonstration purposes.

Even more vital to all archaeological enterprise is overall aerial surveying or mapping. Where in former days it would have taken the tedious labour of weeks or months to produce a more or less accurate map – if the area was in fact at all accessible on foot – the aerial camera can do the same job in just a split second, at an enormous saving in cost and without calling on the specialized expertise of land surveyors and map-makers. Moreover, the photographic product is likely to be far superior. Man-made plans or maps remain at best abstractions and simplifications of the total picture. Not so the photographic record, which registers minute, frequently elusive and transient details that could never have been entered on the most painstaking map. The comprehensive photograph is at once up to date. It gives the whole truth – the thing itself –

whereas a map is always a highly selective reduction of nature to conventions and symbols.

The role of aerial photography in map-making and surface recording is, of course, not confined to the realm of archaeology. Indeed, most modern maps are now based on aerial surveys, and geologists, topographers, mining engineers, demographers, road builders, architects, town planners, foresters, the military, and many others increasingly rely on aerial photographs in their studies. Out of such manifold concern has grown a new science, photogrammetry, which in turn is greatly relevant to reliable archaeological surveying and measuring. While its refinements lie outside the scope of the present book, at least one modern application may be mentioned : the recording of minute contours by stereoscopic photographs from which scaled three-dimensional replicas can be made. In any case, it must be realized that because of their inclusiveness as an accurate simulacrum of the natural landscape, aerial photographs, to yield a maximum of information, call for considerable training and experience on the interpreter's part.

In sum, the bird's-eye view afforded by aerial photography has enormous value in recording and plotting ancient sites and establishing meticulous plans for which operators on ground level can offer no adequate substitute. Since photography from above is eminently suited to a rapid preview before the excavator goes to work, not the least of its services is telling him where *not* to search.

The greatest triumphs of aerial archaeology, however, lie outside mere guidance to the men in the field and the registration of more or less known sites. Originally conceived as an adjunct to ground work and excavation, it has become an independent instrument of discovery. Not only does the observer in the sky (or his camera) record comprehensive designs where previously there had been myopic glimpses, he detects features never noticed before. On a ground which has been ploughed and reploughed for centuries, over which have trampled armies of conquerors, and which may have been traversed many times by curio-seeking antiquarians, he will fix on film (or plate) the virtual blueprint of a long-vanished Roman town, replete with amphitheatre, baths, forum, temples, and insulae (city blocks). The slightest unevenness or disturbance of the surface will all of a sudden hit his eyes as scars boldly carved into the soil. What is more, totally buried sites, given favourable circumstances, will leave marks on the landscape that turn out to be at least as clear. In some notable instances, aerial observation, without ever testing the ground, enables us to 'read' such testimonies to a degree where they can indicate the presence and even the nature of the effaced structure, its age, and the very people who built it. Furthermore, photographs taken by an expert, let us say above the chalk downs of southern England, conceivably will show a cavalcade of overlapping cultures from a Neolithic 'cursus' and a Bronze Age hill camp to an Iron Age fortress and a Roman villa to a deserted village of the late Middle Ages. Again and again when documenting what are in fact palimpsests of cultural landscapes that can readily be deciphered, aerial archaeology has made spectacular contributions. On such occasions the study of material survivals from ancient times becomes a life science, tracing man in his development through millennia. In its finest moments aerial archaeology has the power of recall for the procession and clashing of cultures acted out against and related to their natural scene.

From its inception, aerial photography has employed two basic types of view: vertical and oblique. Both have their uses and their champions. Oblique views are, as a rule, taken with a hand-held camera at any odd angle, preferably from low altitude. With their strong shadows they can best record ruined buildings, earthworks, or walls, which will stand out in dramatic profile. However, it requires great ability to select a revealing viewpoint. On the whole, obliques are far less costly to produce and are ideally suited to the needs of amateurs and one-man operations. In the hands of a master like Major G. W. G. Allen they have recorded some of the most remarkable discoveries made from the air.

Vertical photographs demand more exacting apparatus, since the optical axis should be precisely perpendicular to the earth's surface. Special cameras have been designed for such work. For their overhead view they are usually installed in the underbelly or cockpit of the plane and may be exposed automatically, if need be, at regular intervals along a predefined strip of land to furnish a consecutive series of pictures. Photographs resulting from vertical shots possess, of course, the salient properties of map projections, though allowances must be made for possible sources of error such as tilt, wind drift, and irregularities of speed and altitude during flight. Their scale – a function of the plane's altitude and the camera's focal length – can easily be gauged, just as one can measure the extent of a groundwork appearing on them. Also, with a fairly simple device, features can be transferred from a vertical photograph to a conventional map, thereby helping to locate them in the field. The success of such an operation, however, hinges on one crucial, frequently difficult, problem: the establishment of recognizable control points in the photographed landscape.

The maplike flatness of vertical photos is both a virtue and a limitation. But there is even a remedy for the two-dimensionality of such pictures. If consecutive photographs are taken with an overlap of about 60 per cent, then they can be made to imitate the three-dimensional blending of twin images of unaided human vision. All that is needed is a binocular viewer to produce a stereoscopic effect. Stereoscopic pictures will then display structural surface remains in graphic relief. By exaggerating the contours on the ground, stereoscopic examination of pairs of photographs highlights depressions and elevations and has become a first-rate aid to archaeological detection.

Aerial archaeology as it is commonly understood presupposes two major inventions: flight and photography. Its early history is closely linked with their history. The use of photographs for archaeological research was adumbrated practically at the birth of daguerreotypy when the French physicist D. F. Arago, in a lecture before the French Academy on 19 August 1839, discussed the various applications to which the new invention might be put. First pictures from the air were shot of Paris in October 1858 by that remarkable pioneer photographer Gaspard Félix Tournachon, who affected the terse pseudonym Nadar. Nadar happened to be as enthusiastic a balloonist as a photographer, and his acrobatic feats in combining the two, at a time when clumsy and heavy equipment (including a make-shift darkroom) had to be carried aloft, prompted Daumier to sketch a hilarious cartoon of Nadar riding high in his captive

Figure 1. Caricature by H. Daumier of Nadar's balloon exploits

balloon over the French capital while aiming a monstrous camera at his target. The caption declared that Nadar had raised photography to 'the highest of all arts'.

Nadar, by the way, refused to make his skill available to army intelligence in the war with Austria of 1859. Ironically, however, the foremost advances in aerial photography owe almost everything to military exploitation. Whether one may think of this as a sorry comment on the human race or a confirmation of a pseudo-Nietzschean philosophy of war as the almighty generator of creative forces, there is no denying that, as for so much else in modern technology and applied science, war or preparation for war acted as a decisive stimulant.

Aerial archaeology has had two heroic epochs, the First World War and the Second World War. But some steps, though of little consequence, were taken prior to 1914. As a historical footnote we may mention that the first military use of aerial photography was made in the American Civil War.

In the late 1880s a Major Elsdale of the British Royal Engineers Balloon Establishment introduced free unmanned balloons, which carried self-releasing cameras designed to expose several plates successively. Shortly thereafter, in 1891, another British army officer then serving in India, Lieutenant C. F. (later Colonel Sir Charles) Close, conceived the idea of applying a similar device to photographing from the air the extensive ruins near Agra in order to produce an archaeological map of the area. Unfortunately, his project was frustrated by red tape and fizzled out in a few indifferent pictures taken over Calcutta 'at an unfavourable season'. Only half a century later, during the Second World War, did Close's programme materialize.

Meanwhile, the 'military' history of aerial archaeology entered a new phase in England. During routine practice from war-balloons in 1906, Lieutenant P. H. Sharpe took, more or less by accident, the first pictures aloft of an archaeological site – an oblique and a vertical. The place was the celebrated megalithic ruins of Stonehenge on Salisbury Plain.

These photographs made such an impression that Colonel J. E. Capper of the Royal Engineers exhibited them at the Society of Antiquaries and subsequently published them with a brief note in volume LX (1907) of the journal *Archaeologia*. However, apart from their novel overhead perspective, the photographs did not reveal, at least at the time, any unusual feature unknown to observers on the ground, though they gave a fine glimpse of the entire complex with its adjacent earthworks, avenue, and barrows, and contributed a valuable document of the state of the ruins.

Shortly after the British balloon photographs, Italian army engineers, from 1908 on, embarked on comparable exploits. By 1911, both the Forum in Rome and the ancient port of Ostia had been photographed from above. Another significant enterprise was that of Sir Henry Wellcome in what was then the Anglo-Egyptian Sudan. Just prior to the First World War, this eccentric amateur archaeologist, who was a tinkerer of genius, introduced box kites with remote-controlled cameras to record his own excavations, but the outbreak of hostilities put an end to the ingenious experiments.

The First World War was a turning point on several counts. First, during those four years the airplane came of age, and from then on the major advances in aerial archaeology are linked with heavier-than-air aviation.

The highly mobile airplane all at once opened up a virtually unlimited range to overhead observation. Because of the exigencies of war, the construction of planes, flying itself, and the techniques of reconnaissance from the air were perfected at an accelerated pace. The same was true of photographic equipment, such as lenses and plates or films. In addition, the new methods called for specially trained personnel. By more than coincidence, men with archaeological training were now enlisted by flying corps and were active as photographers, mapmakers, and observers. An odd, if not ironic, symbiosis seems to exist between war and archaeology. Perhaps experts in dolmens, ditches, and decrepit structures of the past were judged well suited to lend a helping hand in producing similar fragments for the *Ruinenschmerz* of generations still to come.

Nevertheless, the First World War precipitated relatively few discoveries in aerial archaeology; rather, it sharpened the wits and pointed up the potential. Quite logically, though several commentators have found it extraordinary, the principal belligerents stumbled on the new archaeological frontier independently and more or less simultaneously. None of the three nations, England, France, or Germany, has yet been able to establish a clear-cut priority. If, as has been argued by Crawford, a discovery has only been made when it has been published, the British might well claim the field. But the same Crawford chivalrously also gives the former enemy his due. It seems the German army was first in launching a mission for the explicit purpose of photographing archaeological sites, while with the others archaeological objects were a by-product of airborne reconnaissance during military duty. As far as is known, a Frenchman, Léon Rey, examined air photographs of ancient sites in Macedonia as early as 1916. The classicist Jérôme Carcopino is also said to have then urged the commander of the French expeditionary force at the Dardanelles to have his air squadron take pictures of near-by Troy. His German colleague Georg Karo, who took an early interest in submarine archaeology as well, at about the same time tried to secure air views of Asia Minor ruins. The last year of the war, 1918, saw some of the most notable results. A prominent German archaeologist, Carl Schuchhardt, who had been associated with Schliemann, had at his disposal air photographs when studying the Roman border wall in the Rumanian Dobrudja west of Constanza. However, these photographs had to wait until 1954 when the composite prints (the negatives had been lost) were published by Crawford in England after they had been rescued by Gerhard Bersu.

Another leader of the archaeological profession in Germany who became intrigued by the new vision was Theodor Wiegand, the excavator of Miletus and later president of the German Archaeological Institute. He had persuaded the German High Command to let him set up a special *Denkmalschutzkommando* (a unit for the protection of historical monuments) in the Near East. Upon his directive, a German pilot on the Gaza front photographed late Roman and Byzantine ruins in the desert lands of the Negev and Sinai, somewhere between the Mediterranean and the Gulf of Aqaba. Wiegand was much concerned about their decay, since natives were dismantling them before his eyes for building material. Technically, the oblique photographs, included in a lavish German army publication of 1920, were of excellent quality, though aside from fine overviews of the old towns, forts, churches, monasteries, adjacent former fields, and rows of cairns (perhaps from vineyards), they added little that could not be tracked down on terra firma. In fact, unknown to Wiegand at the time, much the same ground had been covered by T. E. Lawrence and Leonard Woolley during their 'pedestrian' exploration of the 'Desert of Sin' in January and February 1914. For his initiative alone, however, Wiegand ranks high in the early history of aerial archaeology. Surprisingly, the authorized biography by Carl Watzinger, a fellow archaeologist who was a member of Wiegand's staff at the time, skips the subject entirely. But it reports a curious episode, the bombing of Wiegand's house at Didyma on the Turkish coast, where he excavated for many years. The aeroplane directing the bombardment carried as an observer the Oxford archaeologist John L. Myres, whose main effort appears to have been to protect the adjacent Apollo temple from British and French wrath, while diverting Allied fire to a less sacred structure. Quite a neat example of the uses and abuses of aerial archaeology in wartime

On the English side, the First World War pioneer was a sapper of the Royal Engineers in Mesopotamia, Lieutenant-Colonel G. A. Beazeley, who had been detached from the Survey of India. During his repeated flights over the Tigris-Euphrates plain – much of it then in enemy hands – he sighted sharp outlines of ancient canals, and of towns laid out geometrically on the 'American plan'. How archaeological research could in the future be greatly assisted by air photography impressed him most persuasively when he was charged with a survey of the contested area beyond Baghdad. This assignment was carried out, as he wrote, 'with the result that the remains of an ancient city were disclosed which would not otherwise have been discovered, in all probability...' That large ruined city, some sixty-five miles north-west of Baghdad, was, as is now known, 'Old Samarra', built by the Caliph al-Mustasim, the son of Harun al-Rashid, in the ninth century. It had a life span of little more than fifty years. 'When the air-photographs were printed,' Beazeley continued,

they revealed the faint trace of a vast ancient city some twenty miles long and as much as two and a half miles wide in places, continuous except for a break such as Aski Baghdad, and if it was built at the same time must have housed a population of about four million souls. As it appears to have been built all in one style the area may very well have been one vast town. The air photographs show up clearly the nobles' and rich merchants' estates along the bank of the Tigris, with their mansions, offices, summer houses, and gardens; each estate being arranged on a different pattern according to the whim of its owner. The smaller fry were excluded from the river in much the same way as in the modern city of Baghdad. The centre of the city seems to have been supplied by a system of *karezes* [underground water channels] in addition to supplies led in by canals.

On occasion, hazards of war permitting, Beazeley would supplement his aerial observations on the ground, scouting around palaces, processional avenues, a giant hippodrome, gardens, and underground galleries 'where the royal owners escaped the heat of the long summer days', and investigating an inn where he found thousands of clay goblets. Once again aloft on his way to the war zone, Beazeley made more provocative discoveries, such as a series of forts. They stood out distinctly from above, 'whereas when walking over them on the ground no trace was visible'. He went on : 'Another interesting thing I could plainly see on my flights was the outline of an ancient scientific irrigation system, such as has been introduced in the Punjab only in comparatively recent years.' But in May 1918, on a foray into enemy-held territory, his escorting plane developed engine trouble and had to return to home base leaving Beazeley behind in his flying machine without cover and gunpower. This put an abrupt end to the first venture of aerial archaeology in Mesopotamia, because, in the laconic words of Beazeley's report : 'Unfortunately I was shot down and captured before being able to make a detailed survey of the [irrigation] system during a lull in the military operation.' However, once released, and the war over, Beazeley could relate his experiences in two memorable, richly illustrated lectures reprinted in the *Geographical Journal* of 1919 and 1920. They represent the earliest statements of aerial archaelogy as a tool of discovery and stress the advantages gained from viewing an ancient landscape from above.

That these initial steps in aerial archaeology were made in the arid and semi-arid lands adjacent to the Mediterranean rather than in the other theatres of the First World War is understandable. The Western Front, which was of course the prime zone of military aviation and aerial reconnaissance, extended across an entirely different terrain. Much of it, crossed as a rule at considerable heights, was heavily overgrown or had long been under the plough, and the contours of earthworks, if any survived at all above the ground, could not be perceived with the same clarity as in the desert sands of the Near East. Nor could this European region offer anything comparable to the square miles of abandoned towns characteristic of a region saturated with urban civilizations for five millennia. Besides, few of the Mesopotamian sites had ever been built over. Hence, no special, yet-unknown methods of detection were needed in the Near East.

O. G. S. Crawford, who was a member of the Royal Flying Corps in France and Belgium during the Great War, also suggests that surveying the enemy lines from high altitudes absorbed all the energies and ingenuity aerial observers could muster. Naturally these men may have slighted less obtrusive non-military evidence that cropped up now and then. Yet it was precisely airmen active over the Western Front – foremost among them Crawford himself – who now prepared for their future careers. Crawford, by the way, like Beazeley, had been shot down by the Germans. During his many months of captivity at Landshut and, after an unsuccessful escape, at Holzminden, he could ponder over the archaeological questions that had intensely absorbed him for some time before and during the war.

2. Ghosts of Wessex

'Everything has been invented by someone before, who did not discover it.' In the sense of Whitehead's dictum, Crawford was indisputably the discoverer of aerial archaeology. There were, of course, others before him, and Crawford, who had an abiding interest in the history of the new discipline, paid them ample tribute. Yet only he had the vision to grasp the real importance of the subject. His determination pressed the use of air photographs into the service of British archaeology, and he never ceased to alert his colleagues to their usefulness, both in his own publications and through the journal *Antiquity*, which he founded in 1927 and edited until his death thirty years later. His long tenure as archaeological officer of the Ordnance Survey, for which he produced the famous 'period maps' of British history and prehistory, gave him a key position that he used to the fullest, particularly for the collection of air photographs taken by the armed services over England and the Near East.

From the beginning Crawford assumed a leading part in the development and refinement of techniques. He was ever active in organizing explorations from the air and induced others to follow his example. His enthusiasm fired the imagination of officers of the Royal Air Force and made veteran First World War fliers dust off their wings and reconnoitre on their own. Practically everyone in Britain who embarked on such a career in years to come owed the first impetus to him. Furthermore, it was Crawford who recognized that aerial archaeology could be at least as spectacular an instrument for revealing antiquities of 'barbaric' north-western Europe as it promised to be in the lands of the ancient East. Indeed, he made Britain the very *locus classicus* for discoveries from the air. Thus it remained well into the Second World War, when, largely under the aegis of British explorers, other ancient landscapes at last underwent their aerial awakening. Above all, it was Crawford who laid down the basic principles that govern aerial archaeology. Little has been added since he defined the main categories and phenomena. The terminology he introduced has become universal currency.

The man who helped to usher in a new chapter in aerial exploration was superbly fitted to play this role. Osbert Guy Crawford was born in 1886 in Bombay, where his father was judge of the High Court. Both his parents died when he was in his infancy and he was brought up by two elderly maiden aunts in England. He took pride in his Scottish ancestry, to which he ascribed his tough uncompromising disposition, though his lonely childhood may have been largely responsible for his gruff self-sufficiency and forthright independence of mind; he did not suffer fools gladly. Typical of the man was a statement in his autobiography *Said and Done*: 'Fear of solitude in adults is the mark of ignorance or stupidity. It is a marvellous experience to be completely alone in the desert.'

Such a person was bound to find contentment in activities other than communion with fellow humans. Attending boarding school with boys of his own age was a 'perfect little hell', and he chose life-long bachelorhood. He had the good fortune to grow up in an area of Hampshire that was literally inhabited by the ghosts of a remote past. On his frequent forays into the countryside he was at an early age intrigued by the tumuli, earthbanks, and ditches scattered across the downs. These mute testimonies of prehistoric times excited the impressionable boy, but rather than feeding on local tales of the supernatural, he undertook soberly to investigate: to measure, draw, map, collect, and, occasionally, dig. A school visit to Stonehenge and Avebury converted him once and for all to field archaeology. It was to be in this uniquely British tradition that goes back to John Aubrey, William Stukeley, and such nineteenth-century masters as General William Roy, one of the founders of the Ordnance Survey, Sir Richard Colt Hoare, and General Pitt-Rivers, that Crawford's absorption in all the diverse surface features of ancient Britain and the topographic relations between them and their natural surroundings had its roots.

Like his predecessors, particularly Pitt-Rivers, the founder of scientific excavation in England, he pleaded for the concentration on everyday things just 'because they are common ... and because they are not kept'. With such emphasis went his attention to the geographic distribution of like artefacts, which in his pre-First World War study of bronze and copper axes led to one of the seminal researches in British archaeology.

Crawford went to Oxford to read classics, as we expected of him, but characteristically soon changed over to the unglamorous field of geography, a step which, as he put it, was 'like a son telling his father that he had decided to marry a barmaid' or 'leaving the parlour for the basement; one lost caste but one did see life'. To him geography and archaeology were complementary. Ancient man could be meaningfully studied only in his environment. With good reason he has been called 'the geographer's archaeologist'.

That Crawford should eventually embrace aerial archaeology was almost inevitable. Everything in his career steered him towards it. Given the premise of his concept of the science of antiquities, aerial archaeology was, in a way, the continuation of field archaeology by other means. In fact, even before the First World War Crawford had thought of the benefits that could accrue from an aerial perspective. He shared these 'flights of fancy' with one of his mentors and fellow field archaeologists, a Wiltshire country doctor, J. P. Williams-Freeman. Together they often discussed their longing for overhead photographs. Dr Williams-Freeman later recalled how he had observed from time to time that undulations of the soil, whose outlines were thrown into relief by shadows or snowdrifts, stood out more prominently when viewed from a height while barely noticeable from ground level. During a discussion following one of Crawford's post-war lectures on aerial archaeology, he said: 'I remember thinking that one ought to be a bird in order to be a field archaeologist.' Crawford had felt the same way.

On his hikes into the hillsides near his aunts' home in Hampshire, he came across a great number of low banks which covered the slopes in a maze of rectangular and square enclosures. He learned that the countrymen called them lynchets, and he eagerly tried to find out more about them. Some of the narrow soil shelves were strewn with flints; near by were earthen mounds into which he dug. But the lynchets remained a mystery. Since he had just learned to make maps, he loaded his plane-table on a bicycle and set out to plot the outlines of the embanked fields. The task soon became hopeless, since most of the ridges were ill-defined. All seemed a jumble and he gave up in disgust. If one could only obtain a view of the tangled network from above!

Meanwhile, Crawford had embarked on his professional career in archaeology. In 1913 he joined Sir Henry Wellcome in the Sudan campaign. Here he first came in contact with vertical photographs from box kites of the excavation at Jebel Moya. Then the war intervened. After service with the infantry, when he was engaged in mapping and photography and made the acquaintance of some of the people he was later associated with in the Ordnance Survey, he transferred to the Royal Flying Corps as an observer. The opportunities offered to aerial reconnaissance now took hold of him. Upon his own admission, he had joined up in the war 'rather unwillingly. It became exciting, however, when the first aeroplane went up and took the first air-photographs. I thought of my recent efforts on Great Litchfield Down and how much easier it would be to see a place by just going up in an aeroplane and taking a photograph of it.' Occasionally he would spot a Roman road in France or Germany; in fact, to his knowledge of one such road he owed his safe return to home base. But otherwise there was little scope to make archaeological observations. For him at least the war, 'while it promoted the development of flying, delayed its archaeological exploitation'.

After the war, Crawford made several attempts to pursue the subject. As early as 1919 he tried in vain to gain access to air photographs taken over southern England, but they were withheld for military reasons. A powerful archaeological society he approached showed no inclination to intervene with the Royal Air Force and thus, quite likely, 'lost the chance of a lifetime'. There followed a dig in Wales, where Crawford caused a minor scandal by receiving a committee of ladies in his scant working garb of shorts. Soon after began his employment with the Ordnance Survey. During the war he had met the director, Sir Charles Close, himself a pioneer of aerial archaeology. It was thanks to Close's insistence that the post of Archaeology Officer was specially created for Crawford.

Crawford dated the birth of aerial archaeology from 1922. One day Dr Williams-Freeman, who then lived at Weyhill in Hampshire, the site of a Royal Air Force aerodrome, asked Crawford to come over and look at some photographs that his friend Air-Commodore (later Air Vice-Marshal) Clark-Hall suspected contained 'something archaeological'. Thirty-five years later, shortly before his death, Crawford related the incident in a BBC talk:

I well remember the occasion; Clark-Hall brought out his photographs and showed them to us. They were covered with rectangular white marks which at once recalled to my mind the ones I had started to map nearly ten years before. Here in these few photographs was the answer to the problem, but it was much more than that. The photographs also showed dark lines which were obviously silted-up ditches; they were revealed by the darker growth of corn, which grew better over them and therefore had a darker green colour than the rest. There were also some areas of downland that had not been ploughed since the early fields, with their lynchets, had been finally abandoned some 1,600 years ago. I realised that air-photography was going to be an enormous help to archaeologists in unravelling the marks of all kinds left in the ground and above it by prehistoric man. It was a dramatic revelation, for at that very moment I knew that a new technique had been found, and that I had the means of developing that technique and making it available to the world at large ... It must be remembered that at that time the very existence of those fields was almost unknown, though a few countrymen had seen the lynchets and recognised what they were.

Crawford now set out to produce the kind of map he had unsuccessfully struggled with a good many years before. He then made an exhaustive study of the rectangular lynchets, which he called 'Celtic' to distinguish them from the (post-Roman) Saxon strip system that was brought into England by the Germanic invaders. The result of his investigations was not only a milestone in aerial archaeology; it also helped to establish the archaeology of agriculture.

Lynchets, or 'prehistoric cultivation banks', which played

such a central role in Crawford's researches, call for a brief explanation. They represent a characteristic phenomenon of prolonged farming on sloping terrain. Hence, they are not confined to England but can occur wherever agriculture has been carried on for a considerable time in hilly regions. Crawford observed them in other European countries and on a flight across the mountains near the Mediterranean coast of Syria. Paradoxically, while they are the result of man's working of the soil, they are not actually man-made. The immediate cause for the formation of such earthworks must be seen in the sliding of eroded topsoil, which is gradually deposited at the lower-lying unploughed edges of individual fields. By their outline lynchets will betray the form and size of landholdings, specific stages of agriculture, and even the manner of ploughing. This is why they are an important source of knowledge for ancient economic and social conditions. In southern England there are mainly two types of lynchets. The older ones are the so-called Celtic lynchets bordering on small, more or less square and rectangular plots (rarely of more than one acre in surface), within which a light primitive plough could easily be turned. More recent are the Saxon lynchets which continued into the Middle Ages. They accompany long, parallel strips that had been worked by heavy ox-ploughs.

One must get hold of Crawford's paper 'Air Survey and Aerial Archaeology', which he originally read at a meeting of the Royal Geographical Society on 12 March 1923, to marvel at the amount of information he was able to obtain from a few photographs of Celtic lynchet patterns taken at random by Royal Air Force officers. While some of the data had been verified and supplemented by field work and by the ground research of fellow archaeologists, the masterful re-creation of a whole cultivation system, its specific mode of farming, its age and duration, as well as its origin and relation to other prehistoric monuments, owed almost everything to the aerial vista. Thus, to cite an instance, the camera showed conclusively that lanes issuing from abandoned villages, which had been previously dated from artefacts, threaded their way between the fields in a manner that made it obvious that they were of the same age as the lynchets. Along similar lines,

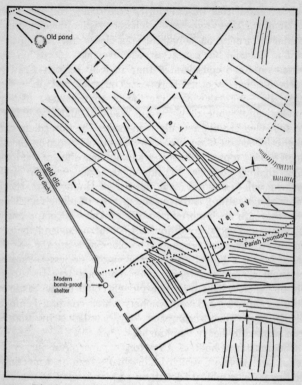

Figure 2. Diagram of 'Celtic' (bold lines) and Saxon (thin parallels) lynchets at Thornham Down, Wiltshire

Crawford could show that one prehistoric camp intersected the lynchets and therefore must have been of a later date, while, on the other hand, Bronze Age disc barrows preceded them. Here are his preliminary conclusions:

A network has been revealed consisting of lynchets, boundary-banks and roads, and associated with upland villages [in contrast to the much later Saxon villages of the valleys which brought a complete reversal of settlements]. Some of these were certainly in existence before the Roman conquest. The network, which I call Celtic, is homogeneous, and the relationship between the parts of which it is composed is such that they form an organic system. Some elements of this system have proved to be older than Roman remains and hilltop camps, but later than the shafts of neolithic flint-mines.

In Crawford's opinion, the Celtic system of lynchets – not the beginning of farming – might well be associated with waves of Celtic-speaking invaders, who were responsible for the introduction of iron into Britain.

Crawford continued to raise the question whether it would be possible to discover when it began, and asserted that the approximate date can be grasped by similar methods. The date he proposed, about 800–700 B.C., he thought might perhaps be one or two centuries too early. Celtic fields lasted in England for close to one thousand years, up through the Roman occupation. The profusion of the system as it stood fully revealed by aerial photographs proved that Iron Age southern England was definitely agricultural. A further aspect of that era was illumined by boundary ditches, which betrayed pastoral needs.

Altogether the findings bore out the scant literary evidence about British farming from Pytheas in the fourth century B.C. to Julius Caesar and Diodorus Siculus. One specific reference by Pliny from about A.D. 70 concerning the use of chalk by British farmers for fertilizing their fields – 'The chalk is dug from shafts, often a hundred feet deep, with narrow tops but spreading out below' – is also corroborated on some air photographs which display round white spots at the end of lynchets, marking most likely the very kind of pits described by Pliny.

Despite his understandable enthusiasm ('It is difficult to express in suitable words my sense of the importance of air-photographs for archaeological study'), Crawford emphasized that the new method was not so much a substitute for excavation and field work as a powerful ally. However, as a key to the relative age of intersecting ditches and banks, the photographs of the Celtic system of lynchets had proved to be of inestimable value. As for uncovering vanished earthworks, observation from the air was vastly superior to any ground investigation. Crawford admitted, with something of a chuckle, that there were, nevertheless, traps. Thus he reports a curious misfortune that befell him. On one occasion he had noted five circular markings on an air photograph. His curiosity aroused, he wasted a whole day inspecting the surface near Winchester only to learn that the circles did not hail from a group of prehistoric barrows but were due to the circular browsing of five very much alive tethered goats!

In Crawford's view of what really mattered in archaeology – and it was his opinion that the treasure-seekers as much as the majority of popular heroes of excavation history were all wrong in their sense of values – the resurrection of the lynchet system of a millennium of British life was anything but a byway of prehistoric exploration. Indeed, judging by the response to his lecture before the Royal Geographical Society in London, he was sure that many in the audience felt as he did, 'that they were gazing, as from "a peak in Darien", upon a whole new world of the past that was now opening for exploration'. But it was another discovery that aroused the general interest and imbued aerial archaeology with an aura of romance comparable to that of flying itself.

Once he had got hold of Air-Commodore Clark-Hall's lynchet pictures and completed his analysis of them, the obvious thing for Crawford to do was to look for more air photographs. Perhaps he might have the good fortune to spy out other footprints of the past. So, with the backing of the Ordnance Survey he now made the rounds of Royal Air Force stations in southern England. His attention was drawn to a deposit of photographs at the Old Sarum aerodrome. And it was there that, only a few months after the alert from Dr Williams-Freeman, when making a rapid selection of what seemed to him the 'most meaty' pictures, he came across several negatives taken near Stonehenge. They had been made two years earlier, in the dry year of 1921 by the School of Army Co-operation at Old Sarum in Wiltshire, but had so far remained unnoticed.

Now, Stonehenge has never ceased to excite the British. The circle of giant stone slabs is probably the best-known prehistoric monument in Europe. Ever since seventeenth-century antiquarians turned them – on the slenderest evidence – into the haunted precinct of hooded Druid priests, the mystery of Stonehenge has become a perennial fascination. Stonehenge, like the Pyramids of Egypt, is always good for another ambitious hypothesis, as illustrated magazines and the publishing industry on both sides of the Atlantic can testify. Even sound research – which by the 1950s disentangled most of what there probably is to know about the age and construction of the monument – draws headlines. Little wonder then that Crawford's findings caused quite a stir.

Two parallel low banks, about seventy feet apart, issue from the main gap of the great circular ditch of Stonehenge. They form the sides of the so-called Avenue, on which, at about a distance of one hundred yards, rests the famous Heel Stone. A person standing in the centre of Stonehenge on Midsummer Day sees the sun rise almost exactly over this monument. Hence, the Avenue has often been connected with the alleged sun cult to which the prehistoric cathedral may well have been dedicated.

Like Stonehenge itself, the Avenue has been the object of much unsubstantiated speculation. William Stukeley was the first to make a study of it, in 1723, and he left some very useful data. Stukeley, a friend of Newton's who started out as a surgeon, was an excellent surveyor, but unfortunately his infatuation with the Druids later turned his head and helped to discredit his fine observations. That is why scholars took with a grain of salt his tracing of the road far beyond its present survival. But there can be little doubt that into the early nineteenth century the Avenue could still be seen running due east for 860 yards to the top of a hill. There it ended between two groups of barrows, which Stukeley fancifully baptized the Old and New King Barrows. The further course of the Avenue – if it did indeed continue – had been entirely lost even when Stukeley made his survey. All the area had long been under the plough. However, Stukeley suggested that the road proceeded in the same direction on to a ford of the River Avon. Astronomic hypotheses also postulated a straight course. Carl Schuchhardt, one of the few foreign scholars to scrutinize Stonehenge, though also persuaded of the sacred nature of the Avenue, thought it had formed a link to Durrington Walls, which he believed was the actual settlement of the Stonehenge people.

Air photography proved all of them wrong. The Avenue was not straight, nor did it follow the shortest route to the Avon or lead to Durrington Walls. It did not fit any pet theory. But there it was, showing up on the photographs as a pair of thin

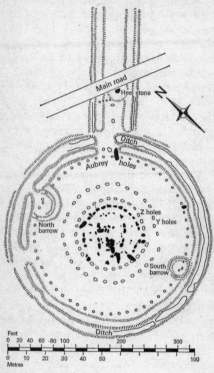

Figure 3. Plan of Stonehenge

parallel lines, even though no surface traces could be discerned on the ground. From the top of the hill it made a sharp turn south-eastward, then, after a straight run over half a mile, terminated abruptly in the hamlet of West Amesbury on the banks of the Avon.

In his report to the *Observer* of 22 July 1923, Crawford wrote:

All this is absolutely new and was never before suspected; and there can be no reasonable doubt that it is correct. Personally I feel quite certain that the marks on the air-photos are those of the Avenue banks; but I do not expect all others to be convinced until trenches have been dug across to prove it. I have just returned from walking, with another archaeologist, along the whole length of the Avenue. We could not see the faintest trace on the surface until we got a mile beyond West Amesbury. But here, between the Old and New King Barrows, there is a bank in a field-track exactly at the point where Stukeley's measurements placed the Avenue, and where one of the two parallel lines on the air-photo comes out. Here, about a mile from Stonehenge, I picked up a piece of 'blue' stone. We could see a double line in a field of potatoes quite plainly – apparently the deeper soil of the silted-up flanking ditches promotes better growth ... The utter absence of other surface indications where the lines appear on the air-photo is remarkable, but in some ways not unwelcome; so much greater will be the triumph of air-photography if digging reveals the flanking ditches besides the banks there. I intend to make this crucial test shortly, if the owners' permission can be obtained.

And this was exactly what Crawford did. Early in September 1923 he set out to dig trenches. To clinch his case he chose three places that were approximately on the strip indicated by the air photograph. Then he cut across to locate the two banks of the Avenue. The topsoil was about six inches thick. At the time of the dig, the terrain was covered by a stubble field. The ground betrayed not the faintest trace even where Crawford knew he had hit the precise location of the ditch. 'It was like steering a ship by means of sounding.'

At half past eight in the morning of 5 September the first test dig began. According to Crawford's description,

a narrow trench had been pegged out to cover the whole width of the avenue. At eleven o'clock, fifteen feet from the starting-point, we came upon the ditch of the western bank of the avenue. It was clearly visible in the side of our trench as a V-shaped cutting fitted with earthy soil. Later on in the morning another similar cutting was observed eighty-four feet east of the first; this was the eastern ditch of the avenue. The width of the avenue near Stonehenge, where it has never been ploughed, is seventy-five feet; and it had already been seen from the marks on the air-photos that where we

were digging the avenue was a little wider. We felt satisfied, therefore, that we had found what we were digging for, and that the
evidence of the air-photos had been vindicated by a severe test.

Needless to say, the other two tests turned out equally successfully. Aerial archaeology had triumphed. It had made the
unseen seen and had shown that archaeological features lost
beyond hope of recovery were suddenly given a new lease of

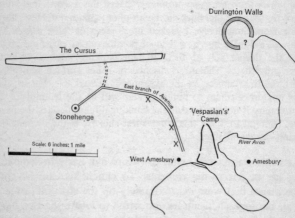

Figure 4. Sketch map of prehistoric monuments in the Stonehenge
area. The three crosses along the Avenue indicate sites where Crawford carried out trial excavations to verify findings on air photograph

life. What is more, it had shown how to reduce excavation to a
brief and speedy trial dig. Without photographic evidence it
would have been a needle-in-the-haystack operation. As Crawford pithily remarked: 'One cannot dig up a whole field or
several fields to find a ditch which after all may not exist.'

The air discovery of the Stonehenge Avenue also gave Crawford interesting clues concerning its original purpose. With the
astronomical theory ruled out of court, the actual course reflected, if anything, pragmatic or technical considerations. It
was now seen to climb from the Avon to the temple via the
easiest gradient, though not the shortest route; and it ended at

the river at a point where the latter came closest to Stonehenge. Such facts, Crawford thought, could be brought to bear
on recent findings by microscopic analysis that the 'blue' or
foreign stones (which form an inner circle and horseshoe of
uprights within the megalithic structure) had been brought by
the builders from Pembrokeshire in Wales some 140 miles
away as the crow flies. The general assumption was that they
had been dragged by a land route all the way. Crawford, who

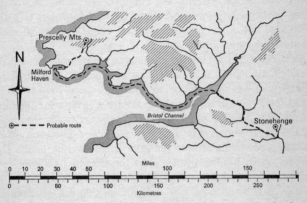

Figure 5. Probable transportation route of blue stones by land and
water from Pembrokeshire (Wales) to Stonehenge

had a high, and well-informed, opinion of the prowess of prehistoric navigators, now opted for a water route along the
coast (via Milford Haven and the Bristol Channel) and eventually up the River Avon – altogether some 240 miles, of which
nine tenths were by water. At the terminal of the Avon the
blocks were then unloaded to be transported along the relatively short, slowly rising road, a distance of one mile and 3,930
feet. Crawford acknowledged the only flaw in his theory: the
Avon might not be deep enough to float blocks weighing more
than two tons. However, in 1954 an experiment was made with
a newly quarried 'blue' stone, which four boys easily poled up
the Avon on three boats lashed together. The land stretch was
then negotiated by fourteen boys pulling the stone on a sledge
with wooden rollers.

The photographs taken by the Royal Air Force, however useful they were to discerning archaeologists, were gathered on military assignments or originated as practice shots by observers in training. The next logical step was for archaeologists to launch their own campaigns. Only by wielding the controls would airborne archaeologists be able to obtain optimal results. So far the new discipline was still a hit-or-miss affair, and the basic principles remained to be fully tested and articulated. Aerial archaeology would not come of age until the archaeologists themselves took to the air. Crawford did not lack the initiative, but a mission of this kind called for considerable funds and lengthy preparation.

To Crawford's aid came a communication from a complete stranger, Alexander Keiller, a man of kindred antiquarian interests who had been flying intermittently since 1909 and who had been a pilot in the Royal Naval Air Service during the First World War. Keiller, too, had been impressed with the possibilities of air photography in archaeological exploration. After reading Crawford's articles on Stonehenge Avenue in the *Observer*, Keiller proposed to shoulder the expense of a joint venture. The target chosen was again Wessex.

Wessex is a region of southern England that has left its mark throughout English history. (In the novels of Thomas Hardy it has also achieved literary fame.) Comprising roughly the modern counties of Berkshire, Dorsetshire, Hampshire, Somersetshire, and Wiltshire, it includes some of the most prominent of prehistoric structures, among them Stonehenge and Avebury. As we have seen, virtually all photographs that had so far made archaeological history were taken over parts of Wessex. And it was here that Crawford himself began as a boy to track down his country's age of dawn in the shelves and shadows of deserted fields. Most important of all, Crawford and Keiller knew that the chalk soil of Wessex was ideal terrain for showing up obliterated antiquities.

Headquarters were established at Andover in Wiltshire and a plane, hired from the De Havilland company, was based near by at the RAF Weyhill flying field. A captured German Ica 25 centimetre focal-length camera, fitted with a 4.5 Zeiss Tessar lens, was purchased from the Disposals Board of the War

Office. The yellow filter and panchromatic $4\frac{3}{4} \times 6\frac{3}{4}$ plates were of English make. To give the operator greater accuracy the camera was installed in the observer's cockpit.

When everything was ready in the spring of 1924 the weather played havoc. Sunny, preferably cloudless, and dry weather making for the most favourable conditions, the exceedingly wet season of 1924 was just about the worst time for this kind of pioneering enterprise. At one point, after three days of continuous rain in May, Crawford and Keiller considered breaking up the campaign. But then there set in a short period of tolerable weather, and work could, intermittently, proceed. Altogether some three hundred pictures were taken. Of these, about fifty of excellent quality were included in the volume *Wessex from the Air*. The text, to which he added valuable references from literature as well as data on soil, crops, and photographic exposure, was in the main written by Crawford and published in 1928 after repeated checking of the terrain on foot.

Considering the hazardous weather and brief intervals when operations were feasible, the accomplishments of the Wessex venture are the more impressive. And while the mission's declared aim was experimental, quite a few far from negligible discoveries could be reported. The team found a great profusion of what Crawford then called 'streak-sites'. These were marks in crops over totally levelled monuments. Indeed, 'not a single flight was taken without our finding several new ones'. What showed up was a number of Roman structures clearly outlined in stripes of darker and lighter coloured oats. At least three lost prehistoric hilltop camps were spotted though not photographed, among them one on Woodbury Hill (Little Woodbury) near Salisbury, which was 'rediscovered' a few years later (1929) on an RAF practice photograph. Expertly excavated from 1938 to 1939 by Gerhard Bersu for the Prehistoric Society, it disclosed in amazing detail what early Iron Age village life in England was like. Subsequently Jacquetta Hawkes re-created it on film. One earthen fortress, which Crawford had come across as 'eorth-burh' in a Saxon charter of A.D. 982, and which had been lost sight of since, was rediscovered as a streak-site. Only this time it was not streaks of oats that proclaimed its presence. Instead, the eye caught crests of poppies growing in a huge semicircle. 'They preferred the richer soil of the silted-up ditch and formed a beautiful scarlet band,' Crawford observed. In addition there were new groups of round and long barrows. Special efforts were devoted to the photographing of lynchets. Their low-lying banks required close attention to lighting conditions.

In his autobiography Crawford wrote modestly: 'Most of our discoveries were quite minor ones. Compared with the results obtained later by Insall, George Allen and St Joseph in Britain, and by Poidebard, Baradez and Schmidt in Syria, North Africa and Persia, ours were very small beer; but they pointed the way.' Pointing the way was the essential contribution of *Wessex from the Air*. No one had shown before how aerial exploration could be systematically applied to the archaeology of one region. In a few days of flying time Crawford and Keiller had restored to the ancient landscape of southern England Bronze and Iron Age settlements and forts, Neolithic burial mounds, and an all-pervading agricultural pattern. Yet, because of its experimental design, *Wessex from the Air* was mainly concerned with establishing untried techniques rather than producing spectacular results. This is what made it a classic in archaeological literature. Quite rightly it has been called the foundation of stone of air archaeology. Forty years later, Irwin Scollar declared the results 'amazing', even by today's standards.

It is now time that we take at least a bird's-eye view of the principles and techniques which Crawford pioneered in Wessex.

3. Contours of Culture

Early in the twentieth century young Leonard Woolley, the later discoverer of the 'Royal' Graves of Ur, was witness to an unusual experience. He was then assisting in a campaign near Wadi Halfa, in the Sudan, below the Second Cataract of the Nile. Woolley and the expedition leader, D. R. MacIver, had busied themselves for several months in digging up a Pharaonic outpost in this African border region. But what was expected to be the major prize, the cemetery of the Egyptian settlement, failed to show up despite their persistent search. One evening, despondent after a hard day's work, the two men walked up a near-by hill to watch the sun descend in tropical radiance across the Nile and to brood over their disappointments. But all of a sudden Aton's divine disc sent them a blessing. The flats below shone up before their eyes specked with darkly outlined rings, none of which they had ever seen. Full of excitement, Woolley charged down the hill, but the circular markings seemed to disappear completely at his approach. MacIver, however, who had remained behind, could direct him from the hill post to where the signs were located, and Woolley thereupon pinpointed them with heaps of rubble. The next morning, native workers were sent out to dig at these spots. Sure enough, below each of Woolley's piles appeared a tomb drilled deep into the rock. More than four thousand years earlier, ancient builders had filled up the crypts with gravel taken from their hollowed shafts. Under ordinary circumstances that material was indistinguishable from the rest of the surface. Yet for just a few moments perhaps during the entire year (as Woolley remarked a bit over-dramatically) light falling on the area at a specific angle accentuated the slightly darker colour and different shapes of the covering stones. And in order to pick out the site at all one had to be placed on a cliff overlooking it, conceivably even, as Woolley later said, from a single point.

Here then is an example of aerial archaeology *avant la lettre*, though Woolley's experience is by no means isolated. Sir Charles Close reported a similar occurrence long known to soldiers who had served in Gibraltar. There, from 'the top of the Rock towards the north front, one could see the remains of the old Spanish lines, which are invisible when one is down near them'. Marks in the soil or its vegetation cover as signs of former human occupation have been recognized in England at least as far back as the eighteenth century. Stukeley was familiar with them. Before him other English field archaeologists traced the streets of Roman Silchester in Hampshire wheat fields. John Bradford in his *Ancient Landscapes* cites the lines of antiquarian-versifier John Kenyon:

> Yet eyes instructed, as along they pass,
> May learn from crossing lines of stunted grass
> And stunted wheatstems that refuse to grow,
> What intersecting causeways sleep below ...

On the continent, particularly in France, the phenomenon had also been known for some time. Ploughed-out round barrows, on which plant growth was sparse, were familiar to local people in Northern France as *danses de fées*. According to popular belief, the agile sprites were responsible for leaving marks in crops from their midnight antics. Several more such unmistakable instances observed on the ground have come to light. Quite a few have made archaeological history. In the 1890s, during exceptionally dry years, F. J. Haverfield, the historian of Roman Britain, and his associates followed plant patterns in order to survey and excavate a site in Long Wittenham in Berkshire. Still earlier a Frenchman, Victor Pernet, who carried out Napoleon III's excavation project at Alesia, where Julius Caesar put down Vercingetorix's revolt, likewise made astute use of growth differentials that he had first perceived from an adjacent summit. In more recent years buried features have been occasionally identified by such means on the ground in the American South-West and in the Near East.

Yet these 'pedestrian' anticipations and applications of a new archaeological method were few and far between. They never matured into a discipline, simply because adequate instruments for consistent study were lacking. Everything was left to accidental discovery. Note how extremely hazardous and unpredictable Woolley and MacIver's illumination of Wadi Halfa really was. An extraordinary set of circumstances had to conspire. Even an elevated view from a surrounding hill – if such a convenient rostrum is at all available – usually affords an unsatisfactory, distorted viewpoint and commands a relatively narrow range. Colour tones, as a rule, will lack in sufficient contrast to distinctly outline subsurface remains. Occasionally marks can be noticed from ground level, but the likelihood, while the viewer's eyes cast about almost horizontally to the surface, is drastically reduced. On the RAF photographs the missing Stonehenge Avenue stood out as clearly as the parallel lines of railway, but even a knowledge of its approximate course did not help Crawford to find it on foot without digging. To register extensive disturbances in the soil, the observer has to be positioned at a considerable distance above the scene. With rare exceptions, it is only then that proper dimensions can be grasped and that the entombed features appear in a recognizable perspective and a sharply defined pattern begins to take shape.

Thanks to the aeroplane chance is replaced by sound and systematic research. This is not to say that archaeology from the air is without pitfalls. On the contrary, it has its share of imponderables. Its success depends, as we shall see, on many variables and their intricate interplay. But it was precisely Crawford's effort to single out controlling factors and to describe how partly or totally effaced monuments could be made to yield an image. No one before Crawford formulated the general principles underlying these phenomena. With him, aerial archaeology assumed the form of a scientific discipline based on rules that are applicable to instances beyond original tests and that are capable of predicting further results. Not the least of Crawford's achievements was to classify the kind of sites which are likely to betray ancient vestiges. In addition he isolated the elements, such as time of year and day, that were essential to the success of the new method.

Analysis of the first aerial negatives to come his way demonstrated to Crawford what he had never expected in the days when he had dreamed of a view from high above: that photographs produced not just vague and fuzzy outlines of archaeological remnants but displayed them in stunning, well-defined precision. A bewildering network of decayed earthworks, barely discernible on the ground, was made conspicuous and could be neatly sorted out. Aerial photographs converted 'chaos into order'. Furthermore, it now became clear that the plough and crops were not necessarily destructive to the tracks of ancient men. Even while levelling structures, they could at the same time help to bring them out graphically. In this way, vegetation acts in somewhat the manner of a chemical developer of exposed photographic plates: it throws up the latent pictures.

One other basic fact is at the root of aerial archaeology, as it is of archaeology in general: to a degree never previously realized, the new medium now demonstrated that virtually any disturbance of the soil wrought by human agency is well-nigh indestructible. Like the inevitable bloodstain in whodunits, it will leave its mark in some way or another. Have your ancestors of two thousand years ago bore a hole to erect a wooden pole or dig a pit into which to dump refuse, let men and the ravages of time fill it and pack it, let it be overgrown by weeds or make the plough run over it for generations, the soil in the cavity will never be the same again as the surrounding undisturbed area. Pithily it has been said that there is nothing so permanent as a hole in the ground. (A recent movement in 'minimal' sculpture, impressed by this very phenomenon, has set out to create so-called earth art from dug and refilled pits that will appear as stark archetypal patterns on the naked ground. Since such works are irremovable, the artist will fix them in scale models or photographs. One artist has embarked on a giant project consisting of mile-long ditches and a square cut into the Sahara, India, and the United States. When the enterprise is completed, 'he intends to take aerial photographs of the three [complementary] sites and superimpose them'. In sum, modern art has embraced instant aerial archaeology.)

All the archaeological marks picked up from the air are

reflections of dislocations of the earth during past ages. According to the way in which they can manifest themselves – either directly or indirectly – and leave definite imprints, Crawford distinguished three principal kinds of site. Archaeological observation from the air centres invariably on these three types. In actuality, however, they will often be found to combine and overlap. Naturally, in the years since Crawford presented the fruits of his researches in *Wessex from the Air* and two Professional Papers of the Ordnance Survey, more study has gone into the various factors which produce these sites and the conditions under which aerial photography will render them most effectively. But his basic categories still stand.

Shadow-sites or shadow-marks were the kind that started Crawford on his road. They revealed to him on RAF photographs, incomprehensible profiles, the ancient agricultural system of prehistoric England. As their name suggests, they depend on shadows cast by rays of light to bring out more or less prominent features. Thus, they trace relics that survive in no matter how fragmentary a shape on the ground as hollows or protuberances. Of course, any ruin or edifice that has not been completely razed can produce shadow-sites. But aerial archaeology is capable of capturing structures that can no longer be distinguished by conventional field investigations. Restricted earthbound vision also fails to gauge the overall design. Most commonly, shadow-sites include ancient earthworks such as furrows, boundary banks, ditches, walls, ramparts, causeways, homesites, abandoned villages, and all sorts of barrows. By and large they will only be encountered in areas that have not been given over to prolonged, intensive cultivation.

For shadow-sites to be adequately registered by the camera from above, lighting conditions have to be exceptionally favourable. The slighter the feature, the more pains have to be taken to render it visible. Long shadows are needed to bring out the relief. Hence the expert will select a time when the sun is low so that its light hits the surface of the earthwork at an angle of nearly ninety degrees, that is, during morning and evening hours. Given clear air, the effect can be striking indeed. Relatively minute irregularities may suddenly emerge sharply etched in black shadows. The same phenomenon is known to motorists driving along a straight, apparently smooth, asphalt highway, which seems all bumps when its minor unevennesses are illuminated at night by the car's headlights.

Just as a site will abruptly rise, it can as quickly vanish. Trial and error will show which are the best moments. Seasons, geographic latitude, and weather all play a part. During the flights over Wessex, Crawford and Keiller found the first hours after sunrise most rewarding. They were in the habit of calling

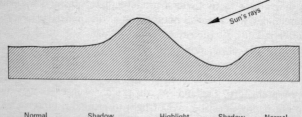

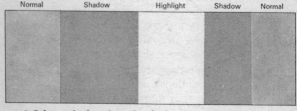

Figure 6. Schematic drawing of a shadow-site produced by light rays falling on an earthbank at a low incline

the early morning 'lynchet time'. 'On a June morning before breakfast,' Crawford wrote, 'the greater part of Salisbury Plain is seen to be covered with the banks of abandoned Celtic fields, but afterwards they "fade into the common light of day".' Most of these earthworks were completely eclipsed three hours after the sun had risen. Of course, with lynchets criss-crossing in various directions, several photographs from various angles may be needed to bring out their entire layout, whereas round barrows will produce markings irrespective of the direction of the sun's rays. Also contributing to superior results in southern England were stands of grass, which throw strong shadows, while the heath that covers earthworks in the moorlands of

Scotland camouflages features and hence tends to be a serious handicap.

Despite their name, not all shadow-sites are strictly due to shadows, but may stand out in glaring white strips caused by more intense reflection of light on inclined surfaces facing the sun. The technique of picking up highlights rather than shadows was used to great advantage by Father Poidebard in outlining Roman remains in the semi-desert of Syria. The French archaeologist was also impressed by the fact that flying under a cloud cover may help to strengthen shadow effects 'from reflected light almost parallel to the soil'.

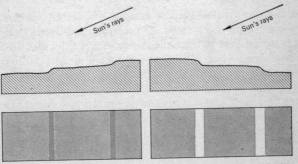

Figures 7a and b. Lynchets can be brought out (a) by shadows, (b) by highlights – depending on which way they face the sun

The value of shadow-sites in archaeological research has already been made clear by Crawford's lynchet studies, the scope of which is largely – but not exclusively – limited to terrain not reclaimed by farmers and builders. Even so, these restrictions leave far more to explore than the deserts and steppes along the fringes of modern civilization. In England shadow-sites have given us, aside from 'new' monuments, an overall view of Neolithic, Bronze, and Iron Age settlements and forts. Furthermore, aerial photographs are likely to clarify the planning, stages, and methods of construction, and sources of material as well as overlaps with previous or later features. A picture of the ancient incomplete Iron Age fort of Ladle Hill showed in detail how the workers moved the earth. At well-known Maiden Castle, on a hilltop near Dorchester, faint shadows registered lines of earlier ramparts. Evidently Maiden Castle underwent various changes, and aerial views gave an incomparable summary of structural developments. 'Air photography', the English scholar Dr J. K. S. St Joseph once noted, 'may recover missing details in known monuments, even the best known.' It also has the power 'to throw different structures into visible relationship, either demonstrating their relative ages or showing where to dig in order to establish the sequence'. This was dramatized at the Trundle, a prehistoric hill fort near the English Channel, where an air photograph led to the discovery of a much older Neolithic occupation site within its confines.

Closely related to shadow-sites are two other, much rarer phenomena in which snow (or hoarfrost) and floodwater take the place of light to trace the low relief of earthworks. Flurries of snow may cling to the more sheltered flanks of shelves or banks, thereby painting them in distinct white bands. By the same token, snow will stress hollows, where it is likely to lie unmelted for a longer time. Low or retreating floods may leave the edges of surface remains above the water level. The dry elevations, even if protruding just a few inches, will then betray a razor-sharp layout of walls, platforms, lynchets, causeways, or entire defunct settlements. Flooding of the lower Tiber valley by the German armies in the Second World War brought out the ancient shoreline and harbour installations of Ostia, the ancient port of Rome, whose complex setting had puzzled archaeologists for a long time.

Unlike shadow-marks, the other two principal kinds of sites formulated by Crawford refer not merely to tangible relics on the surface whose actual relief can be detected, but to differences caused by buried structures. They are soil-marks and crop- or vegetation-marks (Crawford originally called them streak-marks). Crop-marks are by far the more important, but first a few remarks on soil-marks.

Soil-marks entail a coloration of the bare earth, appearing either lighter or darker than the surrounding undisturbed terrain. Those that owe their origin to the filling up of ditches, pits, hollows, trenches, canals, and the like carved deep into the subsoil contain thick layers of earth relatively rich in organic matter. In comparison to the chalk of the English downs they may seem almost black. The fact that they also retain more moisture again makes for a darker shade.

Soil-marks have been shown up by snow also, which sometimes melts faster over man-made excavations, apparently due to the caloric properties of disturbed soil beds.

Since 1960 the Frenchman Roger Agache, on a colleague's suggestion, has followed up with remarkable success damp-marks produced in his native Somme Valley during winter by the different humidity content of the soil. The method is applicable only during brief spells, particularly after the long rains at the end of winter. But damp-marks have the advantage of not depending on sensitive crops, and often stand out with greater precision than crop-marks. Besides, they make features spotted in naked, unplanted fields immediately accessible on foot for further examination without provoking any farmer's ire. While British workers hitherto scored most of their discoveries in spring and summer, Agache has made winter a favoured season for aerial observation as well.

What sunrays at a proper angle can do for shadow-marks, the plough will do with as startling effect for soil-marks. Fresh ploughing in spring brings out the contrast by turning the topsoil, thereby accenting colour differences caused by debris from buildings or humus-filled ditches. In Wessex Crawford found disc barrows which, though completely level, stood out with extreme clarity when newly ploughed. There was an outer white ring from the erstwhile bank (with its admixture of light-coloured grains) adjoined by an inner dark circle from the blacker, more humid silt of the ditch. Sometimes a white spot loomed in the centre indicating an interment. The pure subsoil laid free at the rims of hollows or ditches may add another colour differential.

Soil-marks can also combine with aboveground shadow-marks. Thus, to take again an example from Wessex, banks or lynchets raised from white chalk pebbles will display their whiteness after ploughing. Other curious agents that restore the white coloration of the original chalk banks or ditches are burrowing animals, such as rabbits and foxes, which have a predilection for less compact earthworks.

Eventually soil-marks may well become crop-marks. The latter offer a decided advantage in that they may reappear almost indefinitely, while soil-marks from raised earthworks will become weaker from year to year, particularly after repeated ploughing, and in time will dissipate altogether.

In crop-marks, vegetation is the medium through which underground remains manifest themselves. The basic agent is

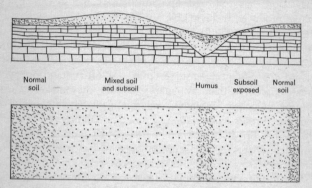

| Normal soil | Mixed soil and subsoil | Humus | Subsoil exposed | Normal soil |

Figure 8. Diagram showing the formation of soil-marks

the same as in soil-marks, only now the modified soil affects the growth of plants instead of revealing itself directly. Hence, vegetation will vary from the adjacent ground that does not contain antiquities. Such growth differentials are revealed by either the colour or physical form – usually both – of the plant cover.

The process sounds simple enough, but there are infinite variations and degrees in the end results depending on as many variables. Obviously, subterranean disturbance can be either detrimental or favourable to growth. Over filled-up ditches and other excavations, where fertility as well as moisture and depth for roots to penetrate is increased, the crop above will display more luxuriant growth and thicker and taller plants, while stone floors, foundations or walls of buildings, and metalled roads will produce stunted growth. Vegetation thriving in a beneficial milieu usually shows up in much darker green during early summer. For this reason, human vision tended to be the best guide until colour photography was perfected. Crop-marks that result from improved soil and which will promote darker lines or patches are now generally referred to as positive; their reverse, caused by growth inhibitors, as negative. This distinction was introduced after Crawford's preliminary observations. However, Crawford's 'parch-marks', which are due to stunted growth – mainly of grass – over masonry or roadbeds, correspond to negative marks, though they are specific to droughts.

Grass is one of the least helpful of all crops and under ordinary circumstances will register no marks whatever. Yet in periods of extreme drought during late summer grass can be as meticulous a delineator of subsurface remains as other plants.

In identifying positive crop-marks, the greatest successes are associated with long-rooted plants which reach deep into the fertile excavated and refilled subsoil. All cereals qualify, but barley and oats seem to react best. Fairly satisfactory results have also been obtained from beets, potatoes, and other 'root' plants. Crawford reported one instance in Wessex where horsebeans outlined a circular ditch more sharply even than oats. In tropical countries, commercial crops like tea and sisal may signal buried remains. Miss G. Caton-Thompson, aided by an aviatrix friend, mapped the irrigation system of the Ptolemaic colonies in Egypt's Fayum from the growth patterns of local desert plants.

In general, cereals will produce crop-marks as neatly defined as an architect's blueprint in late spring and early summer. Later in the season, the taller stems over deep ditches or pits may turn into shadow-marks. Their differential will also be accentuated if bent by storm. After harvest, stubbles of cereals are prone to continue indicating subterranean sites by their thicker stands. At that time – late August or September – weeds or leguminous plants such as clover or alfalfa may renew the pattern in the same fields. Invariably, the growth variations on which crop-marks depend are substantially enhanced by dry spells. Several of the most sensational discoveries were registered in arid years. Many could have never been made had it not been for such climatic upsets.

Ideally, crop-marks should outline buried remains in their entirety. But given large-scale features this is rarely the case.

For one, the area may not be planted throughout with the same 'sympathetic' crop. Indeed, parts may lie fallow. Others will be covered by an altogether unresponsive vegetation. Thus, antiquities are only exhibited in part, if at all, and the aerial surveyor is left with the wishful thought that harvests in future years may eventually help to complete the record. So far, the aerial surveyor's utopian ambition to tell the farmer beforehand what to plant has had little chance of fulfilment unless, like a latter-day Stephens or Evans, he can first purchase the entire terrain. But even without such extraordinary inter- vention, a common cycle of crop rotation can bring about magic results, provided, of course, that the airborne archae- ologist will not tire of taking photographs of the same area for several years.

So complex are the factors responsible for crop-sites that in

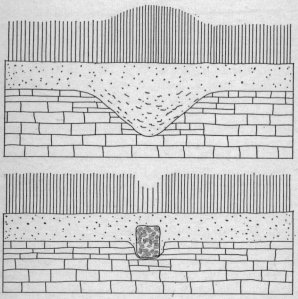

Figures 9a and b. Positive and negative crop-marks caused by under- ground disturbance that may either promote or impede vegetation growth

some instances the same feature depicted on one photograph is known to have brought forth both positive and negative marks. This has happened, for example, when retarded growth over one part of a subterranean structure corresponded to luxuriant crop on another part, apparently stimulated by the lime content of the buried wall that neutralized excessive acidity of the soil.

At best, only a fraction of buried remains will become visible in crop-marks. Conversely, not all crop-marks necessarily betray effaced antiquities. Some may stem from quite recent schemes such as canalization or ploughing, not to speak of conspicuous scars slashed by two world wars into the soil of Europe. On rare occasions, unmistakably geometric shapes must be attributed to more or less natural causes. Like Crawford's tethered goats, fungi spreading out in circles ('fungi rings') have deceived even experienced observers. The frost cracks and 'natural pipes' that Major Allen photographed near Oxford were, appearances notwithstanding, devoid of archaeological significance. Dr Irwin Scollar, active since 1960 over the Rhineland, came across many ring-shaped crop-marks in one photograph he took which at first he thought pertained to a conglomerate of ancient burial mounds. But their great number aroused his suspicion and he questioned the farmer to whom the fields belonged, to learn that the latter had sprayed insecticides from a circling tractor.

However, Scollar could also report an instance in which a break in standing farming practices assisted aerial reconnaissance. One of his remarkable discoveries, that of nine Roman training camps, he made in an area which the previous year had shown no substantial traces. Considering all the other factors present, such a sudden apparition was quite puzzling. Again he made inquiries of the owner of the land, who disclosed that he had not bought fertilizer for his acres as he had in past years. Hence, reasoned Scollar, the roots of the planted crop (rye) had to strike deeper into the soil and thus reacted more sensitively to underground displacements. Had the farmer not lacked money, the walls of the camps would have probably remained undetected.

Just as soil-marks are frequently carried over into crop-marks, so shadow-sites may draw additional attention by their vegetation. The affinity that poppies have for English hill forts is shared by daisies, so that at times prehistoric earthworks are handsomely staked out by white or red garlands of flowers. The reason that certain weeds or wildflowers choose earthwalls is probably their penchant for well-drained soil, while others appear to prefer the more moist ditches; but the pattern may be reversed from season to season.

So far we have in the main discussed plants as principal variables in the resulting crop-marks. However, it must already be obvious that there are quite a few other factors of more or less equal importance, particularly when interacting with each other. The complete mechanism is by no means fully understood. Crawford made a beginning in the determination of salient causes and effects when in 1923 he sent two stems of barley, a large and sturdy one from a crop-mark and its punier fellow from the nearby undisturbed area, to the agricultural research station at Rothampsted for examination. Since then few significant data have been added until the 1960s, when research was renewed through the initiative of Irwin Scollar of Bonn, an American who at last brought aerial archaeology to the same level of competence in West Germany that it had enjoyed in England for several decades.

Together with plants, soil itself – particularly the nature of the undisturbed subsoil – is a foremost element in generating crop differentials. The growth of cultivated plants is in turn a function of the depth of fertile soil and its capacity to store and supply water. It then follows that the greater the contrast between the nourishing properties of virgin soil and displaced-replenished soil, the more graphic the resulting crop-marks. As Dr St Joseph has observed, 'A silt-filled ditch cut in rock or boulder-clay is more likely to promote growth-difference than a trench dug in gravel with which it is itself packed.' Here lies the reason certain types of soil, first analysed in England, are most likely to betray the presence of buried features in their bosom. Among the most favoured types are the chalk downs of southern England, the alluvial gravels along the Thames and other rivers, deposits on glacial terraces in the north, certain limestones, and the silt of Cambridgeshire and the Fenlands.

All these soils share a relatively low rate of water retention and have a fairly thin layer of topsoil – both prerequisites making for greater discrepancy between disturbed and undisturbed sites. Clay, for instance, lacks such qualities, and is far less useful. So is sandy soil, which may quickly fill out ditches, thereby leaving little chance for humus to collect in the excavated section. However, no environment, be it soil or vegetation, can be entirely ruled out. Time was when only the chalk downs of southern England were expected to yield soil-marks; and for many years no crop-marks had been reported from any other European area but the British Isles. Now, through improved techniques and repeated onslaughts, there is virtually no part of England that has not offered vegetation clues to its hidden antiquities.

Needless to say, the degreee of contrast depends on more than the nature of the plants and the surrounding soil. Lighting and atmospheric conditions, camera angle, photographic equipment, and the skill of the observer play a decisive part. So does the altitude of the plane, which for taking oblique pictures ranges between about 400 to 3,000 feet, but has a much higher threshold for verticals. Above all, however, it is the time of year that can make all the difference between success and failure of the airborne mission to trap vegetation-marks. This factor will vary with the crops and the climatic conditions prevalent not only at the time of flight but during the preceding weeks or months. Admittedly, long periods of drought have been most productive of new crop-sites. During such periods a few flights have often led to more discoveries than those made in several consecutive years. Dr St Joseph hit a real bonanza during the drought of 1959, when he sampled new sites by the dozen over various parts of England (1949 was also a banner year). But these are ripe plums, so to speak. In actuality weather conditions are seldom so adverse that they may not yield additional sites to the painstaking observer. Crawford and Keiller's pioneering mission over Wessex is a case in point.

Yet even when taking into account the multiple variables that will affect vegetation and stress its differentials, the outcome cannot be fully predicted. The most stubborn site might well show up unexpectedly or vanish into limbo when all the

breaks seem right. Ronald F. Jessup, another English archaeologist, reported such a crop-site: 'a structure in the form of a
double box, just possibly a Romano-Celtic temple aligned on
the Roman road between Canterbury and Dover'. Though it
has been seen, photographed, and plotted on a map, it refused
to show its scarred face again, 'in spite of seven flights at
different seasons in several years'.

Granting such occasional frustrations from 'phantom sites',
aerial archaeology has nevertheless advanced enough to control
most hazards. This is why Crawford and his successors have
always insisted that success will depend not only on allowance
for the climatic, botanical, and optical factors involved, but on
responsible planning. Before undertaking any flight the aerial
explorer should familiarize himself with the type of antiquities
likely to be encountered and the overall topography and
geology of the terrain. Without such knowledge he may be
unable to tell whether marks seen from above are due to
natural causes or human agents and whether they are old or
recent. To wring the maximum of information from photographs a trained archaeologist has to be called in, but better
still the pictures should have been shot under his direction in
the first place. John Bradford rightly stated that the amount of
significant data derived from aerial photographs is in direct
proportion to the interpreter's experience.

Archaeologically speaking, no ancient landscape can be declared altogether exhausted. Even well-known monuments, including those that have been 'entirely' excavated, have yielded
hidden features to the aerial observer. A bustling twentieth-
century Italian city may display, from above, the outlines of a
Roman Temple or arena of which no stone is standing. As to
vegetation, it must be allowed to respond to the concealed
differences of the soil under ever-changing conditions. Only
then will the surface throw off all its masks – which of course
means that flights must be repeated over several consecutive
years and during almost every season. Like Monet trying to
capture the colour play on the façades of Gothic cathedrals or
lily ponds, the accomplished aerial observer never tires of
snapping still another view. Major G. W. G. Allen, whose main
province was his native Oxfordshire, was the chief exponent of

this principle. He exemplified it in a series of photographs he took of a site near Charlbury. Thus, on one, taken in late fall (November), no evidence of any subterranean structure is in evidence, while another, from the end of June, sketches in crop-marks a Roman villa surrounded by a rectangular dark-lined ditch. Even a former fountain is indicated by a dark patch in front of the villa. Walls of the main building and ancillary edifices, including their chambers, are rendered visible by light lines. Later excavation could add but minor details.

Perhaps nothing proves Allen's point better than the fact that, despite the hundreds of pictures he took over a compara-tively small region of England, after his death others like Dr St Joseph and Flight-Lieutenant D. N. Riley have been able to make substantial additions. It is a true measure of the scope and vitality of aerial archaeology that its work is never com-pleted. Even when it races against time to record sites about to be squashed by the armies of 'progress', who is to say whether such destruction will not offer new opportunities?

4. That Marvellous Palimpsest

Britain's pre-eminence in the new archaeological method remained unchallenged throughout the years between the two world wars. Indeed, until the 1950s no other European country had made any comparable effort to tap the almost limitless store of information consecutive cultures had imprinted on its soil. Crawford and his fellow British archaeologists with commendable humility have accounted for this gap by pointing out the exceptional opportunities afforded by their island's landscape. But more recent results have proved that the techniques of aerial archaeology could be applied with as much success to the lands across the Channel.

No doubt British leadership owes most to the fine, long-standing tradition of British field archaeology and the empirical bent of its exponents, or, as a French commentator, Paul Chombart de Lauwe, has concisely put it: 'à l'intérêt porté dès le début à la nouvelle méthode et la qualité du personnel qui l'utilise' (to the interest taken from the beginning in the new method and the calibre of the people who made use of it). For their full-scale application, aerial techniques required unusual skills as well as resources to match them. Before the Second World War neither was anywhere in abundance. England, at least, could rely on a handful of men who energetically pursued air archaeology from the start.

However, the favourable conditions of the English setting cannot be denied. It was the merit of the British pioneers to recognize them early and make the most of them. England, to begin with, is exceptionally rich in areas that for centuries have never been put under the plough or given over to afforestation. Considerable segments of its cultural landscape have been virtually put to sleep since its ancient settlers left the scene. In this, widespread prevalence of pasturage over farmland played a major part. Furthermore, marginal lands like the Fens of East Anglia or parts of the highlands of Scotland and Wales – all rich in history's material evidence – remained unexplored right into the twentieth century. But even Wessex, strategically located in southern England, in the very centre of things since the human dawn, was far from totally despoiled. Here, where more prominent prehistoric ruins cluster than probably anywhere else in northern or western Europe, aerial archaeology received its first big impetus. Under such favourable circumstances exploration from the air easily evolved from observation of ample surface targets and could then, quite naturally, move on to more elusive features hidden under the topsoil.

Thus, archaeology from the air in Britain has progressed from bird's-eye views of megalithic monuments and the shadow-marks of Celtic fields in Wessex to a gamut of signs in the soil and vegetation all over the Isles. While uncultivated lands were its initial advantage, it benefited more and more from the great variety of English soils and their extensive exposure to different crops. Add to such favourable conditions for the recovery of buried data a more or less unbroken succession of invaders and cultures that have left their mark on the English earth and you may get some idea of aerial investigation's immense potential. The nineteenth-century historian F. W. Maitland spoke of the English landscape as 'that marvellous palimpsest'; large tracts of England are indeed palimpsests, partly effaced, twice-written pages from Clio's notebook whose superimposed symbols can be deciphered. Settlers, immigrant tribes, and conquerors have left us their accounts. The circles, ramparts, ditches, fields, woods, boundaries, dykes, postholes, trails, and walls speak through their hieroglyphic shapes to the knowledgeable scholar. They are the unmistakable manifestations of human industry in past ages and mirror extinct societies. Assembled and interpreted they are nothing less than pages of lost history. The 'scribes' of each age may have tried to erase the testimony of their predecessors, but what ultra-violet rays do to ancient parchments, the airborne camera does for these indelible records: it lights them up, separates their layers, and restores their meaning.

England was also fortunate in having the active support of governmental institutions for aerial reconnaissance. Main assistance came from the Royal Air Force. The collaboration which Crawford had enlisted from the outset soon received semi-official sanction. The RAF not only handed over photographs of archaeological interest, it became an active partner in exploration. Realizing that it required little extra effort or expense to include archaeological objectives in practice shots, the RAF directed its men to be on the lookout for such objectives. At the same time airmen were always ready to follow the suggestions of archaeologists and search out specific sites. Thanks to such arrangements, some remarkable discoveries were made from the air even before Crawford and Keiller's report on their own mission over Wessex appeared in print. Outstanding among these was a discovery by Squadron-Leader G. S. M. Insall, a distinguished flier in the First World War who had been decorated with the Victoria Cross.

In 1925, Insall was stationed at Netheravon in Wessex. On a flight at about two thousand feet he became aware of a large circular earthwork which, he found out later, had long been known to antiquarians as a much eroded, over-sized 'disc-barrow'. A nineteenth-century fieldworker had described it as 'mutilated remains of an enormous Druid barrow'. However, appearing before Insall's eyes together with Stonehenge, which was barely two miles away, it looked very much like that huge megalithic monument. The following year, in July, when it was under wheat, Insall took a photograph. Crop-marks then disclosed its distinctive features. Though there were no stone slabs standing, it displayed an uncanny resemblance to Stonehenge. It too was surrounded by a low bank and an inside ditch. Within its confines Insall spotted some six concentric dark ovals. But, as he wrote to Crawford in a letter published in the first issue of *Antiquity* (March 1927), on climbing 'a hayrick in the same field a few days later, although a few dark patches could be seen in the standing wheat, no pattern was visible, and they would have passed unnoticed. From the air the details of the site were as clear as shown on the photograph, if not clearer.' Insall's photograph caused quite a stir among archaeologists. As early as 1926 excavations were begun by the Cunningtons, a husband-and-wife team, who bought the site in 1928 and eventually published a report in book form.

More or less spontaneously the place came to be called Woodhenge, and an appropriate name it was. Woodhenge stood for nothing less than a wooden version of Stonehenge. Instead of monoliths, its postholes had once held timber uprights. Some scholars have even ventured the guess that Woodhenge served as a model for the more imposing Stonehenge. The correspondence is certainly the closest. Woodhenge, like Stonehenge, is oriented with its longer axis toward midsummer sunrise. Its proportions betray similar geometric principles. In its centre, however, instead of an 'altar stone', Woodhenge had a burial cyst in which the Cunningtons found the crouched skeleton of a child of some three and one half years, its skull cleft in what was undoubtedly a ghastly act of child sacrifice.

Woodhenge in Wiltshire came to rank as the next great scoop of aerial archaeology after the restoration of the missing parts of the Stonehenge Avenue. Scientifically it may well take precedence, because it did not just add to the knowledge of an extant feature, but brought forth a type of monument of which no one had had the slightest notion before Insall fixed it on a photograph. Woodhenge freed Stonehenge from its isolation among prehistoric cult sites and made it part of a larger class without diminishing its stature. In time, as the Cunningtons had expected, other 'Woodhenges' were located. The most imposing of all, situated near Arminghall in Norfolk, which once excavated showed traces of its horseshoe group of giant oak pillars, was also accidentally discovered by Insall in the summer of 1929.

Continuous study, most of it furthered by aerial observation, has extended the distribution of 'henges' into Wales and Scotland, and linked them with Western European traditions of the late Neolithic and early Bronze Ages of about 2000 to 1500 B.C. Grave goods have established their affinity with the so-called Beaker people, who can be traced to the lower Rhine basin. However, on the basis of the many examples now known, henges do not seem to conform to one model but represent interrelated types of religious structures. Perhaps they reflect the different continental background of the original builders, even in the materials they used (stone or wood). The timber circles of Woodhenge, it is now believed, may have actually been roofed. Though most of the circles are closely associated with burials – burial mounds invariably dot their vicinity –

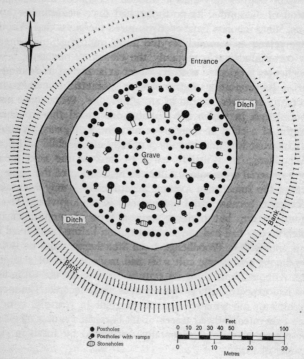

Figure 10. Plan of prehistoric timber circles of Woodhenge north-east of Stonehenge

henges probably served in the main as sanctuaries of primitive cults. So much for these monuments which, thanks to aerial photographs, have opened a new chapter in prehistoric archaeology.

Were we engaged in an exhaustive cataloguing of the field, we would not only have to trace the individual discoveries of the various henges, but do the same for a number of other types of prehistoric structures that the airborne camera found scattered over the English countryside. There are for instance the mysterious cursuses, so named by Stukeley, who thought they served as courses for chariot races. Cursuses (the correct Latin plural is *cursūs*) are frequently encountered in close proximity to henges. In fact, the one known to Stukeley was just outside Stonehenge (there are actually two joined together). In some instances they appear to be older than henges. Cursuses are rectangular enclosures, which may run for miles on end. With their parallel banks they have recalled to several scholars wide processional avenues. They, too, are often adjoined or even intersected by barrows, but nothing definite is known concerning their purpose, though aerial archaeology has established their wide distribution and frequency since Crawford first identified a few outside Wessex in the Thames Valley. (Another one, in central England, was first sighted by a passenger on a commercial air flight.) Without giving a tedious recitation of various finds, it is worth while to note that quantity and distribution go a long way toward accounting for any cultural trait, and it is in this essential though perhaps prosaic task that the coverage and speed of aerial explorations make an essential contribution to the growth of archaeological knowledge.

What has been said about cursuses could be further amplified in the case of the almost as puzzling causewayed hill camps of Neolithic earthworks and a whole range of oddly shaped enclosures and multiple circles like the ones reported from crop-marks near Dorchester (Oxfordshire) in the same first issue of Crawford's *Antiquity* that announced the discovery of Woodhenge in Wiltshire. They too, by the way, had been sighted by RAF pilots during routine exercises.

After Woodhenge, it was an altogether different site that most excited the archaeological imagination. By coincidence, it was little more than a mile removed from the second 'Woodhenge' which Insall was to discover the following year. The place now fully disclosed from the air was the tribal centre of Caistor-by-Norwich, or Venta Icenorum, three miles south-east of Norwich in Norfolk. Venta had never been excavated, but its existence under two fields of some thirty acres next to the church of St Edmund was by no means a secret. From time to time, thanks to the burrowing of rabbits or the plough, Roman coins and fragments of pottery and the like had appeared on the surface. Farmers had frequently complained about the difficulty they had with turning the soil in some places, and a well-known local saying had it that 'Caistor was a city when Norwich was none'.

In the midsummer of 1928, as the barley was ripening, the ghost of this ancient cantonal capital of Roman Britain, settled by the Iceni after Boudicca's rebellion, was reflected in traces of lines that may well have been part of its street plan. The opportunity was too good to miss, and it was feared that it could quickly slip away. The Air Ministry in London was speedily approached in order to clear the way for the RAF to practise their photographic dexterity for once over this Norfolk site, though it was somewhat removed from southern England, where airmen had hitherto so willingly co-operated with archaeologists. Prompt action was rewarded by a stunning photograph which, when reproduced a few months later on a half page of *The Times* of London, was hailed as another triumph of aerial archaeology. An editorial in *The Times* called it 'one of the happiest results so far achieved by co-operation of aircraft and archaeology'. R. E. M. Wheeler, equally enthusiastic, declared it 'the most dramatic example of the potentialities of air-archaeology yet produced in this country'. He added that it 'establishes, once and for all, the desirability of air-photography as a normal precursor to excavation even on sites of known character and extent. Indeed, air-photography may henceforth be regarded as a necessity rather than a luxury in the equipment of the field-archaeologist.'

The RAF photograph of Caistor showed not just a dim web of surmised streets but practically all of Venta. If anything could convey to a general audience the marvel of discovery from the air it was this accurate plan of a totally buried ancient urban complex. Formerly there had been no indications of the town's buildings, and the main reason no excavation had so far been undertaken was simply that no one knew where to start. Now, as a result of a view from 2,400 feet above, the dormant city had been virtually X-rayed. Besides the streets, which were for the first time traced in their entirety, the photograph showed individual buildings, most interesting among them two adjoining temples. Another block (designated Insula X) appeared to include the forum and a basilica. The photograph also hinted that the surrounding wall was a late addition beyond which the underlying streets continued, a further demonstration of the depth of aerial perception. Details of this kind verified what was known about the policy of declining Rome to fortify provincial towns threatened by barbarian onslaughts. Insights gained from a sound interpretation of the photograph were handsomely borne out by the excavation that was started soon after by Professor Donald Atkinson of Manchester University. Two years later, when Crawford flew over Caistor, almost all evidence, apart from excavated sections, had vanished, even though there had been a dry spell.

Caistor-by-Norwich is, incidentally, only one of several Roman towns in Britain that came to be fully revealed by aerial methods. In due time photographs of other centres such as Viroconium or Uriconium (Wroxeter) in Shropshire and Calleva (Silchester) in northern Hampshire proved to be equally effective, furnishing, besides the street grid, plans of all kinds of buildings, and even mosaic floors. Those taken over Verulamium by St Albans helped to guide R. E. M. (Sir Mortimer) Wheeler in his famous excavations. Though Wheeler's campaigns were interrupted by the outbreak of the Second World War, knowledge of Verulamium was much advanced in 1940. An exceptional drought in August 1940 created such propitious conditions that Crawford once again enlisted the help of the Air Ministry, which happily complied despite somewhat more pressing duties elsewhere. Aerial reconnaissance from a height of three thousand feet not only added precision to sites previously dug up but restored missing links of Watling Street (the great Roman highway in Britain), except where it was covered by a modern tennis court. Several 'new' buildings announced their subterranean existence. South of the forum one could track down a small Romano-Celtic temple. A typical Roman corridor house was sketched in the parched grass of a present-day recreation area between an artificially created lake and a tea pavilion.

Tracing of urban grids of classical towns was one of the notable achievements of aerial archaeology in England. Several belonged to smaller towns such as Cunetio (Mildenhall) in

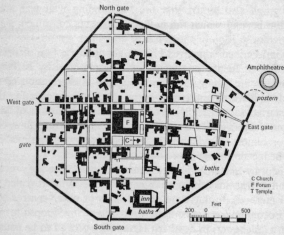

Figure 11. Street net with main buildings of Calleva Atrebatum (Silchester), a Romano-British tribal capital in northern Hampshire

Wiltshire whose site had been virtually lost. It fell upon a British scholar, John Bradford, to apply similar methods to much more rewarding ancient townsites in the Mediterranean. His discoveries at Paestum, from two wartime RAF photographs, and on the island of Rhodes became further milestones on the expanding horizons of airborne reconnaissance after the Second World War.

But to return to our outline of the growth of aerial archaeology in the British Isles, we must now consider the work of another pioneer. Major George W. G. Allen was one of those outstanding British archaeologists who are rather meaninglessly labelled amateurs because they were not originally trained to the profession. By the same token, an archaeologist's archaeologist like self-taught Pitt-Rivers or Flinders Petrie could be considered a rank outsider. (Such facile labels raise a suspicion that every so often the cry of 'amateurism' serves as a device of academic 'ins' to veil their own vested incompetence.)

Allen was by profession an engineer and a director of his family's firm at Oxford. Air photography only occupied his leisure time, which luckily was ample, but his enthusiastic dedication contributed what might have been the lifework of lesser men.

Allen owed his interest to a casual perusal in 1930 of one of Crawford's Ordnance Survey publications, which he found lying on a table in a Southampton hotel. There and then he seems to have been fired by the possibilities of the new scientific weapon. Crawford later commented that the 'chance encounter proves two impossibilities: that the lesser can produce the greater and that neither Government institutions nor English hotels are wholly bad'.

Until Allen appeared on the scene, aerial archaeology in England had, in the main, relied on accidental observations or brief 'one-shot' missions such as Crawford and Keiller's over Wessex and Crawford's 1930 hop to Scotland, in which limited control, if any, could be exerted over conditions of climate, season, lighting, or vegetation. Allen at once saw how one could experiment with these vital factors in order to achieve better results. He developed aerial archaeology into a full-fledged practical technique. He was also the first to stress the use of obliques, which Crawford tended to slight. Possessing the know-how of the engineer and the ingenuity of the inventor, he bent the new weapon to his own will. An expert solo flier, he piloted his private plane, a Puss Moth based at Oxford, and thus was his own master. In his able hands archaeological photography from the air was strictly an individual enterprise. When he found any of the available cameras unsatisfactory for his purposes, he designed and built one for himself. The results were photographs whose quality alone has never been surpassed and which for years made up the bulk of all illustrations accompanying general publications on the subject. His masterly air pictures soon came to be so admired that other archaeologists would ask him to photograph already known monuments, particularly if they were marked for excavation. Allen always obliged, gave freely of his time, bore all the expense, and produced such superb records as that of pre-Roman Maiden Castle which assisted Wheeler in his campaigns. Many of the excavation reports of those years feature Allen's photographs, and they can also be found in profusion in the issues of Crawford's *Antiquity* and in *Oxoniensia*.

As a man of independent means, Allen could dispense with the uncertain good graces of sponsors and officialdom. He went where he wanted to and he flew over the same site as often as he thought was warranted. Only the fullest detail would satisfy him. For nearly ten years, until his death in a motorcycle accident at the age of forty-nine, he sought out promising places, most of them within a twenty-five-mile radius of his Oxford home base. Through his efforts the gravel beds along the Thames were propelled to an area as rich in ancient evidence as the chalk downs of Wessex. In fact, it is largely owing to him that the numerous river terraces all over England came to be recognized as promising antiquarian hunting grounds. But it needed his tireless skill to make visible the traces, which unlike those in the south were almost totally obliterated. Hence, most of the sites he uncovered were revealed by crop-marks rather than by shadow-marks. In the course of less than a decade he literally put the prehistory of his native region on the map. It was said of him that he 'revolutionized our knowledge of the early settlement of the upper Thames valley'. And Crawford did not exaggerate when he declared that 'in mere quantity alone he has discovered more previously unknown ancient sites than any other archaeologist, past or present'.

Allen's discoveries extended over all periods of the English past. They were especially fruitful in Neolithic and Bronze Age sites, including the already familiar types of henges, cursuses, camps, and barrows. In quite a few cases, as in the oddly shaped enclosures (cryptic mazes of rings, dots, and curved and straight lines) he photographed near Stanton Harcourt and Eynsham, Allen produced archaeological information as well as riddles. His comprehensive survey of the successive occupation of the Dorchester area has made this one of the best documented scenes of British prehistory. Probably most famous, however, is his reconnaissance over the Roman villa (or estate) near Ditchley, where, as previously mentioned, he put his subtle technique into full play in a series of pictures. At Ditchley he also made evident his superb use of the oblique airview and exemplified his principle that there is almost always one best angle and position at one time for recording a site. And it was at Ditchley that he proved conclusively that aerial exploration can become scientific if it examines a target throughout a continuum of changes in sunlight, seasons, and vegetation, thereby determining how a lost feature can be most satisfactorily disclosed. Sooner or later the buried truth will out. Reliance on chance, though it had hitherto yielded extraordinary finds, was not enough.

It must not be thought that Allen relied on photographic evidence alone. Whenever possible he re-examined his discoveries on foot. Nothing gave him greater pleasure than watching the excavation of a site.

Ironically, dug-out gravel pits, such as the ones owned by Allen's family company, are among the worst destroyers of prehistoric features in the Thames Valley, wiping out cropmarks and soil-marks for ever. However, as a compensation, some pits on the Allens' property produced Palaeolithic hand axes which he gave to the Ashmolean Museum at Oxford. He also bequeathed his unique collection of nearly two thousand air photographs to that museum, where they are on permanent display. At his death he was engaged in writing an account of his researches, which Crawford and Bradford promised to put into final form in the 1950s. Its release was announced under the title *Discoveries from the Air* in 1957, but because of Crawford's sudden death and Bradford's illness it has so far remained unpublished.

If the mantle of both Crawford and Allen can be said to have fallen on anyone, that man is certainly Dr J. Kenneth S. St Joseph. As articulate an advocate and expounder of methods and their applications as Crawford, he has become something like England's presiding statesman of the field ever since he was appointed Curator of Aerial Photography at Cambridge University in 1948. The creation of a central agency by one of the

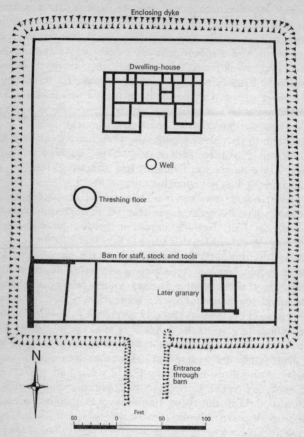

Figure 12. Ground plan, based on air photograph, of Ditchley 'villa' – a Romano-British farm

major universities is in itself proof of the growing recognition gained by aerial photography in post-war England. The importance of Dr St Joseph's work was further recognized by Cambridge University when it converted his office to that of Director in 1962 and in addition set up a Senior Assistantship in Research in Aerial Photography. The discipline had at last achieved academic status. St Joseph's growing collection of photographs, numbering in the ten thousands (all taken by himself), was formerly housed in a small room of the Museum of Classical Archaeology. A move to separate premises became necessary in 1953, and the collection outgrew these too by the mid-1960s. In the meantime, various departments of the University had learned to depend increasingly for teaching and research purposes on St Joseph's unique pictorial record of England's changing human and natural landscape.

Dr St Joseph's active career began during the Second World War when he was attached to the Coastal Command of the Royal Air Force, and continues undiminished. In sheer productiveness it has left Allen's impressive performance of the 1930s far behind. Like Allen, he has an unsurpassed command of the photographic medium; he is as persistent in catching the right moment, has a preference for the oblique view by means of a hand-held camera operated by the archaeologist himself, and has discovered a hundred sites for every one of Schliemann's Troy and Evans's Knossos. It is almost impossible to leaf through any recent book, pamphlet, guide, or learned journal dealing with British antiquities without coming across St Joseph's photographs. *Antiquity*, more hospitable to air photographs than ever since the editorship was taken over by Dr Glyn Daniel after Crawford's death, again and again has reserved supplementary space for St Joseph's researches. Also like Allen, St Joseph exemplifies how much progress in knowledge still depends on individual initiative. Indeed, in this branch of archaeology St Joseph's contributions are so bountiful that they dwarf the work of all others and epitomize aerial archaeology as much as Crawford and Allen's did in the years between the wars. It is therefore the more surprising that his remarkable achievements have attracted relatively few young scholars in Britain to emulate his work.

If Crawford and Allen's researches were somewhat limited geographically, Dr St Joseph's studies know no such restrictions. Year after year he has explored virtually all parts of England, including the apparently unpromising 'lost provinces' of the Midlands, as well as Scotland, Wales, and Ireland. He has also made forays into Northern France and Denmark. And, on a busman's holiday, he reported crop-sites from North America.

Dr St Joseph is a Cambridge-educated geologist. His first and perhaps still abiding interest in archaeology was Roman Britain. Shortly before the outbreak of the Second World War he was engaged in trial excavations of Roman military outposts in Scotland for the Glasgow Archaeological Society. It was then that he joined forces with Crawford, who, both on foot and in short flights in the summer of 1939, had located positions of Roman military advance in the northern zone. During that time Crawford made several discoveries of Roman camps (with Geoffrey Alington as pilot and photographer), mainly in Northumberland and Dumfriesshire. Though he and Insall had explored northern Britain before, in 1930, Crawford realized that so far the surface had barely been scratched. However, he and his pilot were severely limited by time. To Crawford's regret they could not even complete the modest programme he had set himself; that, as he remarked philosophically, is 'the normal fate of programmes'. Also, he had hoped to fly along the 'new' Roman road in Ayrshire that St Joseph had just established on the ground. But on leaving his ancestral land, Crawford was more certain than ever 'that if anyone could carry out a systematic air survey of this area, he would be well rewarded ... It should, moreover, be carried out in a series of successive years, because only when the crop grows in corn do the sites appear as a rule ... The exploration of ancient Scotland from the air has only begun. It is one of the most promising fields of research anywhere in the world.' Crawford's message made a lasting impression on St Joseph, who later acknowledged that he owed his awakening interest in air photography to the older man's 'kindness in providing him with photographs and other material and inviting him to take part in an aerial tour of southern Scotland before the war'.

Unlike Allen, though just as mobile, Dr St Joseph from the start relied on the RAF to supply his reconnaissance with plane and pilot, made available 'in the course of training'. But it was left to St Joseph to make his own selection of sites and to virtually set the course. Thus the co-operation forged by Crawford in the early 1920s was liberally continued into the

1950s by the Air Ministry. However, the RAF's adoption of faster military planes unsuitable for archaeological reconnaissance eventually rang the death knell for this convenient service. Fortunately, St Joseph's labours suffered no interruption. Aided by a grant from the Nuffield Foundation, the University's Committee for Aerial Photography purchased its own aircraft in 1960 (an Auster, replaced by a twin-engined Cessna Skymaster in 1965) and engaged a pilot.

A continuous flow of articles in the *Journal of Roman Studies* covering St Joseph's annual harvests in newly discovered Roman military forts, garrisons, marching and training camps, watchtowers, and roads bears witness to his expansion of our knowledge of Roman Britain. The evidence, completely fulfilling Crawford's hopes for Scotland and elsewhere, is of first importance for all phases of Roman civil and military control of Britain, for which the literary record is extremely sparse. Only since his many finds has it been possible to study in detail the initial phases of the Roman conquest. For the outlying military zones in the West and far North air photography has pinpointed the routes of occupying armies, the bases for advances, and the spearheads and limits of penetration beyond any previous data. The layout and extent of newly discovered military accommodations permit reasoned guesses concerning size of garrisons and armies on the move. Within just a few hours' flying time in the summer of 1945, St Joseph discovered more Roman military sites in the North than had come to be known in the previous two hundred years, during which several seasoned antiquarians and archaeologists had spent lifetimes in their searches. After 1945, St Joseph's further additions advanced in almost geometrical progression. Vastly more valuable than the sheer number of sites, however, are the conclusions that could be drawn from the cumulative testimony. In summing up the implications for just one epoch, Roman Scotland, 'both for the military history of the province, and for the study of individual campaigns', Dr St Joseph stated: 'A picture emerges of the boldness of the Roman strategy supplemented by a wealth of evidence about the technical skill of military engineers at the peak of the Roman army's power and prestige, revealed by a variety of military sites of the late first and second century not easily matched in any other frontier-province of the Empire'.

Take for instance the photographic dénouement of the great Roman stronghold of Inchtuthil in Perthshire, made possible by the exceptional drought of 1949. Inchtuthil is the only site in Britain where the layout of an entire legionary fortress can be examined. One section stood out in such minute detail in parch-marks of grass that rows of timber barracks – in pairs facing each other across a side street – were disclosed, together with their main walls and internal partitions. This one Inchtuthil photograph represents the only plan of a timber fortress so far known throughout the Roman domain of three continents.

The rewarding year of 1949 also found proof of Roman in-filtration deeper into south-west Scotland (Kirkcudbrightshire) than previously suspected. Some thirty to forty new marching camps 'along already known lines of penetration' bespeak massive campaigning in the adjacent area. Other camps spotted beyond the Antonine Wall provide like evidence for the north-eastern Highlands.

St Joseph's researches of the Roman military frontier in Wales were, if anything, even more productive. In the civil districts of Britain additions to the record are as abundant and include much further detail on the tribal capitals at Wroxeter, St Albans (Verulamium), Silchester, and Caistor, in addition to the discovery of entirely unknown Roman villae on the scale of Ditchley, and new information on Roman colonization, land planning, and drainage methods in the silted Fenlands of eastern England.

While 1959 was easily St Joseph's most productive season (yielding three new 'Woodhenges', several cursuses, Celtic settlements in the Nene and Ouse valleys, a Claudian fort in eastern England, some nine Roman camps, etc. etc.), the follow-ing year, 1960, was less so: it was exceptionally wet. Yet it was far from disappointing. A brief dry spell in June prevailing in central England added to the plan of Caistor, even bringing out a system of gutters and confirming that the original street grid was definitely not confined within the visible wall. St Joseph also discovered a larger, undoubtedly older, defensive circumval-lation outside. Here were further hints of the complex history, the development and apparent contraction of a provincial town. The year 1960 also produced an entirely unknown small Roman town in Gloucestershire near the farm of Dorn, clearly outlined by a system of parallel streets within a rectangular enclosure.

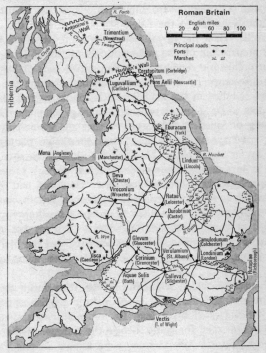

Figure 13. Map of Roman Britain

In the hands of Dr St Joseph aerial archaeology of Britain grew into such a prodigious instrument of research that to describe its achievements one would have to draw up an endless catalogue. To aficionados of archaeological exploration, brought up on more piecemeal rations of one tomb at a time or one burial treasure as the triumph of an adventurer's entire career, the very magnitude benumbs comprehension. Bereft of the traditional romance connected with archaeological discovery, the roll call may seem monotonous. Yet it is the enormous output, its rate and range, that is the very essence of this modern archaeological frontier, and that requires sensibilities of a different kind to grasp its revolutionary scope.

So far we have barely even mentioned Dr St Joseph's equally important contributions to other periods of the British past from the Neolithic to the Anglo-Saxons, and even the age of Cromwell. When the Royal Commission on Historical Monuments prepared an official publication (*A Matter of Time*, 1960) on the prehistoric remains along the gravel beds of England's rivers threatened by 'recent developments affecting the countryside', it relied in the main on aerial photography. The survey's debt to Dr St Joseph was highlighted in the preface by the Marquess of Salisbury, who asserted that 'the whole enterprise could not have begun without the remarkable photographs taken by Dr St Joseph ... Many of the illustrations used were taken by him during flights made especially for this survey and are reproduced here for the first time.' However, had this report, which is a valuable guide to pre-Roman Britain, not been sent to the printers just when St Joseph's startling 1959 discoveries of three more henges, several cursuses and countless enclosures, barrows, Belgic settlements, and the like were being made, the record would have been even more impressive.

The extent to which St Joseph's investigation during the 1959 drought enriched the body of prehistoric English antiquities could be suggested by a long list of monuments. Just one example can stand for many. Before the summer of that year, forty-eight Bronze Age barrows were known in one part of East Anglia. Within a few hours of reconnaissance this number had been increased by about 400 per cent to 250. Once again it was the distribution pattern of these sites rather than their number that yielded novel information on chief areas of settlement, density, and penetration during the Bronze Age in one region of England.

Another facet of the English – and Irish – past in which Dr St Joseph has taken a special interest are the Dark and Middle Ages. Two of his books, on one of which he collaborated with the Cambridge medievalist M. D. Knowles, are devoted to an aerial examination of monastic and other medieval sites. His researches have thrown new light on the much debated problem of the deserted villages of England and their evolution, economy, and decline. Dr St Joseph himself considers the completely levelled Dark Age sites of Yeavering and Milfield among the most remarkable individual discoveries that have ever come from air photography. Their rectangular buildings, including a series of halls 'evidently rebuilt time and again' and an arena-like 'moot', or place of assembly, were perceived unexpectedly on a reconnaissance flight over Northumberland in 1949. What makes the discovery of Yeavering and Milfield so notable is that they could be identified as two seventh-century royal vills mentioned in Bede's *Ecclesiastical History*, and affording 'tangible evidence of the life and social conditions described in *Beowulf* and Bede'.

The extraordinary volume of discoveries made in Britain after the Second World War was particularly opportune, because it produced indelible records of sites that might have been for ever lost to urban and industrial expansion. Records, however, are only valuable if they are systematically collected, catalogued, and made available to scholars and students. Air photographs have become exclusive sources for whole chapters of the English past. As such they are public documents of the first order. As indispensable as any written records, they, too, are historical manuscripts of a kind and deserve the same care.

Britain is fortunate to possess ample collections which help piece together its palimpsest. Though Crawford's library at the Ordnance Survey was destroyed during the Second World War, the loss is partly compensated by the Ashmolean Museum's assemblage of Allen's photographs. The British Ministry of Housing and Local Government harbours all the photographs of Britain taken in post-war years by the National Air Survey. The usefulness of these pictures to archaeology is somewhat limited since they were taken at high altitude and regardless of seasonal advantages. Dr St Joseph has always made it his task to bring together at Cambridge in a central library the thousands of his own pictures of British antiquities. While engaged in annual junkets to make the archaeological record ever more complete, he had been impelled by the urgency of this undertaking. With it grew his conviction that 'the early history and prehistory of Britain can be studied from the air more effectively than in any other way yet available'.

5. Roma Deserta

All over the Western world, from the sun-drenched, sand-swept desolation of the Sahara to the murky, frosty moors of Scotland, imprints abound of the Roman Empire. Around the great inland sea of the Mediterranean, along its indented coastlands, on the islands that dot its shimmering waters, and deep into the hinterlands to the Atlantic fringes, the onward march of the conquerors is sketched by way-stations of the centrifugal power of militant Rome. Storied aqueducts still arch across gulleys in Spain, African wadis, and broad, Arcadian valleys in Provence. Little Romes with their paraphernalia of public baths, forums, pillared temples, mosaics, cloacas, basilicas, amphitheatres, and coliseums mimic in their amenities a standardized cosmopolitan style. Though the unifying order has long departed, ubiquitous ruins continue to proclaim the well-advertised ancient virtues of the imperial taskmaster. They also signal one of history's stunning success stories and the less attractive qualities that make people and nations come out on top. Like Ramesside Egypt, the Roman building furore has crowded out and overshadowed some of the more subtle, and perhaps more precious, relics of their predecessors. Yet, abundant as these testimonies of Roman rule are, monotonous and slightly vulgar as they may sometimes seem, the truth is that we cannot get enough of them. It is also a fact that with all the *embarras* of Roman riches, much needed material – particularly on the frontier provinces – is still missing.

Roman Britain is a case in point. In the preceding chapter we have briefly indicated how much this obscure phase of island history was illuminated by archaeological investigation. Though the British Isles were only a backwater of the Empire's domain, they can be made to mirror the manner of Roman penetration, military organization, civil administration, and provincial architecture in considerable detail. Of this record, literary evidence and prominent surface remains notwithstanding, the evidence was fragmentary at best until the advent of aerial photography. What this method of antiquarian research is able to accomplish was highlighted against the far vaster canvas of another Roman borderland, one flanking the chief combating powers of the East and hence likely to contribute a vital chapter to the annals of the rising and falling fortunes of Roman expansion.

The land was Syria, and the man to whom we owe the titanic accomplishment was a French Jesuit priest, Antoine Poidebard. He virtually blew away the desert sands and pierced the dust storms of the hot *hamad* to glimpse a lively panorama that stretched for some seven hundred miles south-west to north-east, with a width of up to two hundred miles, from around Bostra (Bosra) in the far south to the upper Tigris in northern Mesopotamia. As such the territory constituted a crucial section of Rome's frontier in the Orient. Since then its thousands of square miles had long been in limbo. Until Father Poidebard's arrival little was visible and even less was known of the enormous Roman defence and colonization system that had veined the steppe in a cluster of towns, forts, watchtowers, ramparts, roads, camps, irrigation works, and endless miles of roads. Material was on so immense a scale that it could sum up Rome's military confrontation with the East; the protracted duel with Parthians and Sassanids who, descending from Iran, in turn controlled most of Mesopotamia; and its relations with such satellite realms as the desert Venice of Palmyra, which had acted as buffers until completely absorbed by the Empire. There were also insights to be gained into the more elusive contacts with the partly Hellenized Semitic populace – gradually to be reclaimed by the Orient – and the policies toward roving Bedouins. No wonder that on publication of Poidebard's *La Trace de Rome dans le désert de Syrie* in 1934, the fruit of eight years of intensive surveying, his work could be hailed as 'one of the most important and illuminating contributions ever made to the unwritten history of the Roman Empire'. The reviewer just quoted, Sir George Macdonald, writing in *Antiquity*, further declared that

Hundreds of miles of *terra incognita* have been thoroughly recon-
noitred, so that exponents of the older and less spectacular methods
now know exactly where it will profit them to ply the spade and
pick. And it is certain that their reward will be rich ... Scholars
will then be able to reconstruct with confidence the whole organization of the army of the East, a subject that has hitherto been
well-nigh hopelessly obscure.

For covering so vast a scene the aeroplane was indeed the
ideal instrument. Some of the sand-covered evidence could
probably have been determined on foot – if ever so tediously
and at multiples of the time actually spent – but the enormous
extent of the surveyed land and its difficult access cried out for
airborne exploration. Father Poidebard recognized the potential
of this research method almost instantly and, what is more, all
by himself. Though the principles he evolved are largely identical with those of Crawford, they were independently arrived
at. Like the first full-scale attempts in photographing archaeological objects from the air during the First World War, his is
another of those notable instances when similar advances were
made more or less simultaneously by men who had no knowledge of each other. With Father Poidebard's lifework aerial
archaeology once again took up the promising thread in the
Near East so auspiciously initiated during the Great War. For a
long time Poidebard's was the only name that could stand beside those of the British leaders in the field. Yet, surprisingly,
despite such spectacular successes none of his compatriots followed his example in metropolitan France.

Antoine Poidebard, too, was not trained in archaeology. Born
in 1878 at Lyon, he entered the Jesuit order in 1897 and a few
years after was sent as missionary to Armenia. There he gained
fluency in Turkish and Armenian. Later it was said of him that
next to God, his life had been inspired by two loves, Armenia
and aviation. Poidebard saw active service throughout the war,
first as a chaplain of the French army on the Western front.
Then, in 1917, he was transferred as interpreter to the hotly
contested lands astride the Caucasus, which he knew so well.
Under normal conditions it would have taken him a few days
to reach his post via the Orient Express. Now, with the Central
Powers blocking the way, it meant a hair-raising detour of

nearly five months across Egypt, India, Persia, and Mesopotamia. Once he had reached his destination, he was caught in the seesaw of advancing and retreating armies of the Allies, the Turks, Bolsheviks, and the ephemeral republics that rose after Russia sued for peace. For two years he was attached to the Armenian high command in Erivan. At the same time he made a study for the French general staff of communications across the Iranian highlands between the Persian Gulf and the Caspian Sea. He had barely returned to France in the summer of 1920 when General Weygand made him join the French diplomatic mission to Georgia, a country that soon after Poidebard's arrival succumbed to the Bolsheviks. Meanwhile, in 1923, Poidebard published his first book, *Au Carrefour des routes de Perse*, which won a citation from the French Academy. It clearly foreshadowed his later interests and already utilized aerial inspection. Exposure to past and present in the political ferment of the Near East had also sharpened his awareness of the region's ever-changing scene, for which the road system woven by many hands through the ages served as a reliable log.

In 1924 he was appointed to a professorship at the Jesuit University of St Joseph in Beirut, the capital of French-administered Lebanon. His new post coincided with the influx of a stream of Armenian refugees fleeing their Russian and Turkish conquerors. Poidebard took it upon himself to organize relief work for the thousands of destitute arrivals. Backed by the League of Nations he supervised the construction of housing, set up workshops, and found new trades for his Armenian friends. To further their industry he invented a collapsible chair which in no time swept the Levant.

Continuing his association with the French armed forces, in 1925 Poidebard was named observer in the air force reserve with the rank of lieutenant-colonel. Soon after, the Geographical Society of France entrusted him with an investigation of the economic potential of northern Syria. The enterprise involved the study of the forms of pasturage and agriculture which had formerly flourished in the area. These and the lost watering system that made them possible could best be examined by air.

Poidebard's course was now set. On the very first air survey he was startled by the profusion of tells (ancient conic hills betraying abandoned settlements) and of Roman encampments unknown to anyone who walked the ground. The benefits that archaeological research could derive from aerial scanning of the arid land were now driven home to him. What incredible possibilities opened up for students of the forgotten yesterdays of this once teeming segment of the ancient East! Father Poidebard recalled in his book the impressions he gained on these initial flights, when during his geographic observations 'the airplane revealed itself unexpectedly effective' in the archaeological examination of Romanized upper Mesopotamia.

North of the Euphrates, in the Khabour basin [he continued], the ancient road-net appeared to me neatly marked by the ancient tells of the steppe. The countless tells [raised by successive human occupation] which are scattered across the plain seem, when viewed from below, like a battalion in disorder. Seen from an altitude of some 5,000 feet, they were strictly aligned. A glance at the map which gave the location of former Assyrian and Roman cities convinced me that I beheld the complete network of ancient communications, as traced by vestiges of ancient agricultural compounds and fortified posts. On descending in slow circles to a very low altitude above the ancient tells, I noticed that under oblique light many details appeared on the flat and declined surfaces, while on the ground the grassy vegetation which covered them was perfectly even. Will observation from the air give us precise knowledge of the itinerary described by the historic lanes joining the markets of the extreme Orient with the Mediterranean ports of the Near East? These were problems which had haunted me since my first flight in spring 1918 over the Persian plateau ...

Impressed by the data he had already gathered from the air, Poidebard alerted the Académie des Inscriptions et Belles-Lettres at Paris, a leading learned institution which had long presided over the principal French antiquarian and archaeological researches. The following year (1926) the Academy entrusted the father with verifying his findings on the ground. But ground exploration in this immense waste only convinced Poidebard, as it had other scholars, of the apparent 'ingratitude' of this region to archaeologists.

Between the Tigris and Euphrates, almost all the traces of the ancient Mesopotamian and Roman civilizations have been levelled by successive destruction and by Persian, Arab, and Mongol invasions. The soil carried by the wind for thousands of years has covered the steppe with a uniform mantle which keeps ruins out of sight. Indeed, no ruin appeared where aerial observation had previously revealed quite distinct ancient sites.

Had his assignment turned into a total failure? He had next to nothing tangible to report to his Parisian sponsors. The evidence he thought he had noted from the plane remained unproven. But he did not consider himself defeated. No doubt the ruins existed underground. What was needed was an infallible method of locating and unveiling the buried remains by making use of aviation and documenting the findings on photographs. Poidebard defined that task. Preparations occupied him for two years, during which, in close liaison with the French Air Force of the Levant, he embarked on a minute study of climate and terrain, and the factors that could make aerial surveying a successful research vehicle in the Syrian steppes.

The father's missionary zeal had found a new outlet. It so happens that it was also much needed to dispel the scoffs of learned circles, who, in the country of Voltaire and Anatole France, reacted to the claims of tracking down ancient civilizations from the air with the elegant smile of worldly sceptics for fantasies *à la* Jules Verne. However, the conversion was to be complete when the president of the Académie des Inscriptions declared at a session in 1932 in appreciation of Poidebard's accomplishments: 'L'avion devient un des instruments les plus efficaces de l'archéologie' (the aeroplane has become one of the most effective instruments of archaeology).

Poidebard never made any bones about the obviousness of the idea itself. To debate paternity seemed to him an idle sport. Its general principles were already known to military aviation. Quite naturally it would occur to any observer who flew across the deserted lands once inhabited by the great civilizations of antiquity, no matter how little he might be interested in historical questions. Given only a bit of imagination he could not help being tempted to restore in his mind at least in outline the complex system that the landmarks suggested. 'All of us', he

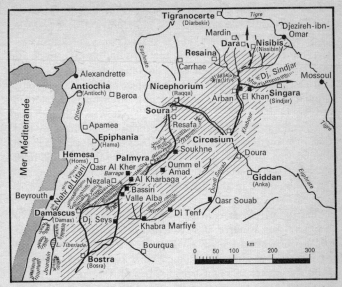

Figure 14. Zone of A. Poidebard's aerial explorations (1925–32) of the system of Roman border fortifications (*limes*) in Syria

wrote, 'who have flown during the war across the desert regions of Asia, Macedonia, Egypt, Mesopotamia or Persia, carried the germs of the method, waiting for a favourable opportunity to develop it fully and to apply it to different terrains.' Others, as he acknowledged later, though he did not know of them at the time, had preceded him in the Near East. Even in India, the director of the Archaeological Service of the State of Jaipur reported an exploration by air of a fifty-mile strip along an old river-bed in the Punjab during the years 1923–4. And in Syria, since the beginning of the French occupation, when archaeology had come into its own, photography from the air had been used (as, for instance, in an airview of Dura Europos, the famous Hellenistic outpost on the Euphrates discovered by British soldiers at the end of the First World War). But on those few occasions it had only assisted excavation; rarely had it added novel features. In the Syrian setting it was left to Father

Poidebard to go beyond rudimentary steps, to look farther than sites along well-known tracks, to hunt down buried remains barely or not at all visible on the ground, to systematically recover an entire region, and, in order to fulfil his task, to devise appropriate techniques. Not until the fall of 1927 did Poidebard hear of Crawford's researches. Until then he was actually only familiar with the work of his fellow Frenchman L. Rey in Macedonia during the First World War. It was still later that he had an opportunity to read Crawford's publications. By that time his own experiments had been completed and the method was firmly established. Needless to say, the conditions for aerial surveying over the Syrian steppes differed considerably from those in the fields of England's rainy and verdant land.

That he arrived at conclusions basically similar to those of Crawford was a source of satisfaction to the padre. Like Crawford he recognized the advantage gained from horizontal lighting in the morning and evening hours, so that long shadows could stress ever so slight irregularities on the ground. He too learned to value the varying colours of vegetation in determining hidden monuments. Vegetation, besides being an independent indicator, could also accentuate the effects of horizontal lighting. Poidebard's observations on growth differentials pertain to wild plant life and not to cultivated crops. They correspond in fact to Crawford's parch- or grass-marks. Two periods of the year favoured their development in the steppe. During the autumn rains, the arid land turned green almost overnight. It was then that the colour of the vegetation would vary 'according to the permeability and undulations of the soil. The colour remains lighter where the ruin is hidden underground, because the permeability is less, or because plant life is hindered by the dissolving of the lime in the old walls. The colour is darker in the depressions due to an old gravel road or trench. A depression of a few centimetres is enough to increase the dampness of the soil'. Similar phenomena occur with the onset of the first hot days in spring, when the merciless sun beating down on the plant cover singes the vegetation within a few weeks and produces colour differences reflecting disturbances under the surface.

Father Poidebard was fond of referring to certain 'actinic' properties of the ground which could register on photographic plates the presence of subterranean ruins quite invisible to the naked eye, even from up high. Early British students never took recourse to such a seemingly occult force. Stated somewhat less mysteriously, all Poidebard probably meant to stress was that the range of colour changes exhibited by disturbed soil and the plant growth it supports is greater than the spectrum perceived by unaided human vision. He himself was an indefatigable experimenter with all kinds of optical equipment. Just as he never tired of testing various filters, lenses, and cameras – often while trained simultaneously on the same object below – he tinkered enthusiastically with several special emulsions for the coating of photographic plates. While sober British workers had espoused the principle that the human eye sees as much as the camera, if not more, and that, despite popular belief, no magic revelation can be ascribed to superior photographic sensitivity, the French priest was in this respect more sophisticated. Indeed, he deserves to be ranked among the pioneers of infra-red photography. In his optical curiosity he was undoubtedly stimulated by the extraordinary lighting conditions of the blinding sun during the hot season in Syria.

The peculiar atmosphere of the arid sub-tropical land presented problems unknown to English aerial explorations. There was, for one, the excessively glaring light reflected from whitish surfaces or, worse still, thrown back from lava outcrops, which acted like mirrors. To this must be added the omnipresence of sand particles, which blurred the view and could turn the customary colouring into a gamut of intriguing opaque pastel shades. The fog created by dust storms was likely to be further modified by water vapours rising from near-by oases, and by air eddies clinging to the ground in the heat of the day. All of these complications were a challenge to Poidebard's optical ingenuity. He found that vertical photographs taken at low altitudes at the end of the day greatly reduced the ill effects of these atmospheric disturbances. But such evasions did not satisfy him. Besides, observations from morning and evening shadows failed to pick up all the marks he had been searching for. As a consequence he developed his technique of 'counterlight', which ran against all common sense yet helped to diminish the ill effects of the sand haze like no other device. Greatly simplified, the procedure was the following: Toward midday, while the upper wing of the plane formed a protecting screen, he faced the camera practically into the sun, though pointed downward at an oblique angle. For photographic plates he chose special orthochromatic anti-halo material, but no filter. The result was *éclatant*. Blurring from sand or vapour was almost nil. Shadows from ancient remains were defined in sharp, unusually black streaks. During one experimental flight over the desert north of the Euphrates, an ancient road was followed for a distance of some sixty kilometres, though it had 'remained invisible to all the observers of previous missions, whether in aeroplanes or on the ground'. Later, in 1936, the counterlight method was successfully demonstrated in Algeria.

In time Poidebard established all kinds of refinements of his technique. Though in his earlier attempts he preferred high altitudes – up to about 8,000 feet – he gradually adopted an approximate height of 1,000 feet as an optimal average for thorough surveying. Flights above 3,000 feet were restricted to general reconnaissance and to overviews of previous, more piecemeal, explorations. However, he was never bound by dogma. In one noteworthy campaign he traced an important road radiating from Damascus for its length of 150 miles from a height that rarely topped eighty feet. Nevertheless, another ancient route linking Palmyra with Hit appeared as a ribbon rimmed by two black lines from as high as 1,200 feet; and – to Poidebard's surprise – when the plane descended any farther the road gradually disappeared. During one low flight, while sighting a Roman milestone, he had his pilot go down to just fifteen feet and, with the propeller barely moving, he read the Greek inscription that gave the time of construction and destination of the newly discovered road. It contained a dedication from the senate and people of Palmyra to a certain Soados, apparently a benefactor of the caravan trade. The date referred to the reign of the Roman emperor Antonius Pius in the second century.

Poidebard never codified his method in full detail. Rather it was his opinion that it is impossible to establish a foolproof set of principles for aerial reconnaissance. Not only must every explorer work out his procedure on the basis of his own experiences, but each region over which he flies presents specific problems which require individual handling. In northern Syria – which geographically belongs to Mesopotamia and which was the principal area of his first researches – one had to consider such hazards as 'the heated air with its pockets which make it impossible to maintain at certain hours an uniform altitude; mirages which, during much of the day, forbid on account of light refraction to gauge exact distances and dimensions; and the gusts rising from the earth which put dust into suspension and thus make high altitude observation and photography impossible'.

However, each flight should be minutely prepared. Before taking off, one's mind must be sharpened to the terrain one is about to survey as much as to its history. Poidebard made a speciality of photogrammetric techniques, and during the flight had charts and conversion tables at hand in his 'moving observatory' to enter sighted monuments. He also developed his own techniques for reliably transforming aerial photographs into maps of known scale. Only thus did later ground work become possible. In order to measure newly discovered features in an uncharted terrain that lacked fixed geodetic points, he made use of an accompanying plane. On the ground that plane, whose dimensions were of course known, provided a convenient scale for the entire photographed scene. Thus, in order to establish the width of a hidden road detected from the air, Poidebard made the plane land on the approximate area. The superimposed wingspan then gave a reliable reading.

Ideally, he once said, one should be able to pilot, survey, draw, take notes, and photograph all by oneself. But, since such acrobatics are next to impossible, the sensible compromise is to find the right aviator, who has made a speciality of the region and is not only an old hand at flying planes, but above all should be as passionately involved with antiquity as his passenger. Poidebard considered himself particularly fortunate to have found several such men among the French air force pilots. To read his many memoirs, articles, and books is to be constantly reminded of his admiration and affection for the men who steered him so expertly over the ancient landscapes of the Near East, penetrating without hesitation into rebel-held territories, coming down on rugged, unexplored terrain without the benefit of landing strips, and frequently adding to the growing body of information through their intimate knowledge of local topography. One eulogy he wrote in 1929 to a pilot killed in an accident movingly evoked – long before the poetry of flight became a literary fashion – the beauty and comradeship of flying in the 'lumière éblouissante du désert'.

In the fall of 1926, fresh from his frustrations on land, he selected an area in the upper Euphrates basin, south of the old fortified town of Nissibin, where according to ancient texts the Romans maintained military stations along the road. Here Poidebard took his first photographs. Previous visits on foot had been fruitless, but now he found from above several Byzantine military camps, their walls finely drawn on the photographs recorded at an altitude of three thousand feet. A year later, flying over the same sites, he was rewarded with the discovery of the fortifications of Tell Brak and its castellum. The flight was made a few hours after the first autumn rainfall. To Poidebard's delight, arabesques of lighter vegetation in the corners of what looked like an amorphous soil terrace announced with unmistakable precision the towers of the castellum. All was buried under a cover of sand, one yard deep, as Poidebard proved by excavations he undertook soon after. Here, too, while standing on the ground, no one could have suspected anything without being guided by photographic evidence.

Further discoveries far too numerous to recite followed in quick succession. Already in 1927 Poidebard eyed, in addition to the Mesopotamian outposts of northern Syria, other areas vital to the total picture of Roman infiltration. A special flight in May 1927 concentrated on the basalt mountains east of Damascus. There, at the edge of a volcanic crater, he found the point where the all-important Via Diocletiana took off toward Palmyra. More flights later in the year yielded details on the construction of this military road, its extension, and all its watchtowers. In 1928 another mission to the north country along the Khabour brought back the complete plan of the ruined Byzantine city of Thannourin, a feat which had eluded all earlier visitors. Just on the right bank of the river Poidebard identified a massive watchtower, known from descriptions by the sixth-century historian Procopius, but lost until then.

Roman and Byzantine landmarks remained the chief targets of all these explorations, whose goal had been defined by the Académie des Inscriptions, the sponsor of all his campaigns, as the retracing of Roman antiquities in this part of the Eastern world. Nevertheless, Poidebard was receptive to the imprints of other peoples. He was keenly aware of the presence and precedence of Hittites and Assyrians, whose foundations Roman town builders and military engineers had often simply incorporated in their plans. A feeling for the antiquity of some of the roads was driven home to him when, during ground exploration, he encountered chipped flint tools of the Stone Age.

Checking the course of roads on terra firma was beset with considerable hazards. Sinking trenches was laborious and wasteful. But where the sand-covered surface refused to disclose any trace to the earthbound examiner, one measure proved phenomenally rewarding; all one had to do was to drive a train of camels over the vicinity, and the desert beasts would file along the hidden road-bed. Such uncanny cameloid proclivities Poidebard had found corroborated in a passage from the Roman writer Vegetius, who observed that these animals seemed to have a natural instinct for following in the steps of their long-departed kin.

Roads as the lifelines of military invasion and consolidation had been from the beginning the leitmotif of Poidebard's researches. Gradually, however, his work assumed a larger and more ambitious theme, which can be summarized under the Roman term *limes*. Now, the word *limes* itself has a variety of meanings, which happen to reflect to perfection the growth and scope of Poidebard's studies of the Roman positions in the Syrian desert. Originally a limes designated just the route of a Roman army into a conquered land. By and by, due to the exigencies of conquest, such a road assumed the character of a fortified line along the enemy borders. It was not yet conceived as the border itself, nor was it static by nature. In fact, the lands claimed by Roman conquest during the Republic knew no fixed boundaries and, if one may say so, frowned upon the Maginot Line mentality. Only with Augustus, during the Empire, do frontiers gradually turn from bases of offensive war into strong and lasting positions of defence against the threat of barbarian incursions. Even then it is only in certain parts that a linear barrier comes to be erected, such as Hadrian's Wall or the Antonine Wall in northern Britain and similar continuous embankments in West Germany and the Dobrudja. However, a limes in its final development, as exemplified in the Syrian desert, is a broad belt of defence in considerable *depth*. According to the nature of the territory and the civil and military needs, it will differ in width and the number of forts, signal stations, camps, strategic roads, and like structures, as well as the quantity of troops that patrol it and the distances within which garrisons are stationed from each other. Naturally, where frontiers coincide with formidable physical barriers, only the flimsiest limes was required, if any.

What Poidebard resurrected was a broad zone of defence adjusted through the centuries to the military challenges and political fortunes of the Roman province in Asia. While he first concentrated on the roads, a realization grew in him of the extent and intricacy of this system. The formidable length of it, in excess of six hundred miles, was indicated by the principal line that ran from Bostra to Damascus, then turned farther inland to Palmyra and beyond northward to Soura at the bank of the Euphrates, which it followed downstream to Circesium, only to make another northern and then eastern turn toward the Tigris near modern Mosul. Parallel and perpendicular roads, which Poidebard traced indefatigably, showed how the enormous territory was penetrated by a network of additional fortifications. In places routes extended out into the enemy territory like antennae reporting to a central nerve centre. Indeed, the whole fabric could be likened to a giant epidermis of protective layers of skin and subcutaneous tissue, supplied by a profusion of nerves, muscles, and arteries. Like a skin it had the ability to withstand shocks. It was also endowed with plasticity and healing power.

Poidebard's supreme accomplishment was to track down this entire system in all its ramifications. The masterful map he drew made a terra incognita, as has been said by Sir George Macdonald, 'as clear as noon day', besides furnishing a conclusive example of the extraordinary ability of Roman planners and builders. The complete outline of the network contributed numerous new sites, many still awaiting the spade. The historical and military information to be culled from it was of the first order. At last it became possible to form a concept of the impact of the desert on the European conquerors, and how Roman engineers deliberately dealt with the threats from powerful Persian horsemen and the almost as irritating incursions of undisciplined Bedouin tribesmen.

The general course of the limes, straddling rugged mountainous terrain where cavalry is hopelessly handicapped, left no doubt as to the wisdom of its designers. Their foresight stood out also in the fact that the limes invariably followed the zone of relatively high rainfall in the extremely arid Syrian desert. That this was due to conscious planning Poidebard could prove by the vegetation pattern on aerial photographs. It was likewise borne out by meteorological charts, on which the isohyetal line trails quite closely the Roman defence zone. Occupation of the more humid region gave the Romans a particularly effective control over the Bedouins, who could thus be cut off from vital grazing grounds unless they submitted to the conqueror. In all likelihood the Roman frontier administration was able to draw Bedouins increasingly into its orbit. Contingents of desert people may have been recruited as auxiliaries; Poidebard had good reason to believe that they were. One of his air photographs of a focal section of the limes showed a quite unusual corral-like enclosure, which looked like no other Roman compound and could never have been built as quarters for Roman regulars. Chances are that it was laid out to accommodate Bedouin clients and their herds.

To give a rounded picture of the complex defence system, one would not only have to describe the layout of forts and camps, of ramparts, of observation and signal posts, and the way in which they were arranged in relation to each other – all lucidly depicted on Poidebard's photographs – one should at least make mention of the sagacious effort that went into providing adequate sources of water to maintain the great number of troops stationed at the border. Poidebard lovingly described the various springs, tanks, underground canals, storage basins, and aqueducts that proliferated. In the northern tier he discovered a number of impressive barrages and reservoirs, feeding large-scale irrigation works.

Roads, too, of course show the skill with which the Romans built. Like the Incas, they freely changed their manner of construction according to the demands of the terrain. Some are properly paved; others, traversing firm and arid areas, needed no more costly material than kerbstones to mark their course.

After completing his exploration of the limes along the eastern boundary of Syria, in 1934 Poidebard took up another project: the investigation by air and on the ground of the Roman organization of the steppelands adjoining it to the west, roughly within the corridor between the Orontes and Euphrates rivers, from Antioch in the north-west to Palmyra in the south-east. It occupied him until 1942. The results – published as *Le Limes de Chalcis* in 1945 – were comparable to the earlier campaign, easily as productive in the yield of data on the administration of the Roman province, and even richer in the epigraphic harvest (which was handled by another Jesuit and long-time associate, René Mouterde), though perhaps not as crucial to the understanding of the fabric and rationale of the Roman frontier.

Altogether Poidebard spent on the two projects some 550 hours in the air during 250 missions. The number of monuments he discovered, from cisterns to citadels, runs into the hundreds. The roads he tracked down must be measured in the thousands of miles. His labours over the Syrian border zone added a profusion of physical detail celebrating the Roman technical and administrative genius which built for centuries. The sequence started with the arrival of Pompey, who made Syria a Roman province in 64 B.C. With minor adjustments, the limes as it had come fully into existence under Diocletian was to last through the Byzantine epoch until the advent of the Arabs in the seventh century. Only then did it fall into decay and come to be blanketed by a layer of sand.

From Poidebard's recoveries of the defence system a whole cycle of history could be reconstructed. The limes was evidently a product of accretion and development reflecting consecutive phases of military advance and withdrawal to stronger positions. To discerning students like Poidebard and scholars interpreting his finds, it illustrated among other things the expansionist policies of Trajan, and the wise containment of his successor, Hadrian; the misfortune of the remarkable queen of Palmyra, Zenobia, and the triumph of her Roman vanquisher, Aurelian; the forceful reorganization under Diocletian, and the misguided campaigns of the apostate Julian, who lost his life in the borderlands. Style of buildings, sometimes just the characteristic shape of the corners of forts, would betray their age or builder. Above all, it was datable roads that marked systole and diastole of a great imperial adventure. Did not the tangle of successive defence lines he had traced here on the outer edge of the Roman territories resemble the streaks of seaweeds washed on ocean beaches by the lapping tides, Father Poidebard mused? Such is the course and vanity of empire.

The flying Jesuit priest's archaeological career did comprise much more than his discovery of the Roman limes in Syria. When he turned away from the desert and concentrated his attention on the lost Roman and Phoenician harbours of Tyre and Sidon, he became the pioneer of an added dimension of aerial archaeology: the photographic examination from high above of lost underwater ruins. With it he inaugurated a new genre of archaeological investigation, which was to be equally proficient on land, at sea, and in the air.

As to Poidebard's consummate study of the Roman border, it showed what aviation could accomplish in the arid stamping grounds of the ancient civilizations of the Near East. The object lesson was not lost on other explorers.

Persia, where Poidebard had first awakened to the effectiveness of aerial overviews, was chosen for one of the most ambitious airborne projects of the inter-war years. Sponsored by the Oriental Institute of the University of Chicago, the 1935 to 1937 campaign was executed by Erich F. Schmidt, a German-born Orientalist who had made his archaeological début with stratigraphic studies in Arizona. Schmidt was, of course, aware of the suitability of the predominantly arid terrain for air reconnaissance, and, not unexpectedly, his forays into all parts of the ancient country, accompanied by frequent landing and ground-checking, bore ample results. Near the Caspian Sea he traced southward a frontier wall (with adjacent forts) of about one hundred miles, the so-called Alexander's Barrier (*Saddi-i-Sikandar*). Though its ascription to the Macedonian conqueror is tenuous at best, it was probably built at an uncertain date to protect Persia from invasions by Central Asia nomads. In addition, Schmidt discovered several enormous sand-covered cities, among them the circular metropolis of Gur on the south-western Iranian plateau, which measured one mile in diameter. On one sortie to the environs of Persepolis, the ancient capital of Darius and Xerxes, during some thirteen hours in the air, he tracked down no less than four hundred ruined sites.

For his time, Schmidt's undertaking was lavishly equipped. The plane and all the apparatus had been specially purchased for the expedition. Nevertheless, he was not as well prepared as he might have been. Upon his own admission, it had simply not crossed his mind that 'aerial operations, in spite of idealistic purposes, have delicate aspects, especially in the troubled countries of the Old World'. Suspicious and slow-moving Persian authorities kept him on tenterhooks. When at last he was given clearance, he had to agree to hand over his plane before leaving the country. A further handicap arose from his own initial lack of understanding of the nature of crop- and vegetation-marks. In fact, one of his vertical photographs of Istakhr near Persepolis, taken in the spring of 1936, was judged to be hopelessly muddled by him and his colleagues of the University of Chicago. Luckily, before casting the picture aside they noted that growth patterns seemed to disclose much of the buried city's layout. The sudden insight came more as a shock than a joyful discovery; it meant that the very location over which a ground party of archaeologists, architects, and surveyors from the Oriental Institute had toiled for eighteen months to complete their costly mapping was now etched in a few snapshots, and with a far greater wealth of features and unexcelled precision!

Similar lessons could be learned from various sporadic efforts in the ancient lands of the Near East where aerial archaeology had taken its start during the Great War. RAF and airmail pilots stationed in the area captured a detailed record of the puzzling web of stone walls, terraces, and hut circles in Jordan and Syria, which had vaguely been known as the 'Works of the Old Men'. Insall, the discoverer of Woodhenge, improved upon Beazeley's pioneering exploration of Samarra with just a pocket camera. Also near Baghdad, across the Tigris from Ctesiphon, he discovered in a dark line of vegetation another former capital, Seleucia, which had been founded around 300 B.C. and which yielded the first complete plan of a Macedonian town. Interestingly, it had been laid out in exact squares with streets intersecting at right angles, like the later Roman cities.

On his visit to the Middle East in 1928-9 Crawford was flown by Insall over Seleucia. He was equally thrilled when shown the site of Hatra, a vast abandoned Parthian centre in the north. Hatra had flourished at the time of Christ; two Roman emperors, Trajan and Severus, had unsuccessfully tried to take it. Thanks to its remoteness it was unusually well preserved. Not surprisingly, it had been repeatedly explored since the 1830s. In 1908 it was assiduously investigated by a top-notch team under Dr Walter Andrae of the Deutsche Orient Gesellschaft. Andrae's detailed ground plan was long considered the *ne plus ultra* in archaeological surveys. He had spent many weeks making it as complete and accurate as possible. Yet Crawford needed only a few glances from the air to realize that there were many blanks on Andrae's map. A whole set of Roman camps, siege walls, and assault works had been missed. 'My own visit', wrote Crawford, 'was a matter of hours only; we left Mosul after breakfast and were back again in time for lunch. We had time to land and inspect the ruins pretty thoroughly, but before we landed, Squadron-Leader Morgan took a fine mosaic from which it is evident that Dr Andrae's gaps are filled in. It took about five minutes to get this mosaic.'

Another archaeologist to explore Hatra by air some years (1938-9) after Insall and Crawford and to add further details on its Roman sieges was Sir Aurel Stein, the twentieth-century Marco Polo who made fairy-tale discoveries in Central Asia.

Stein embarked before the Second World War on airborne missions in Mesopotamia and in the Jordanian territory which adjoined and continued the Syrian limes in the south toward Aqaba. In the course, he completed the survey of the Roman Near Eastern defence system which reached *a finibus Syriae ad Mare Rubrum* (from the far ends of Syria to the Red Sea). However, because of Stein's death in 1943, his researches have unfortunately remained largely unpublished.

Poidebard himself realized that his methods could be applied with profit to comparable conditions in the former North African provinces of Rome. Upon the invitation of the Director of Antiquities of Algeria, Louis Leschi, he undertook several flights in 1937, but his duties in Lebanon kept him from carrying out the thorough research programme that was needed. In 1939, despite his advanced years, he was once again called to the colours and henceforth served in the cartographic section attached to the French High Command.

A major contribution toward the reconstruction of the Roman limes in North Africa 'from Morocco to Tunis', as Poidebard had already envisaged, was wrought by a French colonel, Jean Baradez. His work in sôuthern Algeria was paralleled by the aerial reconnaissance of R. G. Goodchild and other British scholars in Tripolitania and Cyrenaica (Libya), and by Charles Saumagne in Tunisia. These men were to turn their attention also to Roman civil districts in North Africa, notably to the all-pervading residual marks of the chequerboard Roman land division (centuriation).

With Baradez we enter a new era. Not only were his main studies carried out after the Second World War, but all his researches were made under the aegis – and under largesse – of a government department. Furthermore, his starting point was an already existent continuous series of high-altitude vertical photographs, some 120 prints taken from a height of about twelve thousand feet. The pictures had been taken a few years before with modern precision equipment unavailable to earlier pioneers. The initiative to use them for archaeological purposes was entirely his own. It had not occurred to anyone before that these long-range photographs of unusual detail and clarity

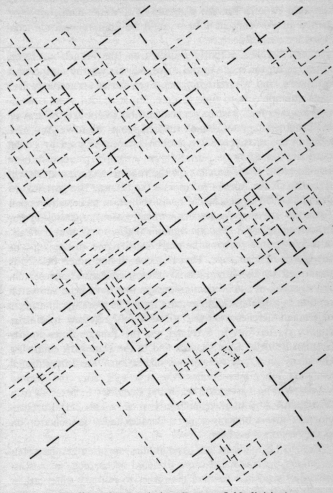

Figure 15. Outline of centuriation (Roman field division) pattern in Tunisia based on stereoscopic examination of air photographs

– made in the course of a survey of the El Kantara district in southern Algeria for the planning of a water dam, but now buried in government files – could be comprehensively analysed for ancient features.

When Baradez, recently retired from the French air force, appeared on the scene in the 1940s, Algeria was by no means a no man's land to archaeologists. Even aerial archaeology had been attempted from time to time. But it needed some convincing on Baradez's part to persuade others of the fruitfulness of his proposed method, which differed from the low-flying missions in the relatively slow, mobile two-seaters used by Poidebard and his followers. However, his amazing results won over Louis Leschi. It set Baradez on the road to restoring an extensive area of the Roman frontier in the Sahara. The feat was to prompt Leschi to declare, in his introduction to Baradez's book *Fossatum Africae: recherches aériennes sur l'organisation des confins sahariens à l'époque romaine* (Paris, 1949), that it meant 'a turning point, perhaps the most decisive one, in the study of the North African past'. That it accomplished much besides is confirmed by the international interest in Baradez's research, not to speak of the academic honours that have been showered on him in England, Germany, and Italy. His work on all aspects of Roman defence was felt to be highly relevant to similar studies carried out in Scotland, on the Roman limes in the German Rhineland, in Rhaetia, and in the Danubian countries. For many years, at the various meetings of the International Congress for Limes Studies (the first met after the Second World War in Newcastle on Tyne) Baradez's lectures were a high point. And in metropolitan France, where aerial archaeology is now a thriving science, Baradez today is looked upon as the Nestor of his field.

Though he relied in his basic studies on photographs taken by others, Jean Baradez came to aerial archaeology as a seasoned flier who had devoted his career to military observation. It was precisely his specialized skill in detecting enemy installations and all kinds of ingenious camouflage that had prepared him for squeezing so many hidden data of antiquity from existing prints. He now applied to archaeological reconnaissance the same meticulous technique of scrutinizing photographs inch by inch, nay square millimetre by square millimetre, for 'suspicious' evidence. An infallible eye for the ruses of the enemy could be as successfully trained on the intricate fortifications of the Romans and the military thinking that went into them. Baradez once again proved to perfection the close affinities that have prevailed between the military and the pursuit of the past from the air. His ventures in Roman Africa profited immeasurably from wartime experience in sound planning, disciplined meticulous method, topographic know-how, and interpretative skill of a high order, as well as an intuitive grasp of the intentions of friend or foe.

Baradez's original interest was civil engineering, particularly hydraulics and forestry. Like Crawford and Poidebard he saw Service in the First World War, but it took him almost thirty years and another war to find his way to archaeology. His military career had started with the French mountain brigade. Seriously injured and almost paralysed, he was laid up for a year and a half. No longer fit for the infantry, he applied for training as pilot, but ended up as observer in captive balloons. After the war, he at last won his wings in the French air force. Commissioned by the Air Ministry to deliver a plane to the newly crowned Haile Selassie of Ethiopia, he flew in 1929 across the ancient lands of the Mediterranean and Near East. The flight over regions saturated with the past filled him with a sense of bygone civilizations and an understanding of historical geography, and resulted in a travel book, *En survolant cinquante siècles d'histoire*. On another airborne mission, he happened to spot unknown prehistoric fortifications in Portugal. After being in command of French air reconnaissance over the German Siegfried Line, Baradez, from 1940 on, lived in semi-retirement in Algeria. With the same eagerness that he had turned to military aviation in his youth, he was now ready to enter his new calling, in many ways a continuation of the old.

On the aerial photographs which Baradez had come to study, one feature commanded his particular attention. This, he thought, was the long-sought *fossatum* (the term stood for a Roman system of ditches). That such a major defensive work existed along the southern gate of the Roman province of

Nubia, with which modern Algeria is roughly co-extensive, was almost certain from references in the fifth-century *Codex Theodosianus*. An air of almost complete mystery ruled as to the nature, location, and length of the ditch, however, despite the lengthy debate the antiquarians had waged over it. There was, for instance, one long trench south of Biskra, labelled a *seguia* (water canal) by the local people. It was widely believed to be part of an abandoned irrigation system of the Sahara district. Folklore had even connected it with the building schemes of a legendary queen. However, early in the century a prominent French archaeologist, Stéphane Gsell, established it as a Roman installation. According to his view the border ditch represented the limes itself. While this opinion was shared by the majority of archaeologists, it was at variance with the *Codex Theodosianus*, which distinguished between limes and fossatum.

What, then, was the fossatum and, for that matter, what was the North African limes? Was perhaps the Theodosian reference ambiguous – were they really one? It fell upon Baradez to solve the dilemma. Besides tracing the fossatum for its entire length of nearly five hundred miles, with minor gaps, he was also to elucidate its function. The fossatum, in turn, led to a thorough investigation of the limes proper and, in fact, amounted to the archaeological exploration of a wide belt of Saharan Algeria, and points beyond, of which very little notice had previously been taken.

We said that Baradez's closely paralleled and corroborated Father Poidebard's findings. Despite his different approach, his discoveries were certainly on the same vast scale and dealt with comparable material, though the Saharan desert, with its tornadoes and climatic extremes, had been more destructive than the semi-arid steppes of Syria, clad as they were with a protective shroud of sand. Also, few scholars had thought that North Africa ever had, or even needed, a limes of the Syrian dimension. No formidable organized armies, like those of the people descending from the Iranian plateau, had threatened its borders; hence the prevalent tendency to identify the limes with a linear earthwork like the fossatum. Unexpectedly, however, Baradez marshalled data to prove that the Roman limes in

North Africa was also of great depth. It too simply bristled with a galaxy of forts, camps, ramparts, and so on. Most of these were first pinpointed by Baradez. Their location and distribution offered him clues to overall Roman defence plans. Here were the same antennae roads probing into nomad territory; the calculated design to cut the transhumance of the pastoral Barbarians and thereby check their movements; above all, the conscious care with which all communication and strongholds were adapted to the nature and strategic requirements of the terrain. Physical obstacles like cliffs and saltlakes were incorporated into defence lines. Wherever possible, ditches, just like walls and roads, were detoured to escape undue attention by the approaching enemy. Signal stations were so placed that they could easily receive and transmit messages.

How circumspectly Roman engineers selected sites for their military outposts was driven home to Baradez on one flight, when he searched for a section of the fossatum. His plane had been caught in a sand storm. As the air began to clear he suddenly saw an unmistakable ditch neatly cutting through the surface. On further examination, however, it did not turn out to be Roman at all; it was a tank trap built by Rommel during the last war. It happened to almost overlap with an ancient defence work. Even a German bunker was lodged on a Roman installation. He had noticed a comparable phenomenon in the beginning of the Second World War over the Rhineland, where a *Blockhaus* of the Siegfried Line was erected smack above the fortifications built by Vauban, Louis XIV's great military engineer. Weapons may change, but the topographic factors determining warfare remain much the same.

After a thorough analysis of the series of high-altitude photographs, Baradez proceeded to investigate on his own by air, on foot, astride a mule, and riding in an old Ford (which he found better adapted to the terrain than a Jeep). To verify previously established evidence and add new material, Baradez now engaged in low-flying missions in a Piper Cub. On more extensive forays he flew a Marauder that had braved the war as a bomber plane.

Baradez's landbound explorations faced the usual problems

of trying to locate the features that had stood out so prominently from above. At the beginning of his involvement with limes and fossatum, when he scrutinized aerial photographs, he was more than surprised that nobody else had made these discoveries before on the ground. But now on his follow-up he had to report that more than once he was to walk across the fossatum without noticing any disturbance whatever. Only with infinite care and with his aerial photographs as constant guide would he eventually succeed. Thus, in the course of repeated air and ground reconnaissance he was able to gradually piece the whole mosaic of limes and fossatum together.

Apart from vital roads and various forts and towers, his discoveries included lost cities like Gemellae, which he was to excavate himself. A by-product of these land operations was a rich epigraphic harvest in stone-engraved texts. A whole bonanza of milestones, first spotted from the air at regular intervals, not only helped to trace an important link of communication, but through their respective dedications to third- and fourth-century emperors, were a reminder of the watchful eye kept by colonial administrators on these arteries. The names, from Heliogabalus and Alexander Severus (both Orientals by birth) to Gordian and Diocletian, and then on to Constantine and Gratian, added up to a veritable 'king list' and were a valuable chronological document. One inscription at Gemellae runs for several lines across a stone block of three metres. It bears a dedication to the great emperor Hadrian, whose omnipresence is so poignantly felt in what was the gigatic defence zone that girded the empire from the Sahara to Scotland, and from the Euphrates to the Rhine.

Hadrian is also evoked by the fossatum. It is more than likely that the system of ditches was initiated by him. Certainly by deliberate design rather than coincidence it closely resembles in its make-up and dimensions – slanted walls with a narrower flat bottom – the so-called *vallum* of Hadrian's Wall in Britain. Like the latter it comprised an adjoining rampart raised from dry rubble.

It is in the grandiose defensive plans of Hadrian and his successors that one can sense the demiurgic intelligence that for centuries unified the Western World. Was it not ecumenical justice that a millennium and a half after Rome's 'fall' men from the fragmented lands that had become heirs to Latin civilization joined with each other to resuscitate its frontiers? In this effort aerial archaeologists played a leading part. The evidence of Rome had been from the beginning one of their chief pursuits. Crawford, who was much absorbed in Roman Scotland, had tirelessly campaigned among his British and foreign colleagues for the compilation of an international map of the Roman Empire. The project had been stalled by the Second World War. But with the stepped-up vigour of airborne studies after the war it was approaching fulfilment.

To return to the fossatum, what were Baradez's own conclusions about it? Certainly fossatum and limes were not the same thing. Aerial investigations in search of the former had revealed the latter in all its complexity and depth. The fossatum, in turn, rather than marking the actual border between Barbarian and Roman territories, was way behind the advance zone. Instead of a first line of defence, as had generally been believed, it appeared to be the final barrier that the enemy had to negotiate once he had penetrated through the array of

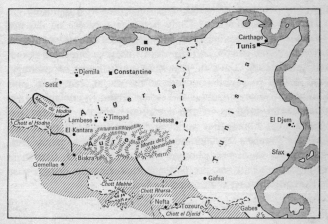

Figure 16. The Roman frontier in northern Africa with its broad *limes* (hachures) and principal sections of *fossatum* (black lines) traced from the air by Colonel Baradez

frontier forts and had overrun all mobile units. If anything, then, the fossatum literally represented a last ditch of the entire limes system.

Baradez's studies made vividly clear that the fossatum had to be seen in relation to Rome's great colonization scheme in North Africa. Behind it stretched a large agricultural region rendered fertile by a water-supply scheme, now unfortunately defunct, that in many respects is as impressive an enterprise of Roman engineering as the limes itself. The peasant-soldiers (*limitanei*) settled in the area were an essential part of the defence organization. Never very far from the fossatum, in case of emergency they could quickly take their positions along it.

Much of the importance of Baradez's aerial survey rests with his contributions to the archaeology of agriculture, a subject close to him as a former student at the French Institut National Agronomique. Where there is today Saharan wasteland, Baradez could show that the Romans maintained hundreds of thousands of acres of cultivated land, irrigated by immense hydraulic works. Though the climate was then as dry as today, Romans truly made the desert bloom. Cereals and olives were the principal crops, of which large quantities were exported.

Here, in the middle of sandy barrenness, where he did not encounter a single inhabitant, Baradez traced countless villages, terraces, walls, canals, and even olive presses, threshing floors, and grindstones. Data of this kind, agricultural or military, were bound to revise concepts of the social, economic, and administrative organization of Roman Africa. In concluding his monumental inquiry in the *Fossatum Africae*, Baradez expressed high hopes that aerial archaeology would point the way for France's 'civilizational' mission in these parts. But, alas, events in Algeria showed that archaeologists, like their brothers the historians, are better at capturing the distant past than in anticipating the immediate future.

6. Italia Aeterna

The Tavoliere of northern Apulia is a large treeless region that lies in south-eastern Italy along the Adriatic coast, between the Fortore and Ofanto rivers. The city of Foggia is in its centre. Roughly sixty miles long and thirty miles wide, the predominantly flat lowland backed by the foothills of the Apennines is the largest plain of the peninsula south of the Po Valley. Here and there a few gentle hillocks, called *coppe*, break the monotonous prairie, which by its climate and starkness has reminded more than one visitor of North Africa. Long dry summers parch the land. The average annual rainfall in Foggia amounts to about the same as that of Tunis – barely eighteen to nineteen inches – and only half that of Rome. Crops have to be harvested by the end of May or early June, before the ground turns into a dust-laden, maroon crust. Yet the Tavoliere is quite fertile. Extensive grasslands and unbroken fields of wheat thrive in spring without the benefits of irrigation. Another renewal comes in September when deep-rooted weeds and wild flowers bloom in intense shades of red, white, blue, and yellow.

Before twentieth-century agriculture returned large parts of it to farming, the Tavoliere, like the rest of Apulia, enjoyed a dubious reputation as one of the least productive and progressive territories of the country. Historians and economists had long thought of it as an undistinguished segment of Italy's underdeveloped, malarial Mezzogiorno (south). That in a land so rich in the vestiges of antiquity as Italy it would have anything novel to offer to students of the past had never been contemplated. Who, indeed, would have thought that the dun surroundings of Foggia were to be revealed one day as a whole sequence of buried landscapes unique in all of Europe for their kaleidoscopic facets and their depth in time? Nevertheless, here 'at the heart of the Mediterranean world' a series of finds reflecting some four thousand years of the human record confronted scholars with the very roots of European civilization. In sheer quantity of sites the Tavoliere ranks (archaeologically) as one of the most crowded regions on the continent. Its underground, frequently intermingling traces were to be deciphered as keys to the evolution of the European peasantry from the Neolithic to the Middle Ages. In importance the newly discovered features by far transcended their local relevance.

How did ancient Apulia come into its own? Once again it started with a war.

Towards the end of the Second World War two British army officers serving with RAF photographic intelligence were stationed in Apulia, where the Allies maintained large airfields. The two men, John S. P. Bradford and Peter Williams-Hunt, had in the course of their military duties gained an intimate knowledge of the topography of the area. Both of them had actively entered archaeology shortly before the war: Williams-Hunt by digging in Berkshire, while near by, also in the Thames Valley, Oxford-trained Bradford excavated an Iron Age site at a gravel pit at Dorchester owned by Major G. W. G. Allen and his brother. Bradford and Williams-Hunt were thoroughly familiar with the achievements of British aerial archaeology. In fact, while fellow officers in the same unit they had for years discussed the possibility of applying abroad 'the principles demonstrated in England by O. G. S. Crawford, G. W. G. Allen, and others'. Though Apulia betrayed no ancient surface features to speak of, they were confident that the Foggia plain would make a rewarding objective for aerial archaeology. They were itching for a chance to test their hypothesis as soon as the end of hostilities would permit them to initiate photographic operations.

They had good reasons for their high expectations. Northern Apulia is covered by quite a thin layer of soil which rests in the main on a rocky substratum resembling porous limestone. Under such conditions, comparable to those in southern England, crop- or vegetation-marks were liable to show up distinctly wherever the ground had been disturbed. Hence, any artificial deepening of the soil by adding more moisture and nourishment to plants over silted-up pits or moats will produce striking differentials in height, colour, and relative luxuriance. Given the acrid climate of the region, contrasts will be much enhanced with the onset of the dry season, when the better supplied vegetation retains its verdure longer and ripens later. A further boon to the registration of underground features in coherent outlines could be expected from the fact that agriculture is carried on here in vast open, unhedged fields, which remain for miles on end under the same crop. Few territories in Europe are as favoured in this respect. While Lombardy, the banks of the Danube, the Rhine Valley, certain areas in the Balkans, and elsewhere may once have been as rich in prehistoric settlements, most have been so split up through the centuries by strip-farming, fencing-in, breaking-up of estates into small landholdings, and crop rotation that it has become nearly impossible to pick up intelligible marks of any magnitude or continuity, not to speak of a whole distribution pattern describing a cluster of sites.

Apart from the uniformity of its present-day cultivation, the Tavoliere counted still another blessing for prospective aerial surveying – large parts of it had long been retained as grasslands, and some had not been put under the plough since Roman times. When the Roman farming system fell into disuse it was not incorporated into or modified by other forms of agriculture, as happened, for instance, in the Po Valley. Nor was it supplanted for centuries to come. Owing to these circumstances, Apulia has remained the only area known in Europe where Roman centuriation has been largely left untampered with since it was abandoned in the early Dark Ages. Nowhere else in Italy can specific details – farm enclosures, field boundaries, walls, ditches, farmyards, and villas laid out along planned roads – be pinned down with comparable completeness. Here a genuine and accurate Roman landscape is fully preserved. It was a unique opportunity to study the life of Roman farmers just as it was portrayed by Virgil in his *Georgics*. Since the Roman Republic planted some of its first colonies in Apulia, the gain for the history of the Romanization of the peninsula is particularly valuable. On the basis of Bradford's aerial survey it is now possible to trace the intricate land divisions with their network of roads staked out around Lucera (Luceria), which was founded as a *colonia* in 314 B.C. The same can be done for four other Roman towns. Grass- and crop-marks were to yield such minutiae as the actual layout of vineyards and orchards, for which beds were cut, row for row, into the rock. At times, individual tree pits appear as distinct patches in the vegetation, while one can compute the exact number of grapevines planted in a given area. Thanks to Apulian centuriated sites, passages in the writings of Roman surveyors and agronomists are now at last extensively illumined by all the physical evidence one could wish for. And yet until two English officers came to Apulia in the Second World War nothing of all this had even been suspected.

Long-awaited opportunity came to Bradford and Williams-Hunt with the armistice in Europe in May 1945. They had to act fast. Planes and equipment needed for their prospective campaign, though at the moment militarily inactivated, would soon be moved to other theatres. Time was also pressing on account of the advanced season in Apulia, which was getting close to harvest and the virtual obliteration of all potential crop-marks. Then there was the danger that the two young officers might be transferred before the cherished project could be launched. Despite such apprehensions, their luck held – at least for a while. Military authorities proved to be most responsive and agreed to lend a hand at every point.

In the four weeks they had at their disposal, both verticals and obliques were taken. The former alone were to amount to several thousand. The RAF subtly justified the vertical missions as 'training flights'; while Bradford and Williams-Hunt produced obliques on their own during 'routine camera tests'. The two types of picture complemented each other to perfection.

For verticals, the RAF used a twenty-inch air camera, which was operated automatically. Two parallel continuous strips were made with overlap for stereoscopic inspection, a system that had become standard for aerial mapping. An altitude of ten thousand feet, which gave a scale of 1:6,000 (or about ten inches to one mile), was found to offer sufficient scope for detailed work. Viewed under a stereoscope, a complex site appeared in life-like relief, and the scale of the prints was considerably increased. Bradford observed that certain crop-marks were so clear that they could still be picked up from as high as five miles, even though their size was no longer satisfactory for minute analysis. Verticals proved their worth by bringing coverage to areas not included in obliques, thereby extending the record of crop-marks nearly tenfold. Equally important, by means of a micrometer scale and photogrammetric tables, sighted features could be measured – and not only large settlements of hundreds of yards but even objects no wider than a few feet! Invariably, when later inspecting a site on the ground, Bradford was gratified to learn how close his calculations from vertical photographs came to the actual dimensions. He could then announce that

in every case where excavation was carried out the expected ditches, wells, etc. appeared clearly with the first trench to be dug. Even when, as at Masseria Vilana, the land had been recently ploughed and there was not the slightest hint on the surface of the twenty-foot-wide Neolithic enclosure-ditch beneath, its position was located in a few minutes by measurements taken from the photographs, which gave its distance from two minor modern boundaries; and the first trench revealed it. This would be equally true of comparable Roman and medieval sites. *If* the photographs are taken and used with precision, we can now say that air photography sites of all the main types are thoroughly reliable for archaeology on Italian soil. The establishment, in Apulia, of this important fact was one more proof that the basic principles of discovery from the air, worked out by O. G. S. Crawford, have a world-wide application under appropriate conditions.

Vertical photographs henceforth also furnished Bradford with a basis for archaeological plans, to which marks were transferred before the difficult task of locating them on the 'featureless' ground was attempted. The largest printed maps then obtainable were of little use because of their scale of 1 : 25,000 (about two and one half inches to one mile). Besides, they were outdated and inaccurate.

Bradford and Williams-Hunt chose a light Fairchild monoplane for their own reconnaissance. That aircraft recommended itself because of its high wing, which would not interfere with their vision. Being manoeuvrable and not too speedy, it also provided room for an observer, in addition to pilot and photographer, who could chart positions of photographed sites on a map.

On their first flights, the two British officers flew about 3,000 feet over most of the Tavoliere without taking pictures. What was needed at this point, of course, was to establish the presence, nature, and frequency of subsurface antiquities. Once they had gained encouraging information and familiarity, they proceeded to take oblique photographs of prominent cropmarks. As to technique, Bradford states that it was basically the same as that employed by Major Allen, using a hand-held eight-inch focal length camera with wide-angled lens while flying at 1,000 to 1,500 feet, except that they used roll-film instead of plates. After the general survey by vertical photographs, which followed the obliques, was completed, further oblique operations were indicated for a follow-up on auspicious sites that had turned up in the verticals.

Whether obliques or verticals, the findings were extraordinary. All high expectations were justified. The Tavoliere was indeed ideally suited for showing up buried sites in its vegetation – right away it appeared that a succession of different epochs had left their mark. The physical factors making for such surprising effects could hardly be bettered. Bradford recalled that

when flying over one particularly good example for the first time, I almost believed for a moment that the outline of ditches and enclosures which I could see below must be due to modern agriculture. When I excavated there, some years later, these proved to belong to the Neolithic period – before 2000 B.C. In other words, we had found one of the settlements of the first farming communities in Italy.

This quotation anticipates the concrete results of Bradford and Williams-Hunt's prehistoric explorations, of which we will soon have more to say. But, by implication, it highlights that northern Apulia was predestined for aerial archaeology by its natural endowments as much as by human associations. Just as in Wiltshire – of which it constantly reminded Bradford – it is

the combination of the two that has made it such an outstanding example of the conjuring trick of the airborne
camera. Neither is enough by itself; otherwise the South
American grasslands, or areas as thick with history as the
Campania or Attica, would have contributed at least as spectacular testimonies to aerial inquiry. It is wise to realize the
limitations as much as the potentials of the pursuit of archaeology from above.

Productive as the Foggia plain turned out to be of crop- and
grass-marks, it would be amiss to think that the territory was
an 'open book' ready to reveal itself to any birdman who happened to scan it in the raking light of a late spring morning or
evening. For one thing, without a preliminary acquaintance
with the kind of ancient features likely to show up, the meaning of some of the marks, if not their very presence, might well
escape the airborne observer entirely. To derive the fullest
benefit from the photographs and thus turn chance discoveries
into a systematic analysis of the total landscape, the expert
needs a real feeling for the setting – its physical geography, its
history, and even its living people. Only through such intimate
knowledge can he adapt his methods to the 'genius' of the
place; concentrate on the significant, and on the abnormal
rather than the normal; dissociate contemporary or recent
features from those long abandoned; unwind and extricate the
manifold marks that betray various past epochs; recognize
their role within the given environment; and train himself to
see not just a few obliterated earthworks but culture groups
with their characteristic economies. Only thus will he be able to
restore a buried landscape and people it with a whole sequence
of humanity which has its origin in the distant dawn but continues into the present. It was aerial archaeology at this mature
stage that Bradford practised with such determination in
Apulia. To it he brought the sensitive understanding of the
artist together with the discipline of the scientist. Aesthetic
perceptiveness is reflected in his sketch of the setting:

On the *Tavoliere* today, the sense of unlimited space and sky and
freedom of movement is saved from monotony by the blue line of
mountains along the horizon that gives a land-locked security and
intimacy, by the fierceness of light and colour, by the sharp con-

trasts of winter cold and summer heat, by the pleasures of a short intense spring and a renewal of spring in autumn, by the long welcoming seaboard that soothes the eye and modifies the impression of a parched hinterland – all these and other things combine to produce that form of harsh yet stimulating landscape which is so often, and so well, depicted in Edward Lear's Mediterranean drawings ... Fundamentally, it is a hopeful environment if properly handled. To the natural potentialities for simple farming, its Neolithic settlers (like those on the plain of Thessaly) were certainly not blind.

The scientist, however, lurks behind the ecological description and evokes parallels and perhaps connections with lands in the eastern Mediterranean from which the first impulse toward farming had probably travelled. As a scientist Bradford followed the prescript of collecting, interpreting, and generalizing; or of analysis and synthesis.

Interpretation was to occupy most of his energies and time. It must be realized that before the coming of Bradford and Williams-Hunt the significance of crop-marks for the discovery of lost antiquities along the Mediterranean had been far from recognized. The archaeology of the Tavoliere was virtually unknown and no aerial investigations had been previously carried out. As a matter of fact, no air photographs were then available of any similar sites in all of Italy. Hence there were no really reliable points of reference. Given the archaeologically virgin character of this province, none of the pictures, no matter how clear the crop-marks, allowed immediate attribution or dating of the sites. Nothing, that is, could yet be taken at its face value. Furthermore, each photograph – displaying, as a rule, a mixed and lengthy record – had to be thoroughly examined in order to disentangle individual data. Though Bradford owned that the 1945 reconnaissance was 'suddenly rewarded by an unparalleled display of buried sites, extensive, complex and novel', he hastened to add that 'at the start their identities were only to be guessed at, until partly reasoned out by photo interpretation'.

Interpretation, which he considered the 'first phase' of study following discovery, occupied him for three years. It was to be followed by a mandatory 'second phase': systematic excavation, to verify and extend the evidence. However, he and Williams-Hunt had already cut a few test-trenches in June 1945 right after they had taken their initial photographs. In this operation they found enthusiastic helpmates in men from their military unit, whose share in the labours military brass consented to as part of 'Army Education'. The brief trial dig at a village 'compound' discovered from the air bore out the favourable surface geology of the terrain, with only one foot of soil overlying a calcareous rock some three feet in depth, which in turn rested above layers of yellow sand. A cut into a presumably prehistoric ditch brought up ample shards of fine quality. They were of two kinds, though apparently contemporaneous: one was brown or black undecorated burnished pottery, and the other, buff-coloured, was painted delicately with broad, tomato-red bands, so-called *fasce larghe*. Here were the first undisputed proofs of a Neolithic context. The distinct style of the hand-made ceramics – without the benefit of the potter's wheel – also pointed toward already known sites in southern Apulia and Sicily, and even to the lands across the Adriatic. Through their affinity with previously dated ware from stratified locations elsewhere in Italy, they hinted at an approximate date of 2300 B.C. Bit by bit Bradford gained a comprehension of the elaborate settlement patterns that had cluttered the Tavoliere two millennia before Imperial Rome. The ways of these pioneers may well have laid the foundations for the sturdy peasantry which was to form Rome's backbone.

Later that year Bradford was named a member of the Sub-Commission for Monuments, Fine Arts and Archives of the Allied Commission for Italy. He then had occasion to contact Italian archaeologists and discuss with them questions relating to the peninsula's prehistory. At the same time he familiarized himself with the field research carried out in Southern Italy some decades earlier, while also keeping an eye on the overall picture of the Neolithic as it evolved and expanded along the European shore of the Mediterranean.

By then he had been separated from Williams-Hunt, who had been assigned to new duties in the Far East in June. For Williams-Hunt, though at first he regretted the abrupt end of his Italian researches, it meant a new beginning, which was to

lead to splendid discoveries from the air of lost cities in Siam
and Indo-China and of abandoned aboriginal camps near Melbourne in Australia. A cruel accident suffered during anthropological work in the Malayan jungle put an end to his promising career in 1953. He was then only thirty-five years old, the
same age as Bradford.

Bradford's major contribution was undoubtedly some two
hundred Neolothic settlements in the Tavoliere, where none
had been known before. In the single year of 1945 the number
of such sites had been more than doubled for all of Italy (including Sicily and Sardinia). Yet this increment came from one
concentrated area, offering, besides sheer numbers, a whole distribution pattern and 'extraordinary opportunities for comparative study'. Unlike previously located sites in Italy, which
were known from just a few artefacts and hazy excavation
plans at best, the new sites stood revealed in clear-cut outlines
which left little to surmise. They all showed a family resemblance, despite considerable range in size and complexity. The
homogeneity of the group definitely set them apart from any
other class of marks in the Apulian soil. All shared common
characteristics in layout. Generally their positions were on
slightly raised levels above the malarial plain. Defensive advantages seem to have been of little consideration, though a
few settlements on the higher western rim were built on the
edge of escarpments like the hill forts of England. Strangely
enough, proximity to water played no decisive part in their
planning. Each of the sites was enclosed by one or more 12- to
25-foot-wide ditches, more or less circular – in one instance as
many as eight, arranged in two concentric groups of four.
Smaller sites usually had only two surrounding ditches, but in
all other respects appeared to be simply reduced or simplified
versions of the larger ones. According to size, Bradford classified them as homesteads, serving one family (or 'extended
family'), and villages. In the majority of instances, both types
consisted of two main sections: an outer one, tentatively
called by Bradford 'farmyard', and an inner 'domestic' enclosure, not necessarily concentric. An entirely novel feature,
never previously reported, was the smaller 'compound', pre-
ponderantly located in the domestic zone. These, too, were

fully or partly surrounded by circular, penannular, or semi-circular ditches. Bradford at first tended to equate these compounds with hut emplacements, but their considerable dimensions (between about 40 and 110 feet in diameter) militate against such an assumption, even though individual homes may have been placed within their precincts. For some unexplained reason, the openings of all compounds of one village pointed in the same direction, usually between east-north-east and west-north-west. Another curious detail, which Bradford was the first to observe, was the presence of inturned, funnel-shaped ditches within the main enclosures. Undoubtedly they represented entrances. Several such corridor-like openings may occur in one ditch. Conceivably they were useful in driving herds in or out of the enclosure, but they could also have had defensive purposes.

Perhaps the most remarkable of all the villages is near present-day Passo di Corvo, eight miles north-east of Foggia. Its oval measures some 800 by 500 yards and is probably the largest of all Neolithic sites known, nearly twice as large as the famous Köln-Lindenthal in West Germany. Bradford thought it displayed the aspects of a tribal centre. Indeed, the more than one hundred inner compounds revealed in the air photograph of its congested ground-plan make it easy for us to visualize how such a Stone Age kraal could eventually evolve into a town of the metal ages. Passo di Corvo assumes even more staggering dimensions if one adds its outer 'corral', which adjoins the village on one side in an eccentric ellipse and is surrounded by one ditch. This annex extends for nearly 1,500 yards.

Despite their variety and profusion, the Neolithic sites did not indicate any significant development or change in style. Homestead and village, with a range of intervening types, probably existed side by side. But while the settlements most likely belonged to one culture, they need not all have been contemporaneous. The mere density of the group made this unlikely. The idea was further suggested to Bradford by analogies with modern African settlement patterns near Lake Victoria, and, above all, by photographic details. On some of his pictures the plan of one Neolithic village was repeated almost identically near by, and the conclusion was warranted that the settlers of one, finding it no longer hospitable because of accumulation of refuse and fouling, removed lock, stock, and barrel to an adjacent spick-and-span replica. Exhaustion of soil must also have made it desirable for the primitive farmers to give up their abodes and move on to untilled fields. Further indication that the Neolithic settlements of the Tavoliere lasted for more than one generation (Bradford came to think in terms of five hundred to six hundred years) was borne out by the fact that crop-marks of related features like ditches of compounds occasionally cut across each other, and hence could not have been of the same age. Sometimes the original plan of a village or homestead was later slightly modified.

It is inconceivable that any other medium than air photography could have picked up a whole homogeneous settlement pattern of which nothing whatever had survived above the surface, and whose very existence was previously unsuspected. With an almost bewildering multiplicity of markings before him, Bradford was able to sort them out, compare them, establish their distribution, and attribute them to one culture phase. Further comparisons helped him to track down affinities with Neolithic centres elsewhere in Italy and in Thessaly and Central Europe. Evidently the Apulian sites were preceded by those in Greece and the southern Balkans, but were considerably older than places in Western Europe like Altheim near Munich, which they also resembled. Their ultimate antecedents, however, were to be sought in the Near East, where the 'Neolithic Revolution' had started around 10,000 B.C. The transplantation of Neolithic culture from Greece to Southern Italy in the third millennium B.C. was strong evidence for the navigational skill of prehistoric people and foreshadowed the seaborne colonies planted across the Mediterranean by Minoans, Phoenicians, and Greeks.

Insight of this kind came to Bradford without any excavation to speak of. Given in the Tavoliere a comprehensive view of what was manifestly one long-lasting culture compactly placed within a challenging environment, he felt he had seen clear indications of 'a methodical, conservative, ingenious people, well-knit together both socially and economically'.

Bradford was the first to admit that when it came to the social and economic characteristics of these remote people, aerial photographs by themselves furnished but tentative conclusions. The ultimate arbiter had to be digging. While field

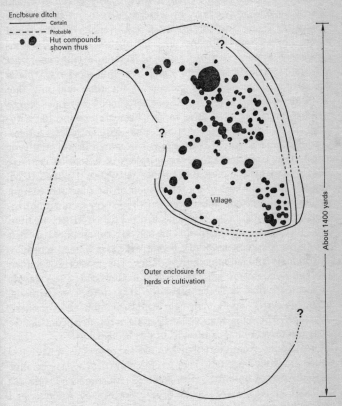

Figure 17. Plan of a Neolithic settlement near Foggia in Apulia, drawn by John Bradford

work was to confirm his preliminary deductions, it alone would eventually answer questions of dating, of racial background, forms of husbandry and agriculture, type or degree of warfare, social make-up of the communities, religious practices, the fate and ultimate eclipse of the Neolithic farmers, and much else besides.

To begin to tackle these problems, Bradford now entered his second phase: excavation. The intensive programme he had envisaged for the Tavoliere never quite came to full fruition. More than one or two seasons were needed to get to the bottom of an entire way of life removed from us by four millennia. Perhaps something on the scale of the exemplary British campaigns at the prehistoric sites of Windmill Hill and Little Woodbury would have been called for. But the Foggia plain was a many-layered landscape, and at the time not only the Neolithic period – and not just one settlement – claimed Bradford's interest. He was active in aerial research connected with other parts and epochs of Italy, and with Rhodes, Attica, Dalmatia, and Southern France (areas in which he was the first to establish from the air surviving traces of extensive centuriated Roman field and road systems), as well as England (East Anglia). After the end of the war much of his time and energy went into the rescue and collection (but also examination) of Allied air photographs, which he had deposited at key institutions in England and abroad. Through his appointment to the Pitt-Rivers Museum in Oxford he embarked on a busy schedule of teaching and administrative duties. His masterly volume, *Ancient Landscapes*, grew out of a lecture course on aerial archaeology that he gave regularly at Oxford. Yet without doubt his aerial survey cum field work accomplished considerably more in Apulia than could have ever resulted from many years of conventional campaigns of dirt archaeology.

Excavations were started in Apulia in 1949 and were continued the following fall. They were sponsored by a specially created Apulia Committee with R. E. (Sir) Mortimer Wheeler as chairman, under the auspices of the Society of Antiquaries, Oxford University, and various other British and Italian learned societies. Work was directed by Bradford, assisted by his wife and two associates.

The Apulia expedition found late summer as propitious for ground work as late spring had been for air photography. At this time the land was free of crops. Instead, it bore a profusion of flowering weeds, which frequently marked underlying features as dramatically as the crops had done. Armed with air photographs or the plans made from them, locating specific sites presented no serious problems. While they obey the same laws as crop-marks, 'the weed-marks', Bradford wrote,

take a far greater variety of forms. Above ancient ditches flowering species grew taller, more thickly and often more quickly; and, thus accelerated, had sometimes flowered, withered and prematurely 'fall'n into the sear, the yellow leaf' before those not so placed. A score of different varieties of wild plants indicated the presence of ditches and other features beneath them. Very often Neolithic and Roman enclosures stood out as bold lines of colour, which could be faithfully recorded by colour-photography. Thus, during our 'ground-check' of sites seen on the air-photographs we frequently found Neolithic village ditches brilliantly outlined as broad bands of chrome yellow by flowering *rugola* (wild cabbage). This plant, which is found everywhere on the Tavoliere, has roots up to two feet long that take advantage of the extra depth, and its superior growth thus reveals silted-up ditches of all periods impartially. The details of the Roman landscape were often delineated in flowers, by mauve wild mint, white 'cow parsley', or yellow-flowering thistles.

Had air photographs been taken at that time of the year, the results would probably have been almost as striking as in spring. But it is noteworthy that, effective as the weed-marks appear to the grounded observer, no one had ever paid any attention to them. It needed the alert from high above before they were used as tell-tale guides. Often, in the course of aerial discovery, it is not so much that buried features are totally invisible on land, but that they fail to catch anybody's eye unless an airborne camera fixes them first on film.

For further examination Bradford concentrated on the site near Passo di Corvo, which had already been revealed as the most prominent prehistoric settlement. Because of its complexity it was conceivably also the most advanced. It so happened that its plan was particularly clearly marked by various weeds. Passo di Corvo of old, which comprised a whole group of ditched villages, was to vindicate its Neolithic horizon completely. Bradford decided to excavate a typical compound, which he hoped would approximate and summarize an inhabited unit. The one he chose was at the centre of the airview.

'When thus directed to the spot the line of its ditch was seen to be clearly outlined on the ground in a strong localized growth of a particular weed, which exactly revealed its course, its width (almost to an inch) and its wide entrance gap. Guided by the photographs an immense economy in excavation was possible and the trench-grid immediately revealed the butt-ends of the ditches and all principal features'. Though he came across traces of a stone wall in the surrounding ditch, he was unable, despite a thorough search, to find any rudiment of a structure inside the enclosure. For a consolation prize a few pieces of 'sun-baked clay with "wattle" impressions' turned up in the ditch. Evidently they had once belonged to the familiar wattle-and-daub hut of prehistoric Italic peasants. But where exactly the hut had been erected and what its extent might have been escaped the excavators.

Otherwise the returns from the dig were quite rewarding. Virtually every article that one could associate with Neolithic village life was dug out from the same compound, with the exception of figurines (which are a common ritual equipment of primitive peasantry both in the Old World and the New) and any kind of weaponry. Yet it would be unsound to argue *ex silentio* that the early Apulians inhabited a utopian realm free of internecine strife and priest-ridden idolatry.

Everyday objects characteristic of Neolithic village life included tools which left no doubt that these prehistoric Italians were indeed farmers: characteristic sharp obsidian flakes showed the gloss that came from their use – probably as blades in the kind of sickles known also from the ancient Near East for cutting grass and cereals. After harvest, grain was ground with pestles on flat stone querns. Needles made from bone and pottery whorls must have served the women for sewing and spinning. Animal bones turned up in copious amounts, giving a hint of the species used for husbandry and food. However, no canines had yet sought the company of Neolithic man.

As was to be expected, pottery was most abundant. The two-week excavation at Passo di Corvo alone furnished some four thousand fragments from a great variety of quite beautiful vessels, dishes, basins, jars, and bowls, admirable in shape as well as texture, colouring and decoration. Despite an unmistakably regional Italian character, the pottery betrayed its source from across the Adriatic.

In summing up the physical evidence from artefacts, Bradford was justified in the conclusion that Neolithic Apulia would emerge as a formative nucleus in Italy's prehistory, 'distinguished aesthetically by the excellence of its pottery and socially by the developed nature of its communities'. Having hit upon the very foundation of Western European farming and the beginning of settled life of about 4,500 years ago, Bradford found it difficult 'to repress a pang of admiration for those methodical and ingenious peasants, whose labours prepared the way for the evolution of cities and nations'.

However, neither air photography nor excavation could determine the exact beginning nor the end of the Neolithic (or Neolithic-Chalcolithic) farming culture in Southern Italy. (Bradford, by the way, does not report any carbon-14 tests.) So far it has been impossible to locate a pure Bronze Age site in the area, and the puzzle remains whether the Neolithic settlements vanished before a new age with new traditions arrived.

The Tavoliere's record of the Bronze Age may be scanty, but thanks to Bradford's aerial reconnaissance it offers unusual opportunities to bring into focus a discussion of other Mediterranean civilizations. Bradford never confined himself to one period. He saw Apulia as a sequence of landscapes, blended into each other, superimposed, and partly effaced. His photographs illumined this cultural cavalcade and archaeological montage. Almost all of them were palimpsests 'more complex than even those to which the late Major Allen accustomed us in his discoveries in the Oxford region'. Out of these composites grew a vision of an organized whole: northern Apulia was a microcosm of the vital stages in the emergence of Italy and Europe. That is not to say that Bradford indulged in a romanticism *à la* Burke that welded the dead, the living, and the yet unborn into a kind of super-blood-and-soul bank. He would, as we have seen, separate the strands neatly, and analyse the dimmest wiggly line if it meant adding to our knowledge of prehistoric animal drives or Latin field partitions. He was as methodical in his reconstitution of the Neolithic peasantry as he was in the elucidation of two other periods that had left their mark in the Apulian soil. Fleeting reference has already been made to his incisive study of Roman field systems and agriculture, which were 'kept on ice' under the Apulian ground. He could take pride in bringing 'some honest country mud into the unresolved and abstract discussion ... which has so often vexed the study of Centuriation'.

His researches into the Tavoliere during the Middle Ages equally revolutionized all concepts. At this stage the landscape was largely remade. Vast tracts were turned over to pasture. Along the coast stretched wild moors, favourite hunting grounds of medieval potentates, foremost among them the extraordinary Hohenstaufen emperor Frederick II (Stupor Mundi). Archaeological evidence also mirrored medieval fragmentation through a patchwork of enclosed fields, a scattering of small castles and fortified villages. From aerial vistas Bradford drew up a comprehensive plan of medieval farms and fields which, like those of the Romans before, had fallen into complete disuse and oblivion but, well preserved underground, could henceforth be reassembled as models for other regions of Europe that were once forced under the feudal yoke. In this inquiry, the peasantry and agriculture – subjects usually neglected by the urban fixations of most archaeologists – again fired his interest, as they had that of Crawford and Baradez. In the course of his investigations he managed to rediscover several once flourishing medieval villages of which not a building was standing. In addition he made a number of important finds that restored Apulia, a favourite resort of Frederick II, to its short-lived place in the centre stage of medieval southern Europe. Thus he could identify more than thirty earthworks of characteristic medieval Norman and Hohenstaufen construction, some with mottes, ramparts, and baileys. At a junction of three dilapidated modern farms, still bearing the name of San Lorenzo, he tracked down an imperial hunting lodge where Frederick repeatedly resided. On a marshy coastal inlet he plotted a complex of deserted streets, walls, and mounds belonging to a forgotten Roman town, and later, as was borne out by documents, to a medieval port (Salpi), which was probably used as a Venetian supply base for the Crusaders. When the 1950 season took him there for trial excavation he gained the melancholy impression that 'today these remote fields and moors are silent but for the birds which wheel and cry above the drying lagoons'.

It was clearly visible that Apulia had begun to deteriorate after the demise of Roman power, particularly as a result of the invasions by Lombards and Saracens. Medieval feudalism

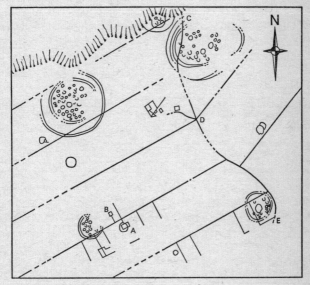

Figure 18. Bradford's sketch – from air photographs – of prehistoric circular villages superimposed by centuriated Roman roads near Lucera, Apulia

and state-monopolized sheep-grazing in modern times brought more calamities, as did earthquakes and malaria. The changing face of the Apulian landscape demonstrates that, strong as the physical factors of climate and topography are, man, if he so desires, can turn deserts into lush oases and blooming gardens into wilderness.

In the air photographs of Neolithic, Roman, and medieval Apulia vital aspects of Italian cultural history had been recaptured. There was, however, one notable gap in that procession: the Etruscan civilization. Unfortunately for aerial archaeology, the 'mysterious' predecessors of Rome had never gained any significant foothold in that region; hence their contribution to the remaking of Southern Italy along the Adriatic was infinitesimal. But why couldn't the winged camera come to the homeland of the Etruscans on the other side of the Apennines? This is precisely what happened. Once more it was J. P. S. Bradford who made spectacular discoveries to enrich the tapestry of the so generously endowed landscape of ancient Italy.

7. Buried Etruria

How the most up-to-date refinements in science and technology have come to elucidate the remotest past has often been demonstrated in our age, but rarely as dramatically as in the spring of 1961, when the Italian state television system brought views from inside an unopened Etruscan tomb into the homes of the entire nation. On hand in the vast necropolis near the ancient centre of Tarquinia, about forty miles north-west of Rome, was the Premier of Italy, Signor Amintore Fanfani. While the dignitaries and archaeologists inaugurated the startling experiment at its source, the far-flung audience was dazzled by the painted walls lighting up from the dark recesses of a subterranean rock chamber. Until Italian technicians had installed their probes, no one, except perhaps ransacking tomb robbers at an uncertain time, could have gazed at the murals since the crypt was closed behind the dead some 2,500 years ago.

The unusual programme was a high point in a series of archaeological researches connected with the revolutionary art of what John Bradford once aptly called 'to excavate with a minimum of excavation'. It marked another advance in the pure vision of buried evidence. No soil to speak of had been turned over and nothing of the underground structure had as yet been dismantled by the spade. Neither had any archaeologist come into direct physical contact with the ancient remains. The novel experience had been made possible by combining several ingenious methods. Basic to all was air photography.

It made good sense for the experiment to centre on the Etruscans. The people who created the first major civilization in Italy, and who had attempted to control the whole peninsula before their Roman disciples began to eclipse them in the fourth century B.C., had remained enigmatic. Despite centuries of discovery, starting with the appearance of magnificent statues and frescoes in the Renaissance (which influenced Donatello and Michelangelo), notions about the ancient people were still hazy. To many the very name of the vanished race that once inhabited Etruria (roughly modern Tuscany), along the Tyrrhenian coast between the Arno and Tiber, evoked legendary figures rather than real men. The riddle of their origin as much as the strangeness of their language, which has no significant affinity to any known idiom, living or dead, continues to pose tantalizing problems to historical and philological scholarship. Even in antiquity the Etruscans troubled the minds of Latin and Greek authors. Livy and Virgil frequently refer to them. But all the extensive studies, like the Etruscans' own literature, are lost, most regrettably Emperor Claudius's grammar of the Etruscan language.

No wonder with the conundrums centring on them that the Etruscans have gained an aura of mystery. In the eighteenth century they had already become a cult which in the learned academies of the cities of Tuscany reached the quaint excesses of *Etruscheria* and *Etruscomania*. Popular imagination has never ceased to be stimulated by their splendid artworks, some of the finest of which are displayed in the collections of the Gregorian Museum of the Vatican, the Museum of the Villa Giulia in Rome, the Archaeological Museum of Florence, and a host of local museums at or near Etruscan sites such as Tarquinia, Cerveteri, Chiusi, Perugia, Cortona, Bologna, Ferrara, etc. There, superb pieces of sculpture, which strike the modern spectator as both archaic and sophisticated in style, dare to deviate from the harmonious proportions and Olympian calm associated with the classical canons of Greeks and Romans. Before the Renaissance, which rose in Florence in the Etruscan (Tuscan) heartland, Italy produced little that could measure up to the terra-cotta Apollo of Veii, the bronze Arezzo Chimaera, the famous Capitoline wolf, or the relief of the Tarquinian horses. The tomb paintings from Tarquinia, depicting Etruscan life and beliefs in spontaneous vitality and variety, have never ceased to excite since they were first unearthed. No doubt the appreciation of exotic art – be it African or pre-Columbian –

has helped to sharpen our sensibilities for all things Etruscan. Their strangely elongated bronze figurines have a special appeal today and foreshadow the creations of Modigliani, a native of Livorno from the northern fringe of the Tuscan coast, and of the Swiss-Italian sculptor Agosto Giacometti. A veritable Etruscan Renaissance can be dated from the international Etruscan exhibition that opened in 1955 in Zürich and then travelled through major western European cities, from Copenhagen to Cologne, The Hague, Paris, and Milan. The comprehensive show was brilliantly assembled from the finest products of Etruscan artistry, including unsurpassed jewellery, delicate ceramics (both Greek imports and characteristic black *bucchero* ware), and an astonishing variety of expertly wrought weapons, ornaments, and household utensils.

Our knowledge of the Etruscans has gained most from their extensive necropolises, veritable cities of the dead, which surround their equally – if not even more – dead cities. The great cemeteries, such as the Monterozzi near Tarquinia and the Banditaccia outside Cerveteri (the Caere of the Etruscans), have been in use for nearly one thousand years, from the eighth century B.C. until well into the Christian era. Covering much larger areas than the cities themselves, they are saturated with burial sites. Characteristic for the environment of the original Etruscan settlements (within a landscape unlike any other in Italy), both cities and cemeteries occupy long, narrow, flat-topped ridges separated by ravines. The parallel escarpments rise above the coastal plain, the Maremma, along which the seafaring people, who waxed rich on the ores of Tuscany and Elba, maintained their ports, and where, if we can believe the generally accepted tradition, they had first disembarked from their Asiatic (Anatolian?) homeland early in the first millennium B.C.

By and large the Etruscans expected the hereafter to be an idealized version of their earthly existence. To secure this blissful state, at least for their pleasure- and luxury-loving aristocrats, was the principal purpose of some of their most enduring art and even architecture. Hence, with the logic of magic religion, like so many other people they believed that by endowing their dead with all the paraphernalia that had made their earthly life joyous and comfortable, they would guarantee the continuation of a happy life eternal. Apparently a painting of the scene or just models of the objects and tools needed would also conjure up the real thing. In their endeavour to provide for the departed they literally stocked funeral chambers with any imaginable goods, not only from their own superb workshops but from other peoples with whom they traded: Phoenicians, Egyptians, Carthaginians, and, above all, Greeks. The latter they admired so much that, at times, their art becomes so strongly Hellenized that it is almost imitative. It is no exaggeration to say that the finest, best-preserved, and most numerous Attic black- and red-figured vases have come from Etruscan tombs, where their deposit in hollowed-out tufa caverns or alluvial sediments kept them pretty much intact. Etruscan women, who, to the shock of other ancient people, enjoyed equal rank with the men, were after death supplied with golden fibulae, cosmetic boxes, bracelets, earrings, diadems, beautifully engraved mirrors, lipsticks, and furniture, as well as 'pots and pans' for cooking chores. In this manner funerary goods offer an almost complete catalogue of the Etruscan mode of living, their tastes, their artistic skill, their economic wealth, their trade connections, their religious ideas, and their forms of entertainment. The swift-moving, boldly outlined scenes in their coloured frescoes, which drew ecstatic praise at the 1955–6 exhibits, bring back a vanished civilization and its preoccupations in a resounding iconography that speaks to us as directly as any testimony could and makes up for the missing literary evidence. So close is the correspondence of funerary provisions to what actual life must have been that the very burial chambers with their adjacent rooms, their columns, roofing, and windows mirror the layout of private houses. (A further proof of this are the clay models of houses found in tombs.) Scholars today look upon the central chamber of Etruscan tumuli as a facsimile of the later *atrium* in Roman domestic architecture.

Since the burials cover the entire span of Etruscan civilization, they also permit us to follow developments and declines in taste as well as in material affluence. Thus, graves of the seventh century, the golden age of Etruria, mark an apogee in wealth. In later centuries, optimism, joy, and indulgence make way for a more sombre outlook. Hence the increasing appearance of images of vindictive gods trying the souls of mortals. By the same token, the underground structures can be shown to undergo considerable modifications. In sum, the Etruscan tombs have provided archaeologists with a prime source for reconstructing a dead but once vibrant civilization. Unfortunately, they have proven as lucrative a quarry to their stepbrothers, the tomb robbers.

By the time scientific excavation got under way in the late nineteenth century, tumuli all over Etruria and the regions of Etruscan expansion had been savagely rifled by illicit diggers. The first to ravage the possessions of the dead were probably their surviving neighbours. Judging by Roman Imperial legislation, looting of graves was even then a widely practised delinquency, as it had been far back in Pharaonic Egypt. In the fifteenth and sixteenth centuries, when the first modern wave of Etruscan discoveries broke, popes were known to replenish their treasury with vast amounts of gold taken from those tombs, just as Central American statesmen and adventurers were to claim the shining metal from opulent pre-Columbian burials in Panama. Cardinal Farnese is said to have extracted objects of precious metal to the tune of six thousand pounds from the Monterozzi in 1546, which he piously applied to the adornment of the Roman basilica St John Lateran.

Gradually the haphazard excavation of tumuli became a gentlemanly sport indulged in, with the same gusto with which contemporary Englishmen dug up 'Druid barrows', by soldiers, churchmen, and local and foreign nobility. It was this profitable pastime that led in 1836 to the opening of the most sumptuously equipped Etruscan sepulchre on record, the Regolini-Galassi tomb at a Cerveteri cemetery, named for General Viricenzo Galassi and the archpriest of Cerveteri, Alessandro Regolini, who presided over the venture. Cleared hastily in a day without any regard for scholarly niceties, it was broken into through the roof. No adequate inventory of the more than 650 articles was kept (an authoritative publication on the discovery had to wait more than a century, till 1947, when the circumstances and details were little more than hearsay), but the fabulous objects that made this veritable Tutankhamen find of the nineteenth century can be admired today at the Vatican. After that, undoubtedly spurred on by greed, discoveries proliferated. The painted crypts of Tarquinia especially never ceased to excite perceptive visitors, though several were soon lost sight of, while others quickly decayed. Paintings flaked off when exposed to fresh air and humidity, or were hacked off by 'art lovers'.

Side by side with these only slightly more respectable exploiters the grave robbers continued in a frenzy which was to turn the solitary grazing grounds of sheep into a moonscape of craters. Aficionados of the time like the English traveller George Dennis, who wrote an early archaeological classic, *Cities and Cemeteries of Etruria* (1848), left painful accounts of the covetous vandals who burrowed through acres of land to extricate valuables. Anything that did not fill their bill was ruthlessly and contemptuously destroyed. Their ire was directed particularly against ceramics, which in those days could not be turned into ready cash. In this respect successive generations of robbers brought a definite improvement, since they were to learn that the international antiquity market was willing to pay its weight in gold for almost any Etruscan artefact. Nevertheless, increasing infatuation with Etruscan art in our time has also made things worse. Aesthetic enthusiasm among the vulgar (i.e. the vulgar rich) inevitably begets acquisitiveness. Italian and foreign dealers conspire with local freebooters to drain the tombs in order to satisfy the greedy collectors of several continents. Today it is believed that of every hundred tombs opened ninety-nine have been plundered. An estimated ten billion dollars' worth of looted antiquities leave Italy annually at a tremendous cost to the national legacy and to scholars, to whom knowledge of the precise location of an object is far more valuable than its material worth. C. M. Lerici has made an authoritative guess that by the late 1950s there were some one thousand tomb robbers, belonging to well-organized bands, at large in the Etruscan cemeteries alone, not to speak of the far more numerous local part-time diggers. At one section of a necropolis, where scientific diggers had been able to excavate on the average one tomb per year, robbers had ploughed through at least three hundred in ten years. 'These figures', observes Lerici acidly, 'represent a remarkable, if disgraceful, success for private initiative.' Against organized crime, aided and abetted by seemingly respectable art dealers and the extravagant bids of their clientele, who seek to gain 'culture' in the eyes of their peers by conspicuously parading stolen antiques in their gaudy mansions, the Italian authorities and the archaeological profession are almost helpless.

But lamentable as the situation is, there is no reason for utter despair. For one thing, the grave goods, no matter how aesthetically pleasing and materially precious, are not all unique. Some of the best specimens, of almost every conceivable type and from known locations, are deposited in national museums. Besides, looted tombs, where robbers have ceased to tread, will quite often continue to yield worthwhile information to science. Furthermore, the regions within the confines of Etruscan expansion – roughly one third of the peninsula, extending from Salerno northward into the Po Valley – are so immeasurably rich in remains that even two millennia of plundering could not have squeezed them entirely dry. Certain once-flourishing areas have been lost track of and may well have eluded both scholars and looters. For all we know, they remain covered by benign layers of soil and vegetation, or even bodies of water. The most thoroughly riddled places, the great necropolises of Tarquinia, Cerveteri, Vulci, Veii, Chiusi, and the like, may yet include sizeable burial grounds which, at least in modern times, have passed unnoticed. It is at this stage that aerial photography has come to the fore. In the nick of time it responded to the burning urgency, when drastic measures were needed to forestall the accelerating rate of destruction from tomb robbers and the equally damaging encroachments of post-war agricultural reclamation.

During his war service in Italy from 1943 onward, that is to say before he turned his full attention to Southern Italy, John Bradford found time to look over photographs taken by the RAF over the territories of ancient Etruria. Unlike the aerial record of his post-V-Day programme over the Tavoliere, none of these photographs had been taken with any archaeological intent. They simply formed part of an enormous, comprehensive coverage of wartime Italy prepared by Allied fliers as a strictly military undertaking. As a matter of fact, the circumstances under which the airborne photographers had operated were not the most auspicious for archaeology. It is extremely doubtful that, given the altitude (up to five miles) from which the survey was made, anything of antiquarian interest could have been spotted only a few years earlier. However, during the war photographic technique and optical equipment had been perfected to such a degree that a whole new range and depth of detail had become accessible. By luck and persistence Bradford was given a chance to examine the most revealing photographs further. At the end of the hostilities, impressed by the wealth of information before him, he made sure that these air pictures were not discarded as had apparently been intended. He then secured them for study and after extracting his first results received permission from the RAF to publish them. With his initial article on the subject, 'Etruria from the Air', in the June 1947 issue of *Antiquity*, begins a new era in Etruscology.

Hitherto, serious archaeological efforts had concentrated on one specific tomb or complex of tombs and their proper excavation. Bradford was above all interested in the plan of an entire necropolis, of whose extent and design no one had a clear concept and for which maps were a dire need, now more than ever, when deep ploughing and the planting of grapes and olives threatened to wipe out any marks still visible from above. The RAF photographs furnished an ideal basis for just such an undertaking. After the laborious work of analysis and ground inspection, Bradford, who, from 1945 on, visited Italy almost every year, was able to produce reliable maps of large sections of the cemeteries at Cerveteri and Tarquinia.

Briefly summarized, the function of air photographs of Etruscan necropolises as he conceived it was threefold: to help in the discovery of unknown tombs and to fix those that, though previously described in the literature, had not been definitely located; to come up with such undetected features as cemetery roads (*vie sepolcrali*) which would suggest the arrangement and interrelation of various sites; and to present a 'picture of the tomb-distribution as a whole' in an overall scaled plan. Once the number, location, and layout of the tumuli had been firmly established, he would at last be in a position 'to determine the course of future excavation with precision and to assess its potentialities in relation to the depredations of the past'. Here was the starting point for a renewed examination of the great cemeteries, one which held out hope for adding not just physical details but new perspectives on Etruscan civilization.

As to the basis of Bradford's explorations, the fundamental principles hold no more secrets for us. Since he made use of those pictures that benefited from favourable seasons in a Mediterranean land with thin layers of soil above volcanic tufa, the success of aerial reconnaissance in spotting underground structures from crop-, grass-, or soil-marks could be predicted. It is the more surprising that before Bradford no air photographs of an Etruscan necropolis had been published, even though shortly before the war a few lone voices had proposed that results comparable to those of Crawford and Poidebard could possibly be obtained in Italy.

The characteristic construction of Etruscan tombs was an essential factor in bringing the marks out 'into the open'. A majority of the sepulchres were built as tumuli with conic barrows piled above them from the excavated debris. Of course, in most instances such mounds had long ago disappeared, thanks to human and other agencies, though they showed up occasionally in slight elevations that could be mistaken for natural undulations of the soil. To air photography these surface features were of little moment. What counted, above all, were the displacements under the levelled soil. The subterranean funerary buildings offered the clue.

Underneath their mounds most Etruscan tombs consist of circular drums carved out of the surrounding rock or erected from blocks of tufa. Often the level of the drum was raised by adding another layer of stones. Excavation around this structure amounted to a depth of several feet, thus forming a ditch that encircled the free-standing foundation of the tumulus. Now, once weathering set in, the ditch began to fill with humus, while the top of the drum would be covered with little soil aside from the pebbles remaining from the erstwhile mound. Under such circumstances the levelled tomb, above which vegetation will grow sparsely and parch sooner, would show up as a pale disc in late spring or early summer when under crops or grass. Since the enclosing ditch, on the other hand, will produce more luxuriant growth due to its greater fertility and thus ripen later, it is bound to appear in a darker green. Contrast between the concentric zones is then responsible for the sharp definition of the tombs in circular vegetation-marks. Their width, once again, could be gauged with surprising precision, even if the diameter on the prints was less than a millimetre. On the RAF photographs Bradford was to detect veritable galaxies of such tombs in whitish blobs or patches that made the meadows and fields of Etruria look like a viscous mass erupting in bubbles and blisters. Yet when seen on the ground, they could hardly be known to exist, particularly off season.

Complementary to vegetation-marks were soil-marks, which can be just as pronounced in the Etrurian fields of the dead, though their outlines are usually blurred due to the scattering of the debris in the course of centuries. In some areas, where the crypts had been hewn out of gypsum or other whitish material, the effect is nevertheless most striking, even when seen at eye level. After fresh ploughing in the fall, Bradford had the distinct impression of snowfall.

Certainly, some of the most remarkable details to impress him on the air photographs were dark wedges cutting from the periphery into the interior of the tomb circle. There was hardly any light-toned patch that did not bear signs of such a cut, and some of the larger ones bore several. On second thought, they left little doubt as to what had caused them. Each one marked the entrance to the tomb, the so-called *dromos*, a stepped passageway leading down toward the centre to the main burial chamber. Sunk deeper under the foundation, the entrances, too, had eventually been filled in by thicker layers of soil which naturally engendered darker vegetation-marks. Bradford spotted more than one hundred in a picture of just one section of a Cerveteri burial ground. The value of signposts of this kind to the earthbound excavator are obvious. Later ground work also helped to explain the proliferation of entrances within one

tumulus. Apparently two or more stood for consecutive burials within the same mausoleum over one or more generations,
While Etruscans originally confined burials within the same
grave to the members of one family, they would in later
periods inter all those who belonged to the same *gens*. Hence,
within what came to be an intricate underground house of
many mansions, the dead were laid out on rows and rows of
stone banks along the walls of the various chambers. It was
that type of halled subterranean palace which was singled out
by Piranesi in his haunting sketches. In the war-torn twentieth
century, they provided spacious shelters for the living.

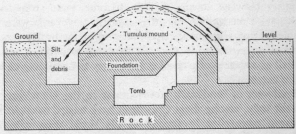

Figure 19. Diagram of an Etruscan tumulus. The arrows show how
levelling of the mound and filling up of the encircling ditch will
produce differentials in the soil and hence in vegetation

Bradford's study of air photographs was to lead to the discovery of no fewer than two thousand levelled Etruscan
tombs. While mapping two of the best-known Etruscan
necropolises, the Monterozzi and the Banditaccia, he was able
to locate some eight hundred virtually unknown tombs in the
former and about half that number in the latter. At the same
time he also considered less famous cemeteries which had
fallen into comparative neglect. Among those he found especially rewarding was Monte Abbatone (Abetone), another vast
graveyard occupying, like the Banditaccia, a ridge across from
Cerveteri, but on the other side of it. This necropolis was even
larger in extent than the Banditaccia, but little was known
about it. In fact, barely half a dozen tumuli had so far been
scientifically excavated. On account of its very thin layer of

topsoil, the plateau of this cliff proved to be most suitable to aerial exploration. Contrasts were exceptionally clear. Large parts were given over to mixed pastures of grass and wild plants. Entrances would infallibly be outlined in the natural vegetation, occasionally by bushes standing like a bunch of flagpoles over the passages. At Monte Abbatone Bradford identified more than six hundred buried tumuli. As at other necropolises, he located, counted, measured, and mapped. In this way it became possible to arrive at a comparative study of several large cemeteries.

Within each necropolis one could distinguish a profusion of individual tumuli, some as large as 135 feet in diameter, but a majority between 20 and 30 feet. In time, there arose from such data a recognition that the immense graveyards were by no means just a haphazard accumulation of tombs. One could perceive an evolution in size and structure among the tumuli as well as a degree of overall organization and planning of the entire necropolis.

Reviewers of Bradford's contributions to the knowledge of ancient Italy, among them Crawford, have tended to slight his Etruscan researches in favour of his signal discoveries of Roman centuriation systems and Neolithic settlements. There may be some justice in this. Etruscan archaeology, after all, was a well-ploughed field long before Bradford appeared on the scene. Tombs galore had already been examined. And even if Bradford's admittedly substantial additions to the number of identified graves should lead the way to fabulous treasures and supreme works of art, the upshot – so the argument ran – would be a quantitative increment in museum pieces but nothing to extend the horizon of science. Such criticism strikes us as unbalanced, and not only because it is perhaps a bit too eager to discount the value of traditional 'gods, graves, and scholars' discoveries. An enrichment of our aesthetic heritage is not to be frowned upon. May it not expand our awareness and creatively impel artists of our own day as rescued Etruscan masterpieces have done in the past? Who is to declare that the newly accomplished chemical synthesis of a hallucinogenic acid is an addition to knowledge and the discovery of a lost Giorgione is not? Besides, there was always the possibility that grave goods would come up with substantial Etruscan inscriptions to add to the meagre corpus of their surviving writings, which, mainly because of their brevity and scarcity (not because the script is undeciphered – it can be read with ease!), have kept us from fully comprehending their language. Even a bilingual of the same text in Etruscan and a known language such as Greek, Latin, or Phoenician could be hoped for.

Yet no matter what the benefits to conventional excavation, Bradford's researches in ancient Etruria were neither in method nor in subject matter archaeology of the old school. As in other areas they lived up to the advanced concept of aerial archaeology as not so much an instrument for the sighting of an individual feature as one for restoring a total ancient landscape in its depth of space and time. We have to see in this light his primary goal of plotting entire necropolises in their topographical context, the relationship of their structures within one cemetery, and the comparison between the various cities of the dead. Discovery meant not just one grave or the other, but clusters of them – their typology and distribution – and also whole new necropolises such as the one Bradford reported at Colle Pantano halfway between Civitavecchia and Tarquinia. Furthermore, together with such observations he was able to gauge, as no groundling with his piecemeal approach could ever have done, the development of the Etruscan graves from the primitive *pozzetti* (little but underground pits and shafts) and the simple *tumuletti arcaici* to the tumuli proper, which grew in dimension as funerary practices themselves changed. In addition, there were traces of formerly free-standing quadrangular *tombe a camera*. The latter, as much as their subterranean counterparts, evoked urban architecture. Indeed, some of the most novel and important results of Bradford's investigations refer to the parallelism between the cities of the dead and those of the living. Since the Etruscan cities, private residences as well as temples, were built largely of wood, they had left few permanent ruins apart from defensive walls. One could apparently learn more of the city of Caere, for instance, from its adjacent necropolises than from the abandoned site, partly built over by an unimpressive modern town. Site plans prepared from photographs showed regular alignments of tombs along roads and silted-up *piazzette*, mimicking oblong city squares, except that the façades of tombs rather than houses adjoined its sides. Concentration on such urban or mock-urban features of the necropolises led to Bradford's discoveries of major arteries, the *vie sepolcrali*, some of which he could trace beyond the cemeteries to the actual town. No doubt, funerary processions had once moved along them, via tortuous gradients, up and down the escarpments between city and necropolis. Major buried roads, whose beds had been originally carved into the rock and hence had a thick layer of humus, stood out for hundreds of yards in the vegetation, while parallel rows of aligned tombs often helped to determine subsidiary stretches of the roadnet. Bradford was by no means oblivious of the Etruscan city sites, by the way, even though the RAF photographs at his disposal could be employed with greater profit on their more sombre satellites. He explicitly stated that for the study of urban remains something more than routine verticals was needed. However, in passing, he pinned down traces of a number of buried roads never reported before which radiated from the ancient Etruscan city of Vulci.

Inevitably, Bradford's discoveries cried for renewed terrestrial explorations and excavation of Etruscan tombs. Whether or not one considers that sequel just a by-product – regrettable or desirable as the case may be – it was bound to come. Bradford himself was convinced of its importance and participated actively in it. What added to the significance, if not the glamour, of this phase was not just its spectacular results or its confirmation of the findings from above, but the fact that it enlisted untried techniques which, almost as much as aerial photography itself, added new weapons and new dimensions to archaeology. It is this sequel which gave a singular proof of the cumulative challenge of science: by conquering new frontiers it introduces new problems and stimulates new solutions. This is not to say that aerial archaeology was in any way supplanted, but rather supplemented. In a book on aerial archaeology we will be necessarily brief in discussing these developments, though they are a direct consequence of airborne achievements and hence bear on its story.

Now, one of the practical applications of aerial photography over Etruria, as Bradford clearly stated, was to pick out and plot those burial areas that, relatively inconspicuous at ground level, might have escaped, at least in recent centuries, the guile of tomb robbers. A similar purpose was served by delineating sites threatened by deep ploughing or planting of orchards and vineyards. Certain such areas seemed to Bradford quite propitious for further excavation, among them one in the south-east

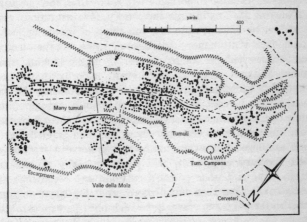

Figure 20. This plan shows hundreds of levelled Etruscan tumuli which Bradford pinned down on an air photograph of the Monte Abbatone necropolis outside Cerveteri (Caere). Wedges within black circles indicate tomb entrances showing up as grass-marks. Thick black lines mark buried cemetery roads (*vie sepolcrali*)

of the Banditaccia. It was there that, before he had an opportunity to see the air photographs, Professor Pallottino, the leading Etruscologist of Italy, 'working from ground indications alone', had recorded only *sepolcri sparsi*. But then, in May 1951, after photographs of that very zone had been published by Bradford, Pallottino, in order to train his students from the University of Rome, directed excavations there for three weeks. Bradford had forecast that 'worthwhile finds' could well be expected. Predictably, too, the tombs had been broken into, though long, long ago. They happened to be moderately rich in a number of goods, especially imported Greek pottery. Pallottino also noted architectural details of interest.

Modern excavation, if it is to maintain high standards, is a costly business. Only on rare occasions can the expense be justified on educational grounds alone. To dig up just one simple tumulus will cost several hundred dollars. Yet chances are that all the money will go down the drain; the grave will turn out to be empty; it will reveal no novel feature whatever; nothing of scientific importance will result from the campaign. Considering the loss in time and money, few institutions, even if backed by affluent sponsors, can think of repeating such a hit-and-miss venture more than once or twice. Yet the Etruscan necropolises harbour tombs numbering in the hundred thousands. Without question, the great majority have been thoroughly ransacked at one time or another during the past two thousand years, several more than once. Intuition may guide one to remoter sites that possibly have gained less attention. But there is no certainty about this, and granted that in such privileged hideaways tombs still preserve a fraction of their funerary equipment, will those be really unique and worth your and your patron's expenditure? Meanwhile the funds could have been much more profitably spent on some other so far unknown grave. But which one? Perhaps a robber, whose less orthodox methods are so much cheaper and who relies on heaven only knows what secret channels of information, besides an uncanny instinct for treasure, may get there first. How, indeed, can one forestall those diggers of darkness? (They usually operate by night.) As if that were not enough, one also has to run a race against reclamation schemes that threaten to wipe out the record once and for all.

There were even more frustrations to come. Aerial archaeology, miraculous as its achievements are, has its limitations, too. These may at least complicate the task of the excavator who has been alerted to a site by photographs from above. Soilmarks, in particular, often become rather diffuse and will be more and more shifted from repeated ploughing of the soil. Hence they do not always qualify as reliable guides and may be downright misleading. Similar disappointments have been experienced with marks of entrances to the tombs. Then there is a group of small burial crypts, so-called *pozzetti*, little but holes in the ground that more often than not the photograph fails to pick up. Should they appear, then several of them or other small underground structures are usually so closely packed together that it will become impossible to single out the individual layout from the shapeless blob on the air picture. Yet, just because these tombs are so unassuming and inconspicuous, they may have been bypassed by robbers and therefore will offer, on occasion, the greater prize. It would be a pity to miss them.

Apart from the small size of a buried feature, its depth may present the most serious limitation to aerial surveying. At a certain level, which, among other factors, will vary with the soil and the kind of plant life it supports, subterranean structures can be seen no more. No matter how sensitive the film, how sharp the lenses, and how selective the filters and range of light rays you turn on them, they remain hidden. Some estimates of the tombs missed by aerial photographs of the Etruscan cemeteries run well above 50 per cent.

Of course, just pinning down a mark on the ground after it has shown up beautifully and distinctly on the air photograph can, as we have already seen, be plagued with difficulties. Everything may seem quite clear on the aerial picture. But when visiting the site one will stare at nothing but weeds or earth. In short, the search has to start anew.

To hope for an answer to all these staggering problems seems sheer hubris. Yet ways have been borrowed from other sciences that go a long way to resolve the dilemmas and to supplement aerial archaeology with formidable tools. What was clearly needed was a method that was more expeditious and cheaper than full-scale digging. If one could only examine a tomb at a glance, or rather examine beforehand as many as possible in order to sift the few that warranted thorough excavation.

It was an Italian industrialist, trained in the techniques of geophysics, who addressed himself to this tall order. He was not the first to apply geophysical techniques to the locating of archaeological material; that honour is, as a rule, granted to a British scholar, R. J. C. Atkinson, and to a German-American,

Helmut de Terra. But even they had antecedents. Lerici, however, was among the earliest pioneers and devised his own procedures and apparatus for Etruscan researches. So enthusiastic was he about the new technological developments he helped to introduce into archaeology that he set aside funds (his family luckily owned a steel mill in Northern Italy) and formed an archaeological division at his geophysical institute attached to the Milan Polytechnic. A branch, from which Lerici mainly operated, was opened in Rome. In years to come, the institute not only directed researches in Etruria, but joined with the University of Pennsylvania in the search for the lost Greek colony of Sybaris in Southern Italy. It also participated in explorations in the Sudan, in Turkey (where tumuli not unlike those of the Etruscans proliferated in the Anatolian highlands), in Bulgaria, Spain, and Jordan.

C. M. Lerici, who was born in 1890 in Verona, received his training as engineer at Turin. Later he was connected with the Milan Polytechnic, where in 1947 he founded the Fondazione C. M. Lerici. This institution devoted itself in the main to geophysical research for the prospecting of minerals, oil, natural gas, and water. Lerici's archaeological interests are said to have been awakened when he was requested to design a family mausoleum. To prepare himself for this enterprise he looked into earlier models and inevitably was drawn to Italy's varied antiquities. There ensued his fascination with the Etruscans that soon became an end in itself. On his visits to Roman collections he was told of the work of Bradford in drawing up detailed maps of the Etruscan necropolises from air photographs of the Second World War. The neatness of the process strongly appealed to his technological acumen. 'It was astounding to me', Lerici later wrote, 'how much could be learned of what lies beneath the the earth's surface by studying shadings of the soil, relative growth of vegetation, shadows and markings revealed in the raking light of dawn or sunset ... Aerial pictures can almost be said to "talk".' But he soon realized that air photographs are not the whole answer. Here was the great opportunity for the geophysicist to apply the tools that had proven successful in the location of underground natural resources.

Lerici and his associates from the Milan Polytechnic made their first test in 1954. They selected a site near Fabriano in central Italy, where an aerial photograph had previously outlined a tomb in a circular vegetation-mark. Though no trace was visible to anyone standing on the surface of the terrain, geophysical 'soundings' at the site registered positive impulses. On digging there they found a stone-lined subterranean grave with pieces of burned human bones and fragments of pottery. Encouraged by this and a few similar tests, Lerici called a conference in December 1954 – the first of its kind – at the Department of Antiquities in Rome to discuss the application to archaeology of aerial and geophysical investigation. Archaeologists and engineers from Italy and abroad attended. One of the participants was Bradford. Another was R. Bartoccini, Superintendent of Antiquities for Southern Etruria, who, despite criticism from the Italian archaeological profession, backed Lerici wholeheartedly in his future operations at the Etruscan necropolises.

Henceforth Lerici and his staff employed three main, consecutive techniques for the exploration of Etruscan tombs. The equipment needed could be easily carried along on a small truck or station wagon. Lerici himself never tired of insisting that all operations had to be preceded by a photographic survey from the air, which as a rule would determine their choice of site. Stage one either corroborates or extends the aerial record by a geophysical test not unlike mine-detecting in wartime. The most common method relies on a simple portable potentiometer which, through electrodes inserted in the ground, will register the relative resistivity of the soil to an electric current passing between them. Since the resistivity naturally varies with the composition of the ground and its artificial or natural enclosures – including air – the precise location as well as depth and dimension of the subterranean structure can be fully determined from graphs. Complementary to electrical tests, and under certain conditions more effective, are methods based on seismic shocks, magnetic fields, acoustic waves, and even radioactivity – all commonly used in the exploration for oil and ore deposits. Thanks to geophysical testing it is now possible to establish the exact location and extent of a tomb chamber.

The stage, however, is not yet set for excavation, since as we have seen the tomb may not justify the effort and expense. It is here that Lerici's approach pulls a real trick: his second step entails the sinking of an electrically powered mining drill (operated by a small generator) through the centre of the crypt's roof. A hole is thus made, causing no damage to speak of. Its width is kept to about three inches. Bradford, whom Lerici invited to direct a campaign of this kind in 1956 at the Etrurian necropolises, where he used his maps as guides, described this phase when 'after a tense period of hard work, suddenly the drill should pierce the tomb's roof. It is a triumphant moment, eagerly awaited! The sound – a resonant "thud" – as it perforates the vacuum inside has a characteristic note.' The test hole, depending on the depth of the chamber, may reach as far down as twenty feet. The drill, apart from making an opening in the tomb, can also be used to extract during that process a stratified sample of the perforated soil.

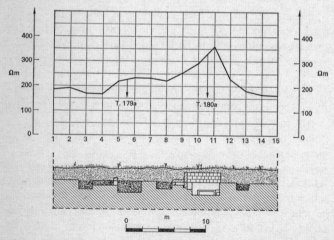

Figure 21. A resistivity graph of two Etruscan tombs (outlined in cross-section below) illustrating how modern 'geophysical' techniques can pick up dislocations in the subsoil

The third step was the most crucial of all and the most exciting. For its execution Lerici had built a special camera tube in his institute's workshop. It consisted of a hollow aluminium valve of some two and a half inches in diameter capable of being inserted into the previously drilled borehole. Its principal fixture was a miniature camera – the German Minox of espionage fame – barely the size of a cigarette lighter. It could take black-and-white or colour pictures only slightly larger than 8-millimetre films. Farther down the tube, also installed behind a waterproof window, was a photoflash which, together with the camera, could be released from the outside. As a general practice the tube was rotated clockwise in twelve turns of thirty degrees each, thus allowing a complete photographic record 'in the round' of the hidden interior. Bradford aptly named this archaeological reconnaissance 'periscope photography', a term now generally adopted. In the following excerpt from a report in the *Illustrated London News*, he described its astonishing achievements:

Every night we examined them [the negatives] through a photographic enlarger, after the day's work. The details were wonderfully clear, and showed to our complete satisfaction if we had discovered a tomb with important contents. While the film unrolled and dozens of pictures appeared, we were privileged to see the interiors of tombs which had been closed for many centuries past. Here were traces of wall-painting, and there lay the vases deposited around the dead! These were some of the most remarkable 'films' ever seen.

The new method was triumphantly vindicated. It was a further extension of aerial archaeology's magic of seeing into the earth. The goal of exploring underground features without digging was fulfilled to perfection. By surveying the remaining artefacts it selected at the same time those sites that definitely called for total excavation. This work phase, too, was aided by the interior photographs, because the films could direct the excavator to exactly where the entrance way led to the burial chamber.

Several technical refinements were later added. A Roman optical manufacturer came up with an improved periscope so

powerfully lighted that it could dispense with time-consuming
photography and permit the archaeologist to gaze directly into
the tomb. (A simple camera attachment above the ground also
provided for the taking of pictures if needed.) From the use of
such an apparatus it was just a small step to the installation of
a television camera peeking into the unexcavated sepulchre.

Lerici's periscope archaeology has proved its worth since its
first major explorations in 1956. By reducing the need for excavation to only the most promising instances, it cut down ex-
penses dramatically while covering enormous ground with all
the thoroughness and speed that was required. Yet no more
than two or three men were required at a time. Benefiting from
and stimulated by aerial archaeology, it took over where
photography from above was no longer at its best. Like the
latter, it performed optical wizardry and achieved amazing
short-cuts that could crowd within a few days labours that
would have formerly meant years, if not lifetimes, of campaigning. Besides it had a fighting chance of beating robbers
and reclamation. It is doubtful whether any other means could
have accomplished so much, even if time, budget, and man-
power were of no concern. Bradford reported that in twelve
days he examined forty tombs in this manner. But this was
only a modest beginning. The 1958-to-1959 harvest was 850
tombs at Tarquinia alone, and this figure includes quite a few
fully excavated. Few and far between, but nevertheless encouraging, cropped up several completely unlooted tombs with
impressive collections of funerary equipment. Bradford in 1957
was bold enough to forecast: 'It is only a matter of patience
before a major group of Etruscan wall-paintings is discovered
by "air-plus-ground" archaeology.' Others were not so hopeful,
considering that no painted burial chamber had been dug up
since the Tomb of Bulls at Tarquinia in 1892, despite so many
labours among the necropolises of Etruria in the past decades.
Yet this is just what happened in March 1958, and also at Tarquinia.

One night, out in the field, the tiny coloured slides of the
Minox camera showed a whole gallery of some of the finest
Etruscan paintings ever discovered. They could be dated to the
sixth century B.C. All depicted athletes indulging in various

sports such as chariot racing, throwing the discus, long-jumping, running, and dancing. Obviously the splendid murals depicted games, most likely staged for religious or funeral events, but still mirroring joyful sporting scenes. No question, the name for the painted tumuli had to be Olympiad Tomb; the

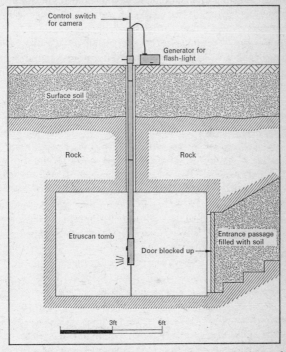

Figure 22. Schematic drawing of the operation of periscope photography within an unopened tomb

name was a natural, both because of the subject matter and by the strange coincidence that the Olympic Games were to be held on Italian soil, in 1960. Since this highly publicized discovery a great many more mural paintings have been brought to the surface by what Lerici loves to call the magic 'Eye of Minos'. In Tarquinia, which has always been the principal source of painted graves, Lerici's explorations had by 1965 recovered some fifty painted tombs, thus doubling within a few years the known legacy that it had taken several centuries to accumulate. Truly, the 'Eye of Minos' searching underground and the 'Eye of Daedalus' roaming high above together have revealed among the dead of Etruria marvellous vistas of one of the most puzzling civilizations of Mediterranean antiquity.

8. Spina: Lost Pearl of the Adria

No matter how much the tombs can tell us about the art, the religion, the economy, and the society of the Etruscans, and how close the parallels are between the abodes of the dead and those of the living, it has long been something of an archaeological scandal that we know so little about their cities. When generations of travellers wrote their impressionistic sketches of Etruscan 'places', they invariably concentrated on the strange structures and splendid contents of the great necropolises. So did the majority of scholars. A visit to Tarquinia or Cerveteri or Vulci still means rummaging around the underground tombs in virtually complete disregard of the ruined town sites near by. For such negligence there are, of course, various reasons, not the least being the time-honoured fixation of antiquarians and excavators on substantial features and removable objects. The real bonanzas were in the cemeteries, so why waste time on indifferent remains of houses or temples of which, because of their perishable building materials, little was left to convey the haunting culture of a vanished race? Admittedly, nearly all we have hitherto learned of the Etruscans – and this is considerable – we owe (apart from literary references) to their treasure-laden sepulchres. But sooner or later the balance had to be redressed.

Fortunately, a volte-face has taken place in recent decades. Even if at first somewhat timidly, as Raymond Bloch, the French archaeologist, remarks, campaigns have been launched at various sites. Employing RAF photographs in the manner of Bradford, the British School of Archaeology at Rome under its director, J. B. Ward Perkins, has in the post-war years probed diligently into the roadnets that once tied Etruscan cities together. Meanwhile, an Italian archaeologist, M. Romanelli, was carrying out excavations at Tarquinia, and, in the late 1950s, R.

Bartoccini, the Superintendent of Antiquities for Southern Etruria, announced his plan to fully investigate the deserted plateau where Vulci once stood. This project was to be conducted with all the devices now available to scientific archaeology, principally aerial surveying and geophysical and geochemical prospecting.

Figure 23. Sketch map of Etruscan Italy. The shaded areas mark the extent of colonization from south of the Bay of Naples to the foothills of the Alps and the coast of Corsica

The Etruscan civilization was, if anything, of an urban character. It was the fame of Etruscan cities that resounded throughout Italy and beyond, so that Livy could write long after their eclipse: 'The renown of their name filled the whole length of Italy from the Alps to the Sicilian Strait.' Cities were the very life centre of the Etruscans. Jacques Heurgon in his instructive volume *Daily Life of the Etruscans* states accurately: 'Though the Etruscans showed themselves to be good agronomists and vigorously imposed their will on Nature, it was above all as builders of towns that they revealed their true genius.'

Unlike the Italic tribes, whose settlements were at best aggregations of scattered buildings, the Etruscans looked upon cities as compact, organic units in which kinsmen were joined under a common spiritual and legal authority. Cities were founded according to strict religious rules (the *ritus Etruscus*), and their hallowed ground was laid out in a prescribed regular pattern. Though concessions could be made to exigencies of terrain, the true city, or *urbs justa*, had to obey certain precepts. Thus, for example, a city had to have three gates and a threefold temple dedicated to the holy trinity of Jupiter, Juno, and Minerva (the Tin, Uni, and Menerva of the Etruscans). Its main streets, the *cardo* and *decumanus*, intersecting each other at right angles, were oriented, like the highways radiating from the Inca capital of Cuzco, toward the four cardinal points. In order to establish precise directions, use was made of a special instrument, the *groma*. Etruscans found Rome (the name is Etruscan) an aggregate of a few hilltop hovels, and left it after their hundred and fifty years' rule a city in the proper sense. Indeed, they bequeathed to Rome the very concept of 'city', or *urbs*. Rome itself perpetuated the Etruscan image of a city with its Capitoline shrine and inviolable *pomerium*, an urban zone that skirted the inside of the wall and could be neither ploughed nor built upon. Until the end of their empire, the Romans would reserve their highest accolades for a city that had been founded according to the Etruscan rite. Roman colonists observed rules, rites, and dedication ceremonies, known to us by the Latin term *limitatio*, in all detail, so that a string of Roman cities and camps in Spain, in Gaul, in Syria and other provinces mirror Etruscan urbanism to perfection. Cosa, an early Roman colony on Italian home soil, recently excavated by Americans (with the guidance of air photographs), is a fine example of a city carved out in the Etruscan manner. Roman chequerboard land division, or centuriation, which has been dramatically revealed from the air in Dalmatia, North Africa, various parts of Italy, and elsewhere, is little but an extension of Etruscan practices. The very unit for square blocks of land (*centuria quadrata*) measuring 710 × 710 metres (776 yards) (or 20 × 20 *actus* = 200 *jugera*), like the surveying methods and theories – Romans translated Etruscan treatises on mensuration into Latin – can be traced back to the planning methods of the Etruscans, who may, in turn, have been indebted to Greek and Near Eastern models.

The Etruscans never merged their cities into a territorial state, and this may well be the reason they ultimately failed to unite the Italian peninsula, while their rude disciples succeeded. Etruria remained a cluster of sovereign cities loosely joined in a confederation of twelve, the *duodecim Etruriae populi*, which appears to have been religious rather than political. Owing to the scarcity of historical texts, we are not even certain which cities belonged to the league, though very likely the most important ancient centres, such as Tarquinia, Veii, Vulci, Chiusi, and Caere, were members. Volsinii, the modern Bolsena, where the French School at Rome under R. Bloch has dug with notable success since 1946, was the 'ceremonial' capital. All these cities had distinguished histories and were held in awe by Romans and Greeks. Before it became fashionable to have their youths study in Athens or Rhodes, Roman aristocrats would have them trained at Caere in the finer things of life.

While ancient authors keep us well informed on even minor squabbles between the Greek cities in Southern Italy, they have next to nothing to say of the course of events in the Etruscan metropolises and their interrelations. Of ruling dynasties, political changes, leadership, social frictions, and military developments the literary evidence is of the scantiest and cries the more for archaeological avenues of inquiry. Though we know at least the general outline of Etruscan expansion into the south and the clashes with the Greek colonies of Sicily and Magna Graecia, and later with Rome, the identity of the newly established Etruscan cities in the Campania (as far south as Salerno) – allegedly joined in another league of twelve – remains vague, aside from powerful Capua on the Volturno, which goes back perhaps as far as the eighth century B.C.

The lacunae are still greater for another vital phase of Etruscan growth, the historic push northward in the late sixth century B.C. across the Apennines into the Po Valley. Here, too, there was created a new Etruria – *Etruria padana* (of the Po) – with a hard core of reputedly twelve cities. Which they were remains largely guesswork. Certainly there was Bologna, a former Villanovan settlement, which the Etruscans called Felsina, maybe Ravenna, and Piacenza (Placentia), where the famous model of a sheep liver has been recovered, and Atria (Adria) once a seaport like Ravenna, which gave its name to the Adriatic Sea. Mantua, the birthplace of Virgil, was most likely another. And there was an unmistakable Etruscan townsite near present-day Marzabotto, some twenty miles southwest of Bologna, laid out in a regular grid. As it was situated on the River Reno, the Etruscan advance route from Fiesole into the north, it was probably the first trans-Apennine city they founded. Undoubtedly of considerable importance, it also happened to be one of the few urban areas thoroughly studied and excavated from the 1860s onward. Nevertheless, its very name (Misa?) is uncertain.

There was, however, no mystery about the name of another northern city: Spina. So famous was this emporium at the mouth of the Po that ancient authors, foremost geographers of the first century A.D., never tired of singing its praise. But it posed a riddle of a different sort. Spina had disappeared from the face of the earth and no one knew where exactly it was located.

Spina had seen its greatest days in the fifth century B.C. when it was the leading port at the head of the Adria and dominated coastal and overseas trade in these parts. From everything we know it was a cosmopolitan centre where Etruscan rulers mixed freely with a middle class of immigrant Greek tradesmen and humble native Venetians, Ligurians, and Umbrians. Just then the Adria and Po Valley had given the Etruscans a new outlet which amply compensated for the setbacks they had suffered at the hands of the Greek cities in Southern Italy. Direct maritime routes were opened to Athens, and the finest Attic ceramics from the golden age of Themistocles and Pericles were unpacked at its piers, both for local consumption and for further distribution. Thus Spina, together with its sister city, Atria, benefited from extraordinary economic opportunities. There was an immensely fertile hinterland along the Po which, thanks to Etruscan hydraulic and agricultural proficiency, supplied abundant crops of wheat. Panning of salt, a profitable export item, flourished along the seashore. Spina must also have played a key role in continental or trans-Alpine commerce. There is evidence that it marketed amber from the Baltic, a product much in demand then by Mediterranean people and still a standard item in the curio shops of Venice. Through Spina and other Padavian centres which came to control the Alpine trade routes, Greek and Etruscan products, in particular vases and jewellery, reached remote Scandinavia, the British Isles, and Gallic France. The Runic script, the first alphabetic writing to be used in Northern Europe, is probably derived from a northern Etrurian variant. Not the least of the cultural effects of transplanting Etruria to the north has been registered in a decisive phase (named after Hallstatt in Austria) of the European Iron Age, the impact of which was felt all over the western and northern continent.

In the humming cultural and economic scene of pre-Roman Northern Italy, Spina, for all purposes, was an Etruscan Venice; and this analogy was, as we shall see, anything but superficial. To the ancients nothing reflected the ascendancy of the city more than the fact that it deposited a tithe of its enormous annual profits in Delphi. The Spina treasury at the pan-Hellenic sanctuary was for long one of the most opulent and could still be seen centuries after the city's eclipse. Such display of wealth helped broadcast Spina's former glory and made people philosophize on its end.

Despite its favoured position, Spina's fortunes were relatively short-lived. Its halcyon days lasted for little more than a century. By the beginning of the fourth century B.C. it began to decline rapidly. Like much of Italy, including Etruria proper and Rome, it was, if not actually ransacked (the lagoons may have shielded her from direct assault), seriously set back by the Gallic invasions from across the Alps. To infer its abandonment at that time, as some modern scholars have done, is hardly warranted. The city lingered on; a diminutive settlement was reported by Strabo in the first century A.D. Rather than the

Gauls, who were partly Etruscanized, what strangled the Adriatic metropolis slowly but surely were elemental forces; or, in
the beloved metaphor of archaeological popularizers, the 'jeal-
ousy of nature', which by jungle growth, flood, earthquakes,
pestilence, and other such apocalyptic agents is trusted to

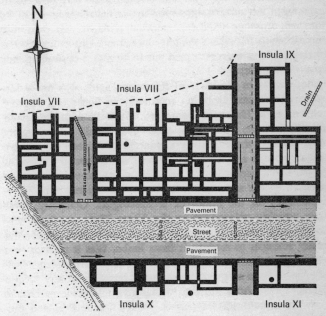

Figure 24. Outline of geometric street and drainage systems of
'Marzabotto', an early Etruscan outpost across the Apennines

eventually make a shambles of proud human handiwork. The
alluvial deposits of the Po removed the city more and more
from the sea. Its vital water routes became clogged. In the
fourth century B.C., Spina was some two miles away from the
coast, with which it was still linked by a navigable port canal.
By the first century A.D. the distance had increased to some ten
miles and, like Ravenna, which was once an Adriatic port
veined by waterways, Spina became completely landlocked. At
last it was entirely abandoned. When the Ficarolo dam broke

in the twelfth century and the Po shifted its course north toward Venice, the whole geography of the delta changed. The area where once Spina's polyglot people bustled and trim white-sailed ships from all over the Mediterranean lay alongside its docks became a lacustrine wilderness of marshes and lagoons. The soil subsided and, presumably, the city was henceforth submerged. All surface signs vanished, as did the memory of its location. Since no fixed landmark survived, it was well nigh impossible to tell where the city once stood. Unfortunately the ancient literary sources turned out to be rather misleading, not to say contradictory.

But thanks to the classical references, Spina was never forgotten. The name crops up repeatedly in Boccaccio. Starting with an early Humanist from Forlì, Flavio Biondo, the search for the lost city became a passion that would occupy many men through the centuries. Carducci, the nineteenth-century Italian bard, in a famous ode did his share to bewail the fate of Spina, that Queen City of the Adriatic, whose voice has been silenced by the mists of time. The sonorous verses rankled reproachfully in the minds of archaeologists. Gradually, however, sceptical voices took up the debate. They wondered why so allegedly great a city could stay so totally lost, despite the many attempts to retrieve it from limbo. Was it perhaps in a class with Atlantis – that beautiful tale of a perished legendary site, endemic to all maritime countries but without any precise factual basis? After all, the ancient accounts made much ado over the nebulous Pelasgians as Spina's first settlers and promoted various scions of Olympian gods to inspired founders of the city. These narratives sounded rather like routine mythology, as did allusions to original landing parties from Greece or Troy. If there had ever been a Spina, one plausible hypothesis maintained, it should probably be equated with a minor port serving Felsina along the mouth of the Reno River near Ravenna. A few scholars felt satisfied with this explanation that more or less fitted the facts and dispensed with any embarrassing challenge to pursue the matter any further. Needless to say, such common sense failed to convince Spina partisans. They held out bravely.

The first crucial step toward a solution of the vexing problem was not at all connected with archaeology. In this instance land reclamation and agrarian reforms, whose public-spirited schemes are likely to raise archaeologists' blood pressure, turned out to be their best friend.

As early as 1913 a plan had been launched to drain extensive waterlogged depressions at the southern fringe of today's Po delta close to Comacchio, a picturesque medieval town built on islets some thirty miles east of Ferrara. Comacchio, which has seen better days, is itself now removed from the coast but is surrounded by marshes and lagoons. The people's mainstay was eel-fishing in the local waters, until land improvements came to yield them both expected and unexpected returns from the reconquered soil.

Reclamation began in earnest in the fall of 1919 in the nearby Vale Trebba. While land slowly emerged between the recently cut drainage canals, agronomists initiated planting in the drier sections. These experiments led them in no time to ancient tombs. Affinities of the graves and their goods with Etruscan burials elsewhere in Northern Italy, particularly those near Bologna and Marzabotto, convinced the authorities of the importance of the site, whose watery shroud promised to have kept it undisturbed. Official excavation under the aegis of the local archaeological administration was entrusted to experts, first to Dr Augusto Negrioli and then to the Superintendent of Antiquities for Emilia, Professor Salvatore Aurigemma. Work continued until 1935. By that time more than twelve hundred tombs had been discovered, aside from an untold number that were emptied illicitly by enterprising Comacchiesi. Of course, it soon became obvious that here was an extensive necropolis. The enormous return in objects included granulated golden earrings and bronze candelabras of distinctly Etruscan cast, amber necklaces, Egyptian vessels of glass and alabaster, and a wealth of red-figured Attic craters. To store all these riches it eventually became necessary to requisition a Renaissance palace at Ferrara, which had been commissioned by Ludovico Sforza. Henceforth called the National Museum of Archaeology of Ferrara, it was soon filled to the brim with one of Italy's most exquisite collections of ancient art.

Archaeologists were not at loss to date the various articles ranging, in the main, from the fifth and fourth centuries B.C. The great amount of Attic ware not only bore out the Etruscans' abiding hankering for Hellenic goods but pointed to many Greeks buried here, a likelihood confirmed by manifold inscriptions in Greek, and the fact that some ancient writers had called Spina and other North Etruscan cities outright Greek. Possibly, Adriatic ports of the time attracted a strong element of Greek artisans and merchants, who formed the middle class, complementing the ruling Etruscan aristocracy and native servants and slaves.

No question about it: a Graeco-Etruscan necropolis of the wealth and dimensions of the Vale Trebba could only have belonged to a major city. Etruscans, as a rule, maintained their cemeteries in the vicinity of their towns, but, irritatingly enough, no such city was anywhere in sight. As early as 1924, Dr Negrioli did not hesitate to declare that the vast new necropolis harboured none other than the dead of Spina. The strong Greek admixture, the literary references to the area, the conspicuous wealth, the mere size, the cosmopolitan flavour of a great international emporium, and the date (fifth to third centuries B.C.), everything fell into line. But where was Spina?

So once more the Etruscans had been revealed through their tombs alone. The more reason why the search for lost Spina had to continue. One thing was certain: Spina could not be very far. Though expectations rode high, for a while nothing came of them. Spina's dead were unceremoniously dug up, the city remained buried. For several years after 1935, the ghost of Spina still slumbered.

Almost two decades later – in 1953, to be exact – antiquities were offered by dealers in increasing numbers, which aroused the suspicions of Etruscologists. They resembled in many ways the Graeco-Etruscan objects housed in the Ferrara museum. The Vale Trebba necropolis was considered cleared. What, then, could be their provenance? This mystery, at least, was soon resolved, since their appearance coincided with another drainage project just taking shape in the Comacchio area in the so-called Vale Pega to the south of the Vale Trebba. Alerted by the experts, Italian officialdom acted promptly. With aplomb that might well be envied by other countries whose antiquities are constantly threatened, a large zone was withdrawn from agricultural utilization and reserved exclusively for archaeological exploration. Italian administrators even ordered the detouring of a projected dam so that the terrain would be left entirely intact.

However, this time the task facing the archaeologists was far more formidable. The new necropolis in the Vale Pega was still under some thirteen to fifteen inches of water. To reach the tombs, of which several were six feet under the surface, one somehow had to penetrate through the mud and slime. Under such conditions, standard excavation methods were futile. Not only this, but just to get to the grave sites from dry land presented more difficulties, considering that the water level was, on the whole, too low for boating, yet too deep, and treacherous besides, to wade through. In such a terrain the cunning local eel-fishers had all the advantages. A visiting American archaeologist (Sabine Gova) has described the unique technique of the 'inventive thieves [who] were attaching wooden boards to their hands and feet and were gliding on all fours across the swamp, probing the mud with steel-topped poles in search of the desired loot'. Eventually most of the area was more or less effectively policed, and with progressive draining professional archaeologists started the tremendously difficult operations, not without adopting certain tricks from their roguish rivals.

In 1954, excavations began under the direction of Professor Paolo Enrico Arias of the University of Catania. He was assisted by Nereo Alfieri, who, from the following year on, became the guiding spirit behind the recovery of Spina.

Nereo Alfieri is himself a native of the Adriatic coast. He was born in Ancona, an old seaport of The Marches south-east of Ravenna. To us it comes as no surprise to learn that this Italian master archaeologist, too, started his career in topography and was to find his way to archaeology via the royal road of historical geography. His doctoral thesis, accepted in 1937 by the University of Bologna, dealt with the topography of ancient Ancona. For some years Alfieri was preoccupied with charting the physical details of historic sites around his native region. One of his first projects was to survey the field at the Metaurus (Metauro) River, north of Ancona, where Hasdrubal, the younger brother of Hannibal, battled the Romans in 207 B.C. and lost his life. Alfieri also learned to take hints from local legends when it came to locating ruins. The story goes that he discovered a remote Roman temple by having a shepherd direct him to a 'sanctuary'. Immediately after the Second World War Alfieri was attached to the Superintendent of Antiquities at Ancona. But once he familiarized himself with the riddle of Spina, he had found his true mission. The region of the old Po estuary, particularly the marshlands around Comacchio, now about to undergo further drastic changes through modern drainage schemes, seemed made for his topographic approach. Few places among the much explored terrain of Italy offered archaeologists greater promise. Somewhere, he was convinced, under the brackish waters and swamps of the monotonous wastes, Spina was hidden. And he was the one to find it. Only a man trained to make his way in a landscape in which all land-marks of the past had been effaced could hope to disentangle the enigma. Alfieri was prepared to face economic and physical hardship. Spina was calling. He left his home town and sought employment in Emilia.

As a reward for his dedication he eventually became director of the Ferrara museum. But first there were years of unreward-ing search. Prior to joining hands with Arias, he was constantly on the lookout for a clue to the location of the lost city. He restudied the ancient sources; again and again he went over the area around Comacchio and the Vale Trebba; he dug trial ditches and test holes; he ploughed through medieval manu-scripts for any possible link between the Etruscan settlement and a Dark Age survivor or successor. Most persistently of all, he pursued his goal of reconstructing the landscape, with its former shorelines and arms of the Po, as it must have appeared at the time when Spina ruled the waves of the Adria. In the latter inquiry he made substantial progress. He identified vari-ous stages of the advancing coast in a series of parallel dunes. There, he was almost certain, the original settlements must have been planted, in addition, perhaps, to raised riverbanks which in sub-sea-level alluvial flats tend to be piled above the surrounding plain. Alfieri also gauged the former course of the Po, the so-called *Padanus vetus*. He saw clearly how the burial

1. The first aerial picture taken in the U.S., this view of Boston was photographed by J. W. Black and S. A. King from a captive balloon in 1860/61, two years after Nadar's pioneer venture over Paris

2. A balloon being readied for aerial photography over Megiddo (Armageddon), Palestine

3. An air view of Megiddo during excavation

4. Extensible ladder (height 9·7 metres) used at Megiddo for observation and photography

5. A low oblique air photograph of Old Samarra, Iraq. In the foreground the Moslem mosque with an unusual, well-preserved minaret. Alongside and behind, some of the vast sand-covered ruins of the short-lived ninth-century A.D. capital are marked in low relief

6. The more or less rectangular 'Celtic' fields on Fyfield Down, Wiltshire, are traced from above in the shadow-marks of its earthbanks (lynchets)

7. Completely invisible from the ground, this section of the Stonehenge Avenue was picked up by air camera in the dark parallel lines of its buried ditches

8. Damp-marks in ploughed fields at Neufmoulin, Somme, revealed this complex of hitherto unknown prehistoric ditches, some superimposed on others

9. The origin of crop-marks demonstrated by a cut through Burcot pit near Dorchester. Over the triangular ditch in the centre the vegetation shows up higher and thicker than on the undisturbed soil

10–11. Site of the Roman 'villa' of Ditchley (Watts Wells), Oxfordshire, photographed by Allen in November and June. Crop-marks in the summer brought out minute details of a completely effaced building, while there were no hints whatever in the late autumn

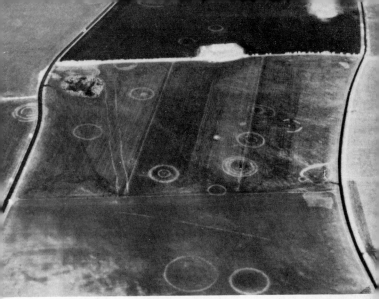

12. Crowmarsh (North Stoke), Oxfordshire. A whole canvas of crop-marks of ring-ditches representing razed Bronze Age barrows with a narrow 'cursus' of two parallel lines running between

13. Wroxeter (Virconium or Uriconium), Shropshire. This near-vertical photograph of the Roman centre on the Severn furnishes almost a blue-print – including street grid and overall layout of buildings – in the crops covering the major part of the town

14. Long shadows of the evening sun depict this deserted medieval village at Newbold Grounds near Catesby, Northamptonshire, with its typical mounds and hollows marking streets and various buildings

15. One of the two major religious circles (henges) on Hutton Moor near Ripon, Yorkshire, turned up in a wheat field in the summer of 1949

16. A small portion of the extensive chequerboard of a Roman field division (centuriation) in Tunisia, charted on vertical air survey photographs over the El Djem-Chebba region

17. In May 1945 John Bradford depicted this huge, *c.* 2500 B.C. Neolithic settlement ('Passo di Corvo') near Foggia, on a low oblique air photograph

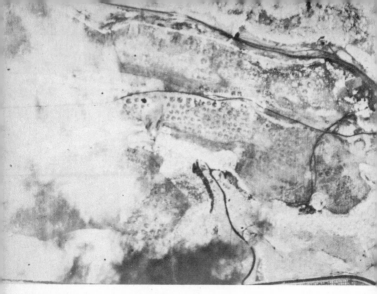

18. The Monte Abbatone necropolis outside Cerveteri, 20 miles north-west of Rome. Whitish blobs disclose hundreds of levelled Etruscan tombs; the dark line top left traces a *via sepolcrale* leading to a road junction. Compare with Figure 20

19. Inside view of a frescoed wall of the 'Tomb of the Olympiad', near the ancient Etruscan centre of Tarquinia

20. Probing an underground Etruscan tomb through a specially constructed 'periscope'

21. Spina, the long-sought Etrusco-Greek city in the Po Valley. The grid of canals and city blocks was neatly sketched in lighter and darker shades of marsh grass. Note the wide black strip, top left, which represents the principal port canal. Superimposed white parallels belong to a modern drainage system

22. Two Maya causeways south of Cobá were registered from the air in intersecting lines by a December 1930 University of Pennsylvania expedition

23. The same airborne team identified unknown pre-Columbian ruins among the overgrown protuberances of the endless jungle of the Petén, northern Guatemala, at longitude 89° 50′ W. and latitude 17° 32′ N.

24. Terraced 'bowls' at Maras Pampa, about 15 miles south-west of Cuzco, revealed in a photograph taken by the Shippee-Johnson expedition

25. A section of the 'Great Wall' of Peru in the Santa Valley, snaking its way through the Andean foot-hills. The rampart is of pre-Inca origin, and probably served military purposes. A number of stone and adobe forts lined it on both sides of its 40-mile length

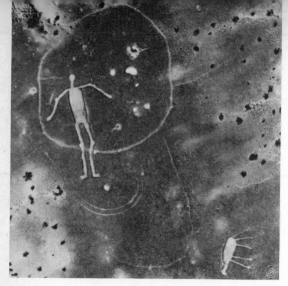

26. This giant 'intaglio' Indian pictograph, probably representing a mythical figure, is one of many similar sand drawings found on the bluffs above the Colorado River. This one, north of Blythe, California, caught the attention of George Palmer, an amateur pilot, during a flight in 1932

27. Geometric network of Nazca 'roads', central Peru. Paul Kosok, who took the picture, thought that these desert markings formed part of the 'largest astronomy book in the world'

28. Poverty Point, northern Louisiana: six enormous concentric banks of earthworks. They once formed an octagon, part of which has been washed away by an arm of the Mississippi

29. Pre-Columbian man-made ridges in the flood plain of the San Jorge River of northern Colombia

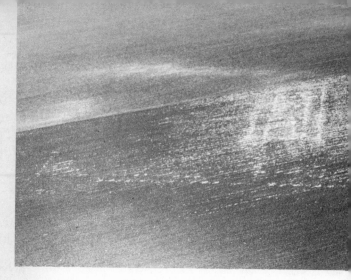

30. The reappearance of this huge Gallo-Roman 'villa' more than 1,000 feet long was aided by hoar-frost in winter. Agache spotted it at Warfusee-Abancourt (Somme)

31. A striking example of the active aerial reconnaissance carried out in Germany's Rhineland by the American-born Dr Irwin Scollar. The oblique photograph shows, in a field planted with rye, two of nine Roman temporary training camps (the first to come to light on the European mainland) which Scollar discovered in 1962 near Xanten

ground of the Vale Trebba occupied the crest of one elongated sandbank. Somewhere in the vicinity, located on similar terrain, and adjacent to the former riverbed, must be Spina. But the area was vast. Much remained flooded. The prize still eluded him.

When the 1954 explorations at the Vale Pega got under way and brought forth magnificent artefacts, lost Spina made worldwide news. Rumours abounded. It was widely suspected that Professor Arias and his assistant had the site all bottled up but chose to keep their intelligence to themselves. Local wags knew better. They insisted that if anyone ever located Spina it would be none other than the agile Comacchiesi eel-fishers, who never failed to get to the region's antiquities first.

Arias and Alfieri's campaign was quite an ordeal. The physical problems faced at the Vale Trebba were multiplied by the muddy state of the soil, in which, in order to 'excavate', one often had to fish rather than dig. Ditches were no sooner dug than they collapsed. The two archaeologists made a humble beginning with the help of 'three workmen, three pails, and three spades'. (In coming seasons, Alfieri could count on a number of enthusiastic volunteers from Italy and abroad.) Gradually they improved their techniques. They learned that a water-hose might free a buried object more expeditiously than the spade. However, painstaking scientific work with minute note-keeping of the precise position of artefacts was nearly impossible. Speed was necessary to forestall robbers operating at night. On occasion, some fifteen graves were cleared in one day. A kind of improvised cofferdam made up of four hinged planks proved helpful in withholding mud and water while emptying an individual burial pit. By the end of the season, when cold weather stopped operations, the profuse contents of 342 tombs were added to the Ferrara museum. In the following year there were even more, and by 1963 they had passed the three thousand mark.

The objects found were virtually identical in type and style with those from the Vale Trebba. No doubt they belonged to the same period and to the same city. If anything, the additional finds only increased the archaeologists' conviction of the size and wealth of the elusive metropolis. Here, too, was the mixture of Greek, Etruscan, Umbrian, and imported Oriental goods. Some of the red-figured vases betrayed the hands of the very same artists represented in the great collections of Berlin, Munich, Boston, and Paris. There were masterpieces that possibly had been painted by the great Polygnot himself; others were closely related to the frieze of the Parthenon. Thematically, the cavalcade of figures covered much of Greek mythology. In some instances they contributed new versions to well-known legends. Obviously the people of Spina had had predilections for certain topics, such as the adventures of Heracles and Theseus, the battle of the Amazons, the Homeric epics, and the struggle between Lapiths and Centaurs. The frequent appearance of Dionysus, particularly in the company of dancing Bacchantes, hinted at the popularity of Dionysian and Orphic cults.

As at Vale Trebba, Etruscan ceramic ware was far less common, but their admirable small terra-cotta *askoi* in animal shapes, probably used as receptacles for perfume, recall the exquisite stirrup vases of the Peruvian Moche. The native Umbrian pottery occurred mostly in the graves of the poor. Lacking the refinement of Greeks and Etruscans, they yet appeal to us by their simple abstract ornaments of bold brush strokes which could be the pride of modern action painters.

An attempt to establish a typology of the graves according to ethnic and social categories, as well as by frequency of inhumation and cremation, has so far not met with complete success. The possibility cannot be ruled out that certain types of tombs are linked with subdivisions of the necropolis, which, as air photography has suggested, was designed in an orderly geometric manner *à l'Étrusque*.

None of the graves, no matter how rich their contents, can in any way compare to the elaborate stone structures and tumuli of old Etruria. Rarely was a sepulchre marked by a stone pillar or even a few pebbles. Burial was probably only on rare occasions in a wooden coffin or cloth, though this is conjectural, because either material is likely to have entirely decomposed. In just two known instances ashes were deposited in small stone sarcophagi. The almost total absence of stone dressing or monuments can, of course, be explained by the alluvial environment, though it is by no means understood why stone slabs or rocks could not have been transported to the Po Valley, if necessary.

Despite their external simplicity, the ditch burials nevertheless reflect the same typical concern for the after-life as at Tarquinia or Cerveteri. In the Po Valley, the Etruscan dead, made to face north-west, were as elaborately equipped. From their accompanying victuals we can still gauge their culinary preferences. Grave goods were placed on the right side of a corpse, just as they were put next to a reclining person at a banquet. Irrespective of class or caste, all corpses grasp a bronze *obolus* in their hands to pay mercenary Charon for their passage across the Styx.

The enormous chores involved in the excavation of the Vale Pega necropolis and the collecting, classifying, and storing of the materials at the Ferrara museum did not keep Alfieri from pursuing his most cherished goal. He knew he was tantalizingly close. There was also a good chance that the southern part of the Pega necropolis, where graves clustered most prolifically, was nearest to the once inhabited site. But all diggings failed to turn up any decisive evidence. For once, no lucky accidental find came to the scholar's rescue.

Alfieri made, however, one fortunate discovery far from the Comacchio archaeological zone – in a library. It was hardly an accident, but rather the fulfilment of his persistent quest for a missing link: a document that reported a settlement or edifice in the neighbourhood of the necropolises from the early centuries of the Christian era, or the dawn of Middle Ages. He argued according to well-known principles of historical geography that names of ancient features (physiographic or human) are frequently preserved in surviving place names, even if the site itself has long disappeared, and that some more recent structure is likely to be built over an abandoned or levelled settlement or shrine. Thus, for example, Buddhist stupas were raised above the pagan temples of the ancient Indus civilization, and the Church of Nuestra Señora de los Remedios rests on the pre-Columbian pyramid of Cholula, just as Mexico City was constructed on the site of destroyed Tenochtitlán. Now, given a landscape like the alluvial marshes of the Po delta, the choice for building sites was severely limited. Hence, in the opinion of Alfieri, the 'law of the persistence of inhabited centres' was more valid than ever. However, if such a 'persisting' centre did ever exist, it would have to precede the cataclysmic shift of the Po estuary in the twelfth century, when all of Spina and its possible successor was drowned under newly formed lagoons. That a written testimony from that early period should have survived was perhaps too much to hope for.

However, Alfieri had previously found a promising lead. Medieval documents in the possession of the diocese of Ravenna repeatedly mentioned a church of Santa Maria in Pado Vetere. The etymology clearly implied its location on the ancient course of the Po. What if this should prove to be the extinct arm Alfieri had traced near the Vale Pega?

On 28 July 1956, Alfieri at last got hold of an old source that mentioned the very church, which it stated was at a place called Paganella near the banks of the Borgazzi (an old river branch). Since both the Paganella and the Borgazzi were known, the approximate location of the church was well established. Could this be the missing link? Alfieri thought it was. 'The moral certainty', he wrote, 'of being close to the site of Spina made me step up the search in that zone.' But there were more frustrations in the offing. All the artefacts that he was able to dig up in the Paganella area were of Roman origin. The vital proof of its Graeco-Etruscan connections was still missing.

In the appropriate tradition of Greek drama, the *deus ex machina* descended from the sky. Just then, in the late summer of 1956, Alfieri learned that a Ravenna engineer, Professor Vitale Valvassori, had been commissioned to take aerial photographs of the reclamation project under way in the Vale Pega. Valvassori, a Second World War veteran of the Italian air force who had photographed Allied targets from his Stuka, had continued experimenting with aerial photography on his own after the war. He constructed a camera with an automatic time exposure. Special equipment enabled him to obtain large colour transparencies, whose tones he brought out artificially in his laboratory through the use of emulsions and filters. The resulting pictures were ideally suited to stress contrasts in the soil or in plant growth.

No sooner had Alfieri heard of these experiments than he rushed to Valvassori's laboratory. It is best to recall the climactic incident in Alfieri's own words:

I went to Ravenna where Professor Vitale Valvassori was developing some aerial colour photographs of the Pega valley. It was not without considerable emotion that, as I glanced at the photographs of the Paganella zone, I perceived, a little more than three hundred yards from the site of the church, the typical outlines of ancient habitations. Not only were there the geometrical outlines of the city blocks, but there were prominent traces of a large artificial channel which the Etruscans, with their noted hydraulic skill, had opened between the maritime dunes for about 1½ miles. From this radiated a series of minor canals and so Spina had the same aspect with its waterways as Venice.

Valvassori's pictures had been taken from an altitude of twelve thousand feet. They were only a beginning. At Alfieri's suggestion, Valvassori now undertook a number of flights in a plane put at his disposal by the Italian air force and piloted by Ugo Cassigoli. These efforts were backed financially by a recently formed society of Spina enthusiasts at Ferrara, the Ente Pro Spina. As a result, Valvassori produced, under various conditions of lighting and seasonal changes, detailed black-and-white and colour pictures at low altitudes – among them some of the most effective aerial photographs ever made of an archaeological site. They show the regular grid of Spina – there could no longer be any doubt about it identity – with its canals and square and rectangular blocks of building sites like an indelible print stamped into the soil. Most impressive of all was the main canal, some sixty-six feet wide, which compared favourably with the recently bulldozed irrigation canals that cut across it. It could well have served as a model to Venice's Grand Canal. The Spina main canal actually turned at right angles to continue farther on towards the former Adriatic coast. The two main arteries, representing watery counterparts to the *cardo* and *decumanus* of the Etrusco-Roman road grid, were paralleled by numerous smaller canals. A lagoon city of the Adria, Spina resembled in every respect the description

Strabo had given of Ravenna as 'built on wood and criss-crossed with strips of water, bridges and boats providing the only access'.

The two-hundred-odd photographs produced by Valvassori during several months showed that Spina consisted, as Professor Arias had already predicted, of a whole conglomerate of settlements with a main centre and several adjacent 'suburbs' and port sections, each one in chequerboard arrangement of canals and insulae. Such a pattern was necessitated by the few scattered portions of land above the lagoons available for building. From the photographs one could estimate the total area of Spina at between 740 and 850 acres. It may have housed a population of around half a million.

What made Valvassori's photographic success possible was in the first place the reclamation project then in process. 'Jealous nature', given a push by man, had generously disclosed buried testimonies of human enterprise. After draining, the risen soil of the Vale Pega remained completely barren for one year and would not have offered any clue whatever. But thereafter tufts of high-stemmed marsh grass gradually covered the surface. It was then that differences in the composition of the soil were minutely registered by this spontaneous outgrowth of plant life. The silted canals, filled with detritus and fertile humus, besides retaining much moisture, were traced by dark-green ribbons of grass, while the squares and rectangles of the building blocks, which stood on what used to be barren sand, supported only a sparse yellowish vegetation. Thus, the basic physical make-up of lagoon settlements was itself a determinant in bringing out the geometric plan. One could not wish for greater contrasts.

The proof for Spina's location and identification was near perfect. After Alfieri's topographic analysis had narrowed the search to La Paganella and Valvassori's aerial photographs made the case for Spina watertight, so to speak, all the circumstantial evidence pointed to Spina of the Etruscans, as had the necropolises before. The widely acclaimed discovery of the long-sought Etruscan metropolis was never seriously challenged, though clear-cut inscriptions naming the city *in situ*, as the excavators of the lost Canaanite city of Ugarit in northern

Syria had been lucky enough to find, have never come forth. However, Alfieri's labours would have been incomplete without corroborative evidence from the spade.

While Valvassori was still extending the aerial documentation to establish the extent and further details of Spina's layout, in

Figure 25. Location map of ancient Spina with adjacent lagoons and present course of the Po

addition to new facets of the two major necropolises, Alfieri began to dig at La Paganella. Almost at once his workmen hit a wooden piling, and very soon a whole row of them emerged. They represented, of course, the stilts driven through the soggy ground into the firmer subsoil to support buildings, as in ancient Ravenna or in present-day Venice and near-by Comacchio and Chioggia. Here at last was incontrovertible evidence of Etruscan houses that rested on platforms above the pilings. Further digging also brought up scattered ceramics. One precious fragment, a handle from an Attic *skyphos* (chalice), provided the final proof, since it could be dated to the fourth or fifth century B.C. The pottery piece was thus of the same age as the ceramics in the Ferrara museum and neatly demonstrated the contemporaneity of city and necropolises. Faced with such persuasive data, Alfieri was fully satisfied and confessed that if he had had any doubts, they were now completely dissolved. In this verdict he was strongly backed by fellow archaeologists, who thronged from all parts of the Comacchio swamps to witness the emergence of the drowned Etruscan city from shallow lagoons.

The epic of Spina's recovery is by no means at an end. Excavations of the immense urban zone had barely been initiated by the 1960s, though considerable efforts were centred on the palaeo-Christian church of Santa Maria and a Roman settlement. Rescue action was still urgently needed at the even more extensive cemeteries, to which aerial photographs added new areas to explore.

Chances are that few remains in the city will match those found in the tombs. And considering that all the houses and public edifices were constructed from wood and bricks, which largely decay when flooded by water, no earth-shaking architectural recoveries can be expected – no Parthenons or Pantheons, no stately mansions or palaces. Yet unforeseen surprises can never be ruled out. Because of its polyglot character, Spina might contain bilingual inscriptions. But no matter how meagre the survivals may turn out, in our present state of knowledge of Etruscan cities, even the plan of a humble private building is a welcome addition to scholarship.

More vital, however, than any buried feature is the discovery of Spina itself in the Mondrian-like geometric planes sketched by the newly sprouted vegetation of the drained Paganella. Thanks to the co-operation of Alfieri and Valvassori, the unnamed ruins near Marzabotto are no longer an isolated and minor instance of Etruscan city planning. In Valvassori's photographs we possess, for once, the immaculate blueprint of an important centre that demonstrates with precision how closely Roman colonists and empire builders followed the Etruscan example. Rome's debt to Etruscan civilization appears in such varied aspects as rituals, ceremonies, political offices, sports and games, engineering, architecture, road construction, even the black arts of prognostication practised by *augures* and *haruspices*, who, incidentally, had a central part in the laying out and ordaining of cities.

Thus, the triumph of Roman urbanization and colonization turns out to be as much a triumph for the Etruscans. After a glimpse of Roman imprints from Britain to Syria and North Africa, Spina has led us to the roots of a great and persistent legacy. To have brought out the original Etruscan contribution, which lives on in all Western civilization, is, in the final analysis, another crowning triumph of aerial archaeology.

9. Lindbergh Searches for Maya Cities

All the United States held its breath one day in February 1929 when wire services relayed that Colonel Charles A. Lindbergh's plane was overdue in Havana. Two years after his famous transatlantic flight, Lindbergh was probably the best-known man on earth and had become America's own 'Prince of Wales'. His recent romance with Anne Morrow, daughter of the American ambassador to Mexico, had added further glamour to the pioneering aviator. The lanky, handsome young man had assumed in the United States the charismatic image of the fair-haired national hero. Day in and day out Lindbergh was constantly in the news. No wonder that his failure to return from his Caribbean flight at the appointed time caused anxiety. The relief was the greater when he and his companion, John H. Hambleton, a vice-president of Pan American Airways, finally landed several hours behind schedule. No one was told what had caused the tardy return.

However, in the following months, the reason for the delay was disclosed. Lindbergh had been more in the limelight than he cared to be, and, understandably, he was in no hurry to account for his every movement. But when in July he visited the American South-West with his bride and flew over Pueblo ruins taking photographs, it transpired that Lindbergh had become intrigued by America's ancient civilizations. Always eager to demonstrate the value of aviation, he had hit upon the idea that the airplane could be of use to archaeological research. The possibility was driven home to him quite unexpectedly during his Caribbean mission in February while he was charting an air-mail route to Panama for Pan American Airways. His assigned programme completed, he went on a detour over north-eastern Yucatán, more or less with the intention of looking around for likely emergency landing fields. During that deliberate escapade, he and Hambleton spotted, embedded in the verdant tropical foliage, a number of high, overgrown, pyramidal mounds from which protruded pieces of masonry. The artificial outcrops were dotted around two glistening green lakes which stared at them like watchful eyes of the enigmatic jungle. The extensive ruins, some eight miles in diameter, undoubtedly belonged to an abandoned pre-Columbian city. Excited by the find, Lindbergh swooped down to take a closer look, circled the complex several times, made notes, took compass bearings, and scanned the adjacent area. Had he come across a long-lost Maya centre? If so, it would almost certainly be the first such major discovery ever made in the Americas from a plane.

The experience took hold of him. Was not the flying machine ideally suited to scout across the vast virginal areas of Central America, which had remained unmapped and most of which had never seen a white man? How many abandoned cities built by what were probably the continent's most brilliant indigenous people might be located from above? And what if among the crumbling unknown monuments of the dark forest scientists were to find clues to answer the riddles of the rise and fall of the extraordinary Maya?

Since the days in the late 1830s when a Yankee lawyer from New York and his gifted English artist friend had made the world aware of the existence of great ruined sites in the primeval wilderness of the American tropics, fascination with the aboriginal civilization of the Maya never abated. After John L. Stephens and Frederick Catherwood there came a string of adventurers and explorers who brought back spellbinding tales of architectural wonders and who spun around them lianas of imaginative theories. Even when the scholars began to arrive to search and to study, the wonders did not cease. Men began to learn of the intellectual achievements of this native American race, whose mathematicians were conversant with the concept of the zero long before Europeans adopted it from the Hindus via Arab intermediaries, and who had developed astronomical knowledge and calendrics to a stage that compared favourably with that of their Spanish conquerors. Here were a people who, without metal tools, wheeled transportation, and beasts of burden, constructed enormous temples, palaces, and pyramids that must rank as masterpieces of art as well as engineering. Virtually alone among pre-Columbian people they developed an advanced script that was moving towards ideographic and phonetic symbols. They produced books and kept records. But, alas, most of their manuscripts were destroyed by Spanish fanatics. Few of their inscriptions except calendrical notations can now be read. Despite the progress made, substantial gaps remain in our knowledge.

The Mayas lived in one of the globe's most unsalubrious and adverse regions, comprising roughly what are today the Mexican states of Yucatán, Campeche, Tabasco, Chiapas, and the territory of Quintana Roo, in addition to most of Guatemala, British Honduras, Honduras, and parts of San Salvador and Nicaragua. Modern explorers under the spell of the magic Maya have roamed far and wide over these lands, yet large tracts of jungle are left which they have never penetrated. Tropical forest and hostile Indians present a formidable barrier that is only slowly receding.

Lindbergh's first accidental venture into American antiquities led to further efforts. On his return to the United States he stopped over in Washington. There he sought out information on the Maya and was referred to Dr John C. Merriam, the president of the Carnegie Institution, which had for years been engaged in archaeological investigation. Merriam was much impressed by Lindbergh's outline of the airplane's potential in archaeological research and wholeheartedly accepted the aviator's offer to co-operate with the Carnegie Institution along such lines. Since Lindbergh was soon to embark on another flying mission across the North American continent, Merriam suggested that the airplane's effectiveness be tested among the United States' own imposing Indian ruins. Those sites were near Lindbergh's intended westward course.

Dr Alfred V. Kidder, the head of the Institution's archaeological division and a leading authority on both Maya and Pueblo, with many years of experience in the field, was just then carrying out excavations in the South-West. He drew up a list of Pueblo places that Lindbergh might photograph on his transcontinental flight. The few glimpses Lindbergh gathered en route were judged to be quite encouraging by Dr Merriam, whom the Colonel met again in San Francisco. Thus, on his return from the Pacific, Lindbergh decided to stop over at Kidder's camp in Pecos, New Mexico, for a more exhaustive survey. With Pecos as their base, Colonel Lindbergh and his wife set out on several consecutive mornings for flights across the Pueblo region, particularly the rugged arid plateaus and jagged gorges in the Four-Corner land, where the states of Utah, Colorado, New Mexico, and Arizona meet. Here Lindbergh took photographs of precipitous cliff houses and of deserted pueblos (villages) with their characteristic communal compounds.

Though American archaeologists were then almost totally oblivious of the scope as well as technique of aerial surveying of ancient remains, it was immediately evident that the airplane could be of immeasurable aid to them. In the broken terrain of the South-Western mesas, where one may spend weeks on horseback or foot exploring a limited area, the observer from above can encompass more in a few hours. When comparing some of Lindbergh's data with those previously obtained below, Kidder could bear out that Lindbergh had not only detected virtually all the ruins registered on the ground, but was able to gaze on antiquities that had remained entirely unnoticed. On one mesa that Kidder had crossed a few days before on horseback without being aware of any traces, Lindbergh picked up the outline of an extensive Pueblo ruin. Furthermore, the perusal of the more than one hundred photographs taken by the Lindberghs made Kidder intuitively grasp a chief contribution of aerial reconnaissance: to demonstrate the dependence of former settlements and their occupants on nearby topographical features. 'Some of the photographs taken by Colonel and Mrs Lindbergh', he reported, 'show clearly the relation that existed in ancient times between water supply, land available for farming, and easily defensible house site, matters which are of great importance to scientists as they try to picture the conditions under which prehistoric peoples lived.'

The photographs were developed at the laboratory of the School of American Research in Santa Fe. Professor Edgar L. Hewett, then the dean of South-Western archaeology, saw them there and declared that they were the first successful application of aerial photography to archaeological purposes in America. With his students from the University of New Mexico, he successfully followed up several photographic leads to prehistoric dwellings in the Chaco Canyon of New Mexico.

Meanwhile, the Lindberghs were reconnoitring on their own. They had sighted and photographed Pueblo cliff houses high up

Figure 26. The area covered by Colonel and Mrs Lindbergh on their pioneering aerial survey of the Pueblo region of the American South-West

under the rimrocks of the Canyon de Chelly and Canyon del Muerto in Arizona. Several of them had so far remained un-known and unseen. Though their wind-hollowed recesses were sizeable and permitted the construction of perched houses several stories high, the ledges on which they stood blocked the view from the bottom of the canyon. But to the observer from above they were fully exposed. In fact, on low flights he could peek into the rooms of decayed buildings. One such ruin on the edge of the Canyon de Chelly near its junction with the Can-yon del Muerto caught the Lindberghs' fancy and they resolved to explore it on foot, so they set down their plane on the precarious mesa not far from a cave where archaeologists were then campaigning.

Edward Moffat Weyer, Jr, and his associates were quite sur-prised when one late afternoon they saw a strange phantom-like figure descending the trail down the canyon. Extraordinarily tall, it appeared to be humped. Was it a spectre of the desert air? The creature came closer, crossed the river at the canyon's foot, and turned out to be an unusually big man carrying some kind of rucksack. Soon after, the man set down his pack, which proceeded to walk energetically by itself. It was a petite woman. The unannounced visitors were none other than the celebrated newly-wed young Lindberghs who asked to spend the night in the cavern so that they could embark on their search in the morning. Weyer and his party were as much enchanted by the presence of their glamorous guests as by the fact that the Lindberghs had taken to archaeological exploration. Like Weyer, they had sought out this remote canyon to look for dead villages. While the Lindberghs' observations were of a most recent vintage, and cursory at that, they could unlock secrets of the cliffs that had escaped him. Here he was, painstakingly trying to draw a map on which every ancient cliff-dwelling of the region should be entered. But how incomplete it was became only too obvious once Lindbergh showed him photographs from a previous flight. They proved unmistakably the point made by the aviator that 'from my ship I can find one undiscovered ruin for every one that has been located from the ground'.

Early the following morning, the Lindberghs and their fellow archaeologists set out for the cliff dwelling which Weyer had already decided to mark on his map as 'Lindbergh Cave'; that is, as soon as it had been definitely located. The 'hike' was to be long and arduous, across rocky terrain and patches of desert scrub, up and down cliffs and along vertiginous ledges. Nowhere did the setting fit the aerial photograph which Lindbergh constantly consulted as a check. The morning was almost gone and no cave was in sight. It grew unbearably hot. The little water that had been taken along was soon exhausted and the explorers had to quench their thirst from rock pools. But for Lindbergh's own confidence and their trust in his uncanny sense of distance and direction, they might well have given up. Close to noon, Lindbergh could at last assure them that they were near the cliff house. Indeed, as Weyer later wrote in an entertaining magazine article,

A little farther on, from an overhanging ledge, we could look right down into the ruin, no more than seventy-five feet away. Shelves of rock in the cave divided the masonry rooms into three tiers, one above another. One of the upper rooms, on a difficult ledge, contained a skeleton. Unfortunately, there were no grave deposits with the body, and I do not think it could have been very old. That the cave had been occupied quite early, however, was indicated by the types of pottery which were represented in the scattered shards. We had not been able to carry digging tools to the cave so we had to content ourselves with simply poking around. Some day Lindbergh Cave will be worked thoroughly.

In September of the same year, Lindbergh was once again undertaking a Caribbean flight for Pan American Airways. This time he was charged with inaugurating the first regular service from Miami to a South American destination, the then Netherlands possession of Surinam (Dutch Guiana). The venture was to be synchronized with a full-scale exploration over the Maya country. Pan American Airways, which supplied a twin-engined Sikorsky amphibian flying boat, and the Carnegie Institution of Washington had agreed to sponsor the campaign. At the time, the Carnegie Institution was heavily engaged in Maya research, chiefly in connection with the restoration of some of the prominent buildings of Chichen Itzá in northern Yucatán. Scientists from that society were involved in all aspects of Maya archaeology, from the deciphering of inscribed stelae to the tracking down of ruins, whose discovery they often owed to *chicleros* (native or half-caste gatherers of chicle) for the promised premium of twenty-five dollars 'per city'. Carnegie Institution workers shared their president's enthusiasm for the novel research too. They too were fired by the promise of an expansive overview and the freedom of air and space only flight could give.

In much of Central America, explorers had hitherto laboured so close to the ground in areas which could only be reached on trails hewn with machetes through the dense tangled maze of the rain forest that they were virtually trapped, rarely seeing the sky above. Thus, they were confined to a twilight zone when searching out buildings buried under the matted blanket of tropical vegetation, with roots and foliage spreading voluptuously above and between the piles of stones of even the highest structures. Under such conditions they were likely to come within an elbow length of long-sought or unknown monuments and remain completely unaware of them. Ruins that have been cleared once may be swallowed a few months later by the omnivorous forest, and in the absence of recognizable fixed landmarks are as lost as a volcanic island sunk beneath the Pacific. Scientists who have toiled for years at major sites like Palenque reported that on a return visit they were hopelessly lost. The extent of many well-known cities is still unknown. At Uaxactún, the important city of the Petén in northern Guatemala, discovered by Sylvanus Morley in 1916, the Carnegie Institution was engaged in intensive excavation for five consecutive years, yet no one had an inkling of a high natural ridge towering a few miles from the site until Lindbergh spotted it from the air.

It need not be stressed any further that archaeological work in the torrid zone is ridden with immense problems. Travel even within the shortest distances may be excruciatingly slow and perilous. A daily progress of ten miles is considered a good average. When flying from Tikal, probably the largest and oldest of 'classical' Maya cities, to near-by Uaxactún in six minutes, Lindbergh could not believe Dr Ricketson that it had taken him a whole day to make the trip by mule train.

The truth is that in 1929 – in 1971 for that matter – archaeologists have little more than nibbled at the vast Maya network of decayed cities and shrines spread across some two hundred thousand square miles of Central American lowlands and highlands. How much lies still hidden is indicated by the astonishing discoveries that continue to be made in our day, such as Bonampak in Chiapas with its fabulous murals; the vast site of Dzibilchaltún continuously occupied for some thirty-five hundred years, with its *cenotes* and causeways and temples, which had remained completely unknown until the mid-twentieth century, though only a few miles north of Mérida in one of the most accessible areas of Yucatán; or the number of splendid ruins, artificial waterways, and roads along the Caribbean coast of Quintana Roo (eastern Yucatán Peninsula), which were located by the twenty-year-old French amateur explorer Michel

Peissel and by members of CEDAM, the Exploration and Water Sports Club of Mexico.

Lindbergh's airborne expedition, inspired as it originally had been by the aviator's sighting of massive ruins pushing through the green canopy, naturally hoped to report the finding of lost cities, but, above all, conceived its goal as providing just that comprehensive view of the Maya country that the myopic explorer trailing in the dark so sorely needed. Not only were considerable sections totally unexplored and left blank on the hopelessly inadequate maps available, but apart from the coastal strips, none of the inland areas were reliably charted, precise locations of some of the well-established features or places were in doubt, and concrete concepts of the physical geography of the land were lacking. Again it was Dr Kidder who got to the crux of the matter by saying:

Above everything else, we wished to get an idea of what the Maya country really looked like … Archaeologists have pieced together a fairly consistent outline of this history but of the Maya country as a whole, of the 'lay', so to speak, of the land, we have had, until Colonel Lindbergh's flights, only the scantiest knowledge. Our problem was clear. We must cover as much of the area as possible, and learn all we could about it.

Belize, the capital of British Honduras on the Caribbean, once a notorious buccaneer's nest, was chosen as the expedition's base. Here Pan American Airways maintained major installations. From Belize all Maya centres were within a radius of some four hundred miles. The Lindberghs arrived there on 5 October after blazing the air route to northern South America. They were shortly after joined by William I. Van Dusen, a Pan American Airways representative who was designated as 'historian', and Dr Alfred V. Kidder. Both men had flown in from Miami. Another Carnegie Institution archaeologist, Dr Oliver H. Ricketson, who was an expert on the Petén area, came overland from Guatemala City. Additional members of the team were a radio operator and, for the final stretch, a co-pilot. Mrs Lindbergh acted as official photographer.

Soon after their arrival at Belize, Lindbergh and the two archaeologists huddled together over maps to chart their intended flights. The maps offered only vague data on the interior and were most valuable in highlighting unexplored areas. The plane was equipped with a radio transmitter and a collapsible rubber boat. Though it was stripped of all non-essentials to increase the flying range, Lindbergh saw to it that the plane carried emergency rations, machetes, first-aid kit, and make-shift sleeping and cooking facilities should the need arise 'to live off the land'. He left orders that search parties should be dispatched twenty-four hours after their plane had been reported missing, but no earlier.

For five days, covering some two thousand miles during twenty-five hours in the air, the Lindbergh party forayed into the little-known or unknown hinterland of Central America, over most of which the Maya once held sway. The Yucatán Peninsula was crossed three times in its entire length along roughly parallel routes. On the first day, 6 October, the initial course was set westward from Belize toward the focal area of the 'classical' phase of Maya culture history (about A.D. 300–600) in the northern Petén. In no time all signs of modern civilization were left behind. Soon even the natives' thatched huts – probably unchanged for thousands of years – faded away. The plane was following the curling Belize River. But unless Lindbergh kept directly overhead, the silvery serpent would be lost amid the tall trees that lined its banks. At last the lagoons of Yaxha appeared and they knew they were approaching the Petén heartland. Yet though Maya ruins were known to exist here, no scrutinizing from high and low revealed the slightest trace. A few minutes beyond, however, and the sun-bleached roof-combs of the grandiose temple-towered pyramids of Tikal, the highest of Mayadom, raised their silhouettes above the forest mantle. Then followed the brief hop to near-by Uaxactún and a glimpse through a clearing of the pre-classical squat white pyramid with its grotesque masks, which Ricketson had uncovered a few years earlier. Ricketson commented facetiously: 'It is not good for an archaeologist to fly over this region, especially if he is going back. The thought of all day on a mule in contrast to six minutes in an arm chair is unsettling. Besides, the ticks don't fly.'

Throughout this flight, as on all subsequent jaunts, everybody was fully occupied. Lindbergh, at the controls, was busy checking the course, gauging distances, referring to the various maps he had piled on his knees, and making meteorological and other scientific observations, besides keeping his eye on any unnatural eminences that might light up on the horizon. Mrs Lindbergh, most of the time in the cockpit beside her husband, proved to be as keen a ruin watcher. She took most of the

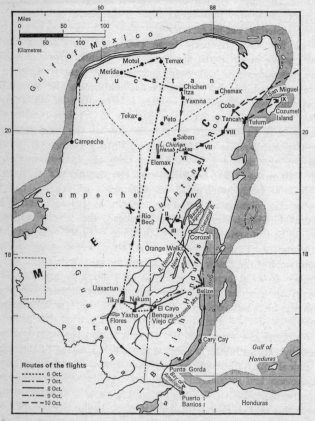

Figure 27. Map of the Maya territory on the Yucatán Peninsula with the routes of the Lindbergh-led Pan American Airways-Carnegie Institution archaeological flights in October 1929

aerial photographs and also looked after the explorers' culinary needs. Ricketson and Kidder, in rotation, jotted down running notes on any kind of detail they noticed concerning the nature of the terrain, the distribution of plant growth, and, above all, the shape, style, dimension, and location of ruins. Van Dusen kept a log of his own and composed the dispatches that through Ehmer, the radio-operator, and via Pan American Airways receiving stations at Miami and Belize, would reach the wide world in a matter of minutes.

After gliding over Uaxactún at a low altitude for Mrs Lindbergh's picture-taking, Lindbergh turned due north. His destination was Mérida, Yucatán's capital, where that day's flight was to end. On this long stretch of approximately four hundred miles the plane cut across the Yucatán Peninsula in southeastern Campeche. Before Lindbergh and his party spread an extensive uncharted region whose coverage was one of the expedition's principal goals. Far and wide, all around them, a virtual ocean of vegetation, a monotonous, unbroken expanse of eternal green. Not one open space was in view. There were no rivers or lakes, no landmark but an endless blanket of proliferating chlorophyll. Even Ricketson's indefatigable scribbling came to a standstill.

About an hour after leaving Uaxactún, Lindbergh broke the lethargy that had settled over the party with a promising nod. He had spotted in the distant east above the treeline an irregular shape that so far looked little more than a bump. Nevertheless, in this flat green desolation it loomed as conspicuously as a tiny white sail above the immense blue sea. On coming closer it more and more resembled a ruin, and a fairly well preserved one at that. A heavily overgrown square pyramid was crowned by two temples or towers like the spires of a cathedral. Numerous smaller mounds emerged in the vicinity as Lindbergh carefully scouted the area. The site, quite unexpected in such an unlikely landscape, was announced as a new discovery. However, later checking with various sources makes it probable that it should be equated with Río Bec (Rio Beque), whose peculiar architecture had given its name to a Maya style. But the double-turreted temple pyramid is not unique to Río Bec and conceivably Lindbergh's find may have belonged to another, so far unrecorded, ruin in the region. Of course, a precise geographical location was not available for Río Bec in 1929. And Lindbergh, who oriented himself by compass reading and flying time, was not much better off. Hence, it is extremely difficult to establish identities of inland sites reported from the air to be absolutely certain whether they represent a new discovery or not, unless descriptions or photographs are so accurate that confusion is impossible. In any case, the south-eastern corner of Campeche, as it is now known, is not as bare of aboriginal sites as Lindbergh and his associates may have thought at the time.

Somehow, a once heavily peopled south-eastern Campeche did not quite fit the then prevalent ideas about the evolution and spread of the Maya. The numerous mounds they saw, even though they did not discern any masonry, could have helped to undermine such preconceptions. In 1932, the Carnegie Institution of Washington announced that ruins of very difficult access had been discovered on foot by a young botanist attached to the American Chicle Development Company in the region over which 'Colonel and Mrs A. Lindbergh and Dr A. V. Kidder of the Carnegie Institution flew on their air survey in 1929'. Given the name Calakmul (Kalakmul), it ranks today among the most extensive of all Maya cities. Dr Sylvanus Morley, a specialist in Maya epigraphy, lured by the reported wealth in inscribed stelae, sped to it and spent two weeks in mapping and decipherment. Tikal alone exceeds it in number of stelae but must take second place in the quantity of those that carry hieroglyphs.

Some fifty miles from the Río Bec region the landscape became less forbidding. Once the state of Yucatán was entered, typical *milpas* (cornfields) and huts of the Mayans' twentieth-century descendants began to appear. The dense jungle gave way to sparser savanna-like vegetation. Several villages were crossed, from which the inhabitants could be seen seeking cover in the bush when the monster bird approached. Though some of these settlements were of considerable size, with stone-built houses and Spanish-style churches, none were marked on any of the maps carried aboard. At last the explorers reached Mérida, where they were to be fêted by the governor of the state.

The following day, 7 October, on the return to Belize, Lindbergh flew farther east through the Yucatán Peninsula. South of the impressive Chichen Itzá ruins, of which Mrs Lindbergh took several photographs, he entered the interior of the territory of Quintana Roo, to this day Mexico's least explored part. Again the green hell swept by endlessly. The country was so densely overgrown, Kidder declared, that 'no trace of ruins could be discerned'. No one knew whether it held any secrets. At last a large stream wound its watery loops through the forest. But all the probing failed to produce the slightest sign that a living or bygone race had reached its shore.

Soon after, Lindbergh steered towards a series of lakes. The maps showed only one lake in the general area and that did not resemble any of those sighted, besides having a different location. However, the setting was most encouraging. Maya settlers liked to pick out lake sites. Indeed all kinds of water bodies – *aguadas* (natural reservoirs that collect rainwater), *cenotes* (underground pools whose limestone roof had collapsed), and actual lakes – have served chicleros and explorers as guideposts to pre-Columbian settlements. Near the banks of the largest lake Lindbergh saw unmistakable mounds. Hopes ran high that the Maya, had they ever reached this region, would have found the locale congenial for building a major centre. All expedition members agreed that such an ideal setting called for further investigation. The lake was big enough to permit the amphibian to land, so Lindbergh decided to bring the plane down in order to scale the surrounding hills and search for ruins. Van Dusen well described the expectant moments:

Everyone was immediately tense at the prospect of setting foot in the heart of this pathless dominion. One final arc, the motors were cut and the lake came rushing up to meet the ship. A flood of rich blue water, gorgeous, transparent, raced past the windows for an instant; the plane glided smoothly over the calm surface and came to a stop. Climbing out of the cockpit under the motors, Lindbergh brought the anchor from the front hold and dropped it over that side. Next came a rubber boat, to be inflated, and Ricketson lent a hand with this, while the rear hatch was opened in the roof of the cabin. Camera first, Mrs Lindbergh drew herself up through the opening and came out into the sunshine ...

Machetes, a compass and fire-arms were loaded into the boat, and Ricketson was rowed ashore first to look over the ground, while Lindbergh returned for the rest of the party, one passenger at a time.

Alas, though the natural scene was perfect, the Maya had apparently missed it. The expedition members cleared a path, climbed the hills, and examined the ground meticulously. But their search through the bush for masonry was fruitless. Greyish pieces of stone that could have been taken from the air for fragments from a decayed building proved to be 'moss rocks'. None of the mounds appeared to be man-made. Here was a sobering lesson for believers in the infallibility of aerial observation or, for that matter, in the omnipotence of environment. The sum total of physical factors may set the stage for cultural development, but you cannot rule out human perversity.

But the time was not wasted. If anything, it helped to prove the feasibility of one of Lindbergh's pet projects: to search out and test landing areas to which explorers and their supplies could be transported and from which a ground survey could then proceed.

The landfall cost the party but two hours. Once aloft, Lindbergh spent another hour coursing to and fro 'across the broad plain, exploring every change in colour and formation that might suggest the presence of data valuable to scientific study'.

That evening, back at Belize, a conference was quickly convened to review the by no means earthshaking accomplishments of the past two days. Almost certainly prominent sites had been missed. How were they to master the art of spotting shrouded ruins and camouflaged temple platforms between the treetops of the jungle? Were there indubitable signs of man-made structures in the green wilderness? The explorers realized that here they were treading on virgin territory. Indeed, they were ill prepared for it. In the little time they had left, they thought the dilemma could be resolved by a crash programme. All that was needed to perfect the novel technique of 'sky-spying', they argued, was more practice. They must learn from experience.

So, next morning, 8 October, they made their way once more to the Petén to see whether they could not sniff out ruins known to exist in or near certain areas. Everyone eagerly participated in the crash course. The test was to be launched over Yaxha and Nakum, which had escaped them on the first day's flight. Lindbergh directed his plane towards the approximate site and then whirled it around in various angles. At one moment he was circling high above, and then swiftly he dived down to almost touch the treetops. Admittedly, no clear-cut principles evolved from such drastic empiricism, which the partners seem to have weathered without any constitutional upsets. Nevertheless, at some point jagged outlines could be made out. What exactly did the trick in those instances and why the same features had failed to show up previously is left rather vague by Kidder's laconic and Van Dusen's more colourful account, though both seem to have been convinced that no inscrutable phenomena were involved and what was needed above all was a set of sharp, tireless human eyes adept at scanning the forest and its horizon. In fact, Van Dusen stated confidently: 'From hours of constant peering into the depth of the foliage we had all become expert in detecting important variations of bush and topography.' After the third day the team hoped that they had reached this postgraduate stage. And while such rapid advance in aerial detection may seem presumptuous, the results of the fourth day perhaps vindicated Van Dusen's claim.

On that final crossing of the Yucatán Peninsula from Belize northward closer to the coast of British Honduras and Quintana Roo, by far the most notable observations of the entire campaign were made. At least three sizeable cities and a host of smaller ruins were sighted. Up from the swamplands along the Caribbean, Lindbergh struck an inland route across uncharted wilderness towards Lake Bacalar, a large body of water in northern Quintana Roo. That landmark, too, turned out to vary considerably in shape and location from its outline on maps. Flying over the flat Yucatán jungle west of Lake Bacalar, Lindbergh suddenly smiled as he turned around to his passengers. With his fingers (the droning engines made communication by speech impossible) he signalled the emergence of three prominent sets of mounds above the green carpet. They belonged to a major complex of Maya pyramids and temples around a raised plaza, some, Kidder thought, as high as 120 feet. The massive grey stone structures were, as usual, engulfed by the roots and branches of bushes, and even the masonry of steep pyramids was cleft asunder by tall trees. Though this extensive city was the top prize of the day's flight and gave the explorers a great thrill, it was soon followed by other monuments. Thanks to their newly gained expertise and self-confidence – not to speak of favourable conditions for observation – the discovery of new ruins now became a kind of game in which everyone sooner or later scored a winner. In the flat country of the northern Yucatán Peninsula, pyramid mounds could often be noticed when still miles away.

Kidder at last had a field day. Here was material to fill several writing pads with his random notes. Except when a large pyramid came into focus or the plane tumbled through air pockets, he scribbled almost continuously. The following is a sample from his 'air notes':

Steep pyramid on N. horizon (12.05); small lakes to N. (12.07); another small lake about 6 mi. E. (12.16). Now coming over pyramid (it was visible 20 miles away). Drop to about 100 feet – group contains one large pyramid with three smaller ones. 100 yards E. of it on a plaza (?) Indian village (6 palm-leaf huts in clearing) just (2 mi.) W. (12.20) Off N., bush dry and grey, low, and can see ground now and then between trees. High bush seems to have ended at last site. (12.29) Circled low over Indian huts, people running into houses and into bush. (12.35) Six-house village. (12.37) Bush dry and deader looking than ever, think some of these trees must shed leaves at this season. Small rain-squalls all about, air bumpy. (12.39) Large, low mound directly below in Indian clearing. (12.43) Turn due W. toward high pyramid sighted by Mrs Lindbergh and now heading for it across uninhabited country. (12.49) Another pyramid to N. of first one.

As can be gathered from this brief selection from his notes, Kidder paid particular attention to the vegetation associated with ruined sites. Out of this came remarkable insights which, had they been systematically followed up, might well have given aerial surveying of the tropical jungle a scientific basis. It had already been known that modern natives purposely sought out the vicinity of Maya ruins, because of the greater fertility of the ground. (It is not clear whether this fertility is a result of settled life or whether the area had for that very reason been picked by the Maya.) Chicleros were also aware that sapote trees, from which they extracted the sap for chewing gum (the wood was used by the Maya for their carved lintels), were likely to occur in greater profusion near the ancient mounds. Surprisingly, Kidder could distinguish from the air different species of trees and thus bear out that the tropical jungle, even though it may mask and dismantle once splendid cities, can also be made to yield clues to their hidden presence. Here were tantalizingly close analogies to Crawford's vegetation- and crop-marks. (Though instances of unusual species of trees or shrubs crowding around former sites of human occupation have been reported in several countries, little organized research has yet been done along those lines. In Greenland, for example, plants apparently not native to the island were found to signal defunct colonies of Norsemen. Growths of that kind point either to human agents who imported the original plants or to the transformation of the soil by organic matter, which rendered the locale hospitable to species not otherwise common. In either case, such vegetation – even if it does not trace any buried features and although it grows irregularly – could conceivably be used as beacon in airborne reconnaissance.)

Most of the sites that had been examined during the day were probably new; however, Kidder later believed the first large city spotted had been approached some years before on foot by a British medical officer-archaeologist of Belize, Dr Thomas Gann, who fell sick on reaching its outskirts and was forced to turn back. Substantial ruins between the already reported centres of Tuluum (which had been sighted by the Spanish as early as 1518), the impressive walled Maya-Toltec city overlooking the Caribbean, and Cobá, were at least in part unknown. The largest inland city of the area, now known as Chunyaxché, appears to have been briefly visited by Herbert J. Spinden and Gregory Mason on their 1926 land expedition, even though they may have actually gone to near-by Muyil. Michel Peissel 'rediscovered' it in 1958, and since then it has been the target of several scientific explorations.

Peissel, by the way, was oblivious of the Lindbergh aerial

campaign on his first expedition, but after familiarizing himself back in the United States with Mrs Lindbergh's photographs he came to realize that for a good number of ruins he had to grant priority to the airborne exploring party of 1929. Writing of the Lindbergh survey, Peissel fully acknowledged that it 'yielded photographs of many yet unknown temples'. He continues with the comment:

Looking at these aerial photographs, I spotted the tall pyramid of Chunyaxché, easily recognizable by its position close to the lagoon. I could see the site of Yochac, and among the photographs I recognized the ruins of Puerto Chile, which no foreigner had reached by land until my passage some twenty-nine years after the photographs had been taken.

In little more than half an hour after Kidder made the quoted mid-day entry in his notebook, Lindbergh was guiding the plane to the magnificent place that he had accidentally hit upon in February and which was the 'true begetter' of their present venture. A glance by Kidder was sufficient to deprive the Colonel of his tentative title of discovery. The city was Cobá, a site that had so far been only seen by a handful of white men, among them Kidder himself. Kidder was astonished to find it far from where he judged it to be according to his recollections of three years ago. Yet there could be no mistake. There was only one Cobá; it was unique. Already it was making archaeological history, not only because of its impressive architecture and exceptional setting between several lakes. For one thing, there was the comparative antiquity and wealth of inscriptions from the 'classical' epoch of this northern city which were about to change accepted concepts about Maya history. Until Cobá had been studied it was virtual dogma that the Maya had originally founded an 'Old Empire' in the south, and only after its fall did the survivors migrate to the northern Yucatán Peninsula to establish a 'New Empire' which, like the 'New Kingdom' of Pharaonic Egypt, revived some of the ancient glories without ever recapturing the purity of style and lofty spirit of its model. Cobá, more than any other site, helped to disprove all this. Even if the Petén may have seen the finest flowering, the north was settled by Maya people at least as early. No shred of evidence pointed to an exodus, which the various accounts by members of the Lindbergh expedition still took for granted. Indeed, to reconstruct the mythical migration route of the Maya and to find missing links in unexplored zones between allegedly Old Empire and New Empire cities became an almost obsessive leitmotif of the aerial endeavours.

Cobá also inspired another pursuit of the Lindbergh-Carnegie survey: the tracking down of Maya causeways or *sacbeob*. Several expeditions which had recently visited Cobá on foot had come across a net of raised highways radiating from the city. The most formidable of all Maya roads known had been followed for forty-five miles by Kidder, though its terminal at Yaxuna, south of Chichen Itzá, had not yet been established. That the Maya had built extensive roads, mainly for the procession of priests and sacrificial victims, was widely known from early Spanish accounts, but their study had been neglected until Cobá emerged in the 1920s.

Cobá certainly called for a close look. Everyone was itching to tread its ground. Lindbergh made an attempt to land on one of the lagoons, but after gliding over the waters he decided that the surface was too small and the high trees too close to take the risk. So he quickly lifted the plane, circled over the temple mounds, and crossed, as Kidder relates, 'in a split second a swampy lowland that three years before had cost Eric Thompson [the outstanding British Maya scholar then also associated with the Carnegie Institution] and me a full hour of bitter, sweating struggle'.

The eventful day climaxed instead with a landfall at Tuluum. There, incidentally, the party had an unlikely encounter with chicleros, who wanted to know who the various members were. When Kidder introduced Colonel Lindbergh two of the natives became ecstatic but the third registered no surprise. His companions screamed at him; did he not know who *el coronel* was? His embarrassed confession of ignorance prompted the instant reply: 'El Coronel Lindbergh is the man who flew around the world in a single day.' Thereafter, Van Dusen wrote, 'the three Indians watched Lindbergh's every move'.

The last night of the campaign was spent across the narrow

Yucatán Channel on Cozumel, a Caribbean island where Pan American Airways maintained a base. Cozumel turned out to be more than a convenient stopover. Once a sacred place for Maya pilgrimages reached via a *sacbe* from Cobá to a cross-channel point of embarkation, it had yet been disregarded by archaeologists. Before diving down to a landing in the tiny harbour, Lindbergh was able to spot several ruined mounds at the southern end and near the island's centre that had never been heard of before.

Once the official business and courtesies were taken care of, the party hastened to visit the unfinished Pan American airport, where substantial relics belonging to a typical Maya temple city had cropped up during clearing operations. There were columned walls and remains of a most unusual round tower, of plazas and ball courts, and of remarkable stone-carved images. Curiously, not the least of aviation's contributions to archaeological knowledge is connected with the construction of airports; incidental finds made in this manner are legion. Cozumel is only one of the earliest in a chain of discoveries due to the increase of military and civil landing fields in the Old and New World from Roman villae in Italy to Neolithic camps in England.

Cozumel was the last stop of the Lindbergh-led aerial survey. The next morning the plane was bound for Miami via Cuba. But to end the whole adventure where it began, Lindbergh wanted to fly once more over Cobá. Like the archaeologists on land, he and his companions were intrigued by the Maya highways. It should be possible to gauge from above some vestiges of the formidable system. Main target was, of course, the artery extending westward from Cobá, built like a levée of compact boulders and once covered by cement-like stucco at an average width of thirty-two feet and a height of over two feet (more than eight feet in swampy areas). Unfortunately it remained completely invisible despite repeated crossing in the air of an imaginary east to west line between Chichen Itzá and Cobá. Kidder then suggested searching for the roads known to radiate south from Cobá. But again the matted forest betrayed no sign whatever. According to Van Dusen, 'A shifting mist and the soft light of early morning conspired against us.'

Regretfully Lindbergh swung the plane away from Cobá toward home.

Remarks like Van Dusen's on the unsuccessful search for Maya roads suggest with how rudimentary a knowledge of the principles of aerial observation the expedition executed its survey. Nowhere in the published reports or articles, except for some afterthoughts, is there a hint that any of the members understood how the angle and nature of light and the lengthening shadows of morning and evening may help to bring out features. The advantages of a vertical, or even oblique, view from considerable altitude were, on the whole, disregarded. Instead Lindbergh more or less haphazardly wheeled his plane around in precipitous curves, tacked back and forth, rising high to a thousand and more feet at one moment and diving down the next until he skimmed the jungle. Somehow, it was hoped, an unregistered ruin would thus come into focus. On the whole, the explorers seem to have been convinced that proximity bestowed optimal visibility. Yet Kidder felt that for the observation of high-rising shrouded monuments an elevated view from about five hundred feet was the 'most advantageous' for a comprehensive picture. Almost invariably, they were concerned with ruins that either pierced through the green canopy in a profile recognizable on the horizon or which could be scanned amidst forest clearings. That buried structures, not by themselves visible from above, could conceivably produce striking effects to announce their presence and dimensions was just barely suggested by Kidder's acute botanical observations, which were never properly worked out and applied. Furthermore, all flights were geared to scouting by the human eye. Despite some occasional lip service to the sensitivity of the photographic plate, the camera was neglected as an independent agent of discovery. There is no word on experiments with filters, optic lenses, and photographic materials. True, fine photographs were taken at dramatic inclines, but only to fix a site already established by the unaided human viewer.

Critically to evaluate a scientific performance of forty years ago may be odious and amount to little but unfair hindsight. Yet so significant an effort as the Lindbergh-Carnegie flights has to be related to the growing knowledge in that field. It must then be admitted that in its approach and method – or rather lack of method – it fell far short of the work carried out by contemporaries in Europe and the Near East. Innocent and evidently ignorant of the sound 'laws' formulated by Crawford or Poidebard, it proceeded naïvely by trial and error alone. Nevertheless, for the Americas it was in every sense a trail-blazing achievement. Unfortunately for the development of aerial archaeology in the New World, it had picked the most difficult target imaginable: tree-shrouded ruins buried in a welter of tropical jungle. A Crawford or a Major Allen would have shied away from this area as the least susceptible to the scrutiny of the winged camera, and to this day, experts are not at all agreed on the complete efficacy of the aerial approach. Instead of continuing in the infinitely more suitable South-West, Lindbergh's party decided to concentrate on the glamorous Maya country. Here, they declared, lay the real test. Here was the lure of lost cities and vast forested territories never explored by white men. They may have swept in five days over ground that, as they insisted, it would have taken five years to cover on foot. Yet the returns were relatively minor, if one weighs them against the findings of earthbound students working, naturally, at a much slower pace. The Lindbergh-Carnegie discoveries – not all of them fully verified decades later – are easily overshadowed by such one-man earthbound enterprises as those by Dr Thomas Gann or of the Danish archaeologist Frans Blom, who alone had at the time of the Lindbergh expedition some sixty-seven new sites to his credit.

After all this has been said, it must be acknowledged that Lindbergh and the Carnegie scholars defined their mission primarily as a general reconnaissance of uncharted territories. If, as Kidder said, they wished above all 'to get an idea what the Maya country really looked like', then their experience had been enriching and worthwhile. They brought back vital data on the topography of the dark, dank forested lands in which the Maya civilization flourished. In recording natural features and fixing landmarks they helped to pave the way for future explorations to follow on foot. Lindbergh, with his interest in airborne transportation, was particularly eager to prove the value of the aeroplane in ferrying and supplying archaeologists at work in the deep jungle. In this he achieved complete success as shown by his repeated nimble landings on inland and coastal waters. Notwithstanding imperfect techniques, the aeroplane promised to become at least an auxiliary agency for archaeological campaigning in tropical countries.

However, the true achievement of the 1929 aerial expedition in Central America is not completely reflected by its scientific or technical results. Disregarding a few isolated and incidental investigations from the air such as those of Indian earthworks in the American Midwest and of ancient Eskimo dwellings in subarctic snowdrifts, this was the first major, exclusively archaeological enterprise of its kind in the Western Hemisphere. As such it made history. Since it was instigated and directed by so celebrated a personality as Colonel Lindbergh, it was destined to gain wide publicity for aerial archaeology.

In the long run the measure of a pioneering effort lies in its setting an example to spur on others. In the wake of the Lindbergh-Carnegie mission, successive ventures by air in the Americas were to hasten archaeological revelations of the pre-Columbian past.

Where the Lindbergh-Carnegie campaign failed, another flying expedition succeeded a year later, in December 1930. It not only garnered the first air pictures of Cobá, but more notably gave conclusive evidence of perceptible changes in the plant cover over a hidden structure in forested Central America. It managed to sight several of the Cobá causeways and nail them down on photographic plates. Fairly well defined as dark lines crossing each other at an oblique angle above the lighter green blanket, two intersecting *sacbeob* south Cobá were disclosed on one striking photograph. It appears that the darker shade was caused by the shadow thrown by the higher trees growing on the raised roads, rather than indicating species different from the trees in the surrounding jungle. Otherwise the trees were probably little affected by the limestone blocks of the roadbeds, and grew neither better nor worse than the unobstructed forest. At least, this explanation was endorsed by Crawford, who later republished the extraordinary photograph in *Antiquity*, remarking that 'there is an essential difference between this photograph and one of a crop-site in England, though at first glance they seem similar – and though the *results* are in fact similar'. Crawford also recalled that Major Allen had observed a comparable phenomenon when surveying a section of Wychwood Grim's Ditch that passed through a wood in Oxfordshire. However, he thought that the Maya roads would have shown to better advantage if the photograph had been taken facing the sun.

The enterprise that scored a further advance for aerial archaeology in the Maya country had been launched by the University of Pennsylvania in Philadelphia under Percy C. Madeira, Jr. The *New York Times* and *Philadelphia Bulletin* defrayed part of the cost against promised dispatches from the field leader, Gregory Mason, a journalist turned archaeologist, whose rhapsodic books on pre-Columbian civilizations enjoyed a vogue before the Second World War. Additional members were J. Alden Mason, a leading authority on ancient America, and Robert A. Smith, an expert flight photographer from the Fairchild Aerial Survey Company. Though intentionally following the Lindbergh-Carnegie example, the Pennsylvania University expedition expected to add data on the Maya, 'from both air and land', that had been missed by their predecessors. In their eight-day flights they covered more ground; crossed the base of the Yucatán Peninsula east to west; penetrated large

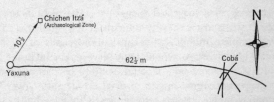

Figure 28. Drawing of the Maya causeways radiating from Cobá in north-eastern Yucatán Peninsula. For the intersecting roads just south of Cobá, sighted from the air by University of Pennsylvania explorers in December 1930, see also Plate 22

untouched areas, particularly in Chiapas and Campeche; marked unknown geological features; refined geographical positions and outlines of sites such as Cobá and various inland water bodies; and landed their plane repeatedly on lakes and swift rivers in order to continue exploration on land. But when it came to discoveries of cities, they fared little better than the Lindbergh team. The only sizeable new ruins were pinpointed in the same general area of Quintana Roo.

Their method, too, was much the same: flying as low as possible to discern from a distance bulges against the horizon, belonging, they hoped, to palaces or conical pyramids. Smith declared outright: 'The only way to pick out new pyramids was to fly very low over the treetops, clearing them by about ten feet.' Such an approach worked only in flat country; it was a complete failure in the rugged, broken southlands. Indeed, until turning to the level terrain on the peninsula farther north and closer to the coast, the expedition members judged their flights to be a flop. Even then they agreed that the returns hardly warranted the effort and expense of flying.

In drawing a balance sheet, G. Mason had to confess that 'it is not an unfair guess that, for the four cities we discovered, we missed from twenty to forty others'. In addition, there was the familiar predicament that an allegedly new site had limited value until its exact location was known so that it could be reached by ground parties. That was hardly possible from a moving plane in uncharted regions, unless an observer could be dropped to take bearings of latitude and longitude on terra firma.

Several remedies suggested themselves. The obvious one, extremely costly and technically difficult at the time, was to produce a complete mosaic by vertical photographs of all Maya territory. The coverage would then serve as an inclusive map on which some fixed points could possibly be plotted; though even that procedure might prove problematic over the monotonous jungle. It was also proposed that landfalls in less accessible areas by a manoeuvrable autogiro plane (the predecessor of the helicopter) might profitably be adopted. But this plan presupposed an opening in the jungle near ruins, which was the exception rather than the rule. More ingenious and practical were Madeira's plans to mark the site by destroying some of its vegetation with chemicals or, better still, to drop a device which for some time to come would send out electromagnetic or other waves. Groundlings might then find their way to the location by tracing the signals to their source.

While the expedition made an undisputed contribution with an aerial recording of Maya roads and at least gave a hint that sophisticated techniques had their validity in the forested tropics, it hardly improved upon what was known from land surveys. None of the sixteen-odd Cobá causeways were followed to their end. The major highway west from Cobá, according to Madeira, failed to show up at all, though G. Mason, in his flamboyant account, says they were able to sight it for twenty miles from Cobá.

Of all archaeological features, the Maya causeways nevertheless seemed the most susceptible to aerial investigation. If they did not stand out as completely as one might have wished, this was perhaps not so much the fault of the aerial approach as of the observers' inexperience. All the more regrettable that little was done in years to come to pursue the study of the *sacbeob* from the air – or on land for that matter. The subject certainly deserves the attention long devoted to its Inca counterpart. However, incidental discoveries by air, mainly from photographs taken by oil geologists, have since increased our concept of the road system and its magnitude. Victor W. von Hagen, who spent years investigating Inca highways (repeatedly resorting to aerial observation) and of late has concentrated on the Roman roadnet in the Old World, has isolated from air photographs a number of *sacbeob* taking off from Chichen Itzá. Other causeways were spotted not only along and near the coast of lowland Yucatán, but in the interior of Campeche, Chiapas, and the Petén. It has now become certain that communication links existed between the major Maya centres, bearing out early colonial reports. Yet a great deal remains hypothetical about the extent and organization of the system. Even the suggestion that the Maya marked distances and built way-stations along their roads like the *tampus* of the Inca has so far not been substantiated.

Both the Lindbergh-Carnegie and Pennsylvania University flights raised doubts whether a sound technique for depicting jungle-buried and overgrown ruins from above was within the realm of possibility. Hence, for a long while these pioneer efforts were not matched by any comparable aerial campaigns over Central America. Significantly, as late as the mid-1950s, the husband-and-wife team of Betty J. Meggers and C. Evans tried in vain to locate mounds in the tropical wilderness of the Amazon delta, but 'became fully convinced that aerial photography has nothing to offer as a means of locating archaeological sites in the Amazon area'.

Of course, unhampered by such uncertainties, aviation in the torrid zone progressed by leaps and bounds. With it grew the photographic coverage of tropical America for various non-archaeological purposes. Mexican and Guatemalan civil and military authorities boasted an increasing number of aerial pictures. As in other areas of the world, archaeologists, while hesitant to launch programmes of their own, have frequently found it useful to consult such records. But the initiative to enlist aerial photography for exclusively archaeological reconnaissance, on no matter how small a scale, was rarely taken in the Maya lands – that is, until a moderately conceived venture by a scholar from Brigham Young University in Utah, an institution engaged in Maya research for somewhat bizarre religious reasons, did most to rehabilitate the aeroplane's effectiveness for jungle survey and discovery in the Central-American tropics. (In a somewhat similar medium, the South-East Asia of the fabulous Khmer ruins, which resembled those of the Maya in more ways than one, successes were registered as well.)

Presented with the need to map the area of Aguacatal on the Gulf Coast of Campeche, where he had campaigned for two seasons, Ray T. Matheny realized that heavy jungle growth hindered him from establishing on the ground the actual extent of the ruins and details of their natural setting. Progress continued to be slow. 'One could walk within twenty feet of an archaeological structure and not see it.' Why should examination from above offer a short-cut?

A partial answer is that this was the 1960s and a whole battery of aids, such as the hand-held K-20 aerial camera, Super-XX, infra-red, and special chromatic films and filters, were available at little expense. A Mexican-owned Piper Tri-Pacer could be rented for a nominal fee from a near-by airport at Ciudad del Carmen. Aerial interpretation of photos made on various sensitive materials, including colour film, had made great strides since the days of the Lindbergh flights and so had the knowledge of the effects of human occupation on soil chemistry and vegetation in the tropics. Even though there was relatively little profit to be derived from other scholars' archaeological work over the jungle, guidance could be got from the aerial researches of ecologists, geologists, or plant biologists operating under like conditions. Thus Matheny learned a great deal from perusing articles on esoteric subjects such as 'An Evaluation of Aerial Photography for Detecting Southern Pine Beetle Damage' in a 1959 issue of *Photogrammetric Engineering*. A booklet issued by the Eastman Kodak Company was invaluable: *Kodak Data for Aerial Photography*.

Aside from a brief foray in 1956 by a Utah colleague, Ross T. Christensen, none of the many ruins in the region's Xicalango Peninsula had been archaeologically surveyed from the air. However, high-altitude photographs existed, made by CIA Mexicana Aerofoto in 1938 and 1943. Meticulous examination of the Christensen and Mexicana photos found traces of light-marks in the jungle vegetation that Matheny thought might stem from walls surrounding Aguacatal. Here was a promise of what judicious employment of modern photographic means might accomplish over the bush forest.

Matheny experimented with Kodak Super-XX Aerographic, Infra-red Aerographic, as well as 35 mm. Kodachrome and Ektachrome films. They all had their specific uses. But Super-XX (particularly in combination with a Number 12 (minus blue) filter to reduce the haze) was on the whole most satisfactory for registering the colour differentials of the vegetation attributable to ruined edifices. Consecutive examination of the ground furnished convincing explanation of the factors that produced patterns on the aerial photographs.

'In lowland regions,' Matheny wrote in his brief communication to *American Antiquity*,

vegetation specializes itself according to the dryness and chemistry of the soil. At Aguacatal four species of mangrove tree grow in the wet latosolic soil. Within the mangrove stands are found archaeological structures which rise a few inches to 30 feet above the ground level. The soil on the structures is better drained, has considerable sand, and is chemically different from the surrounding soil. The soil chemistry was changed by human occupation. Pottery clays, ash, food refuse, and building materials such as sand, shells, and stone were introduced by past inhabitants. It was found that 14 species of trees grow on these structures but do not grow in the lower wet lands. Even the worn-down structures a few inches high have grasses and other plants that the lower ground does not have. Patterns of the structures were easily traced on the photographs by their light gray tones in comparison with dark gray representing the mangrove stands.

How good were the overall results of aerial photography when verified on land? Matheny reported that not all details can be expected to be picked up from above. For instance, the numerous small hummocks on major temple platforms failed to appear distinctly. But larger mounds, separate from the platforms, stood out prominently, among them those that had been left unnoticed during previous ground explorations. Of two recently discovered Maya ceremonial sites not far from Aguacatal, the photographs fully revealed their plan and dimension. Building complexes on a near-by island, which had remained totally unknown even to local inhabitants, were now spotted thanks to aerial photographs. In terms of time spent, aerial reconnaissance once again proved its economy. Matheny expended no more than two hours in the air to photograph the area of Aguacatal which, he asserts, would have required two seasons to survey from below.

In the thirty years that it took airborne reconnaissance of pre-Columbian civilizations to mature, aerial archaeology, as was to be expected, made greater progress in other parts of the Americas. However, it is not without paradox that the new archaeological approach, dependent as it was on the successful construction of a flying machine by modern American inventors, was only intermittently applied to their continent's past. (The first archaeological air photographs of any American site are believed to have been taken of the Cahokia mounds, Illinois, by Lieutenants A. C. McKinley and H. R. Wells in 1921 to 1922. But they revealed nothing new.) Unlike Britain, the US has no key agency or scientific leadership to continuously preside over and launch such 'lofty' research. The first flurry of enthusiasm, which led here and there to noteworthy finds, petered out for no good reason in the 1930s. In 1952 Crawford could write with some justice: 'Air-photography has not as yet been much used in America for archaeological discovery'. However, his additional statement that he does not know of 'any published illustration of a crop-site anywhere in that continent' reflects Crawford's limited knowledge of American publications.

In one of the rare pre-Second World War articles written by an American and devoted exclusively to the application of aerial photography to archaeology, a major of the US Army, Dache M. Reeves, in 1936 reproduced pictures of earthworks in

Ohio which, though obliterated, reappear on air photos as patterns in cultivated fields.

At least as early as 1930 unmistakable vegetation- or grassmarks were photographed in United States territory and reproduced in *Exploration and Fieldwork*, the annals of the Smithsonian Institution. The pictures resulted from a carefully planned campaign centring on the same South-West where Lindbergh had made his initial tests, only this time the target was not the decayed dwellings of the Pueblos in the Four-Corner Country, but features even better geared to exposure by the roaming lens of the aerial camera. The area was southern Arizona and the sites scrutinized were the ancient irrigation canals that ingenious aboriginal agriculturists, the so-called Hohokam (a modern Indian name), had built on a truly gigantic scale.

The waterworks had been abandoned before white settlers appeared on the scene, and so it was by no means common knowledge that a system of hundreds of miles of prehistoric canals had existed in this arid country, tapping the Salt and Gila rivers and rendering extensive tracts of parched earth fertile. The new arrivals, inadvertently following in the footsteps of the ancient farmers in the nineteenth century, would often just incorporate canal beds. Otherwise, few people gave the remaining sections much thought, and if they did they ascribed them to Spanish colonists rather than 'primitive' Indians. How could any but Europeans with their Iron Age tools have cut deep lengthy ditches through volcanic rock, built dams, and directed and controlled the flow of water through hydraulic devices? By the time archaeologists fully recognized the pre-Columbian origin of the extinct farming culture and pursued its study, it was almost too late. Of some estimated 230 miles of canals still in evidence in 1922, only some 10 per cent could be observed in 1929. This sorry state of affairs was faced squarely by Neil M. Judd, a Utah-born archaeologist of the Smithsonian Institution who specialized in the South-West.

We wanted maps of these latter, hand-made Indian canals [he wrote]. We wanted to know their extent, their position relative to each other, the approximate acreage they once watered. Similar desires on the part of other observers had prompted surveys which were not altogether successful for the simple reason that so little is now visible of the ancient ditches. Modern agriculture has been too destructive; it has ploughed and planted until the aboriginal farming communities and their works were pretty thoroughly obliterated. From the ground, one's range of vision is too limited; from the air it might be possible to recover data for the maps we had in mind.

A public-spirited United States Senator of Arizona, Carl Hayden, the son of one of the first pioneers of the region, used his influence to promptly mobilize an aerial survey. In its execution the Smithsonian Institution was joined by the War Department, which furnished the plane, pilot, and photographer. Judd acted as scientific leader.

Operations began in late January 1930. Owing to winter haze over the valleys, flights had to be confined to two midday hours. This meant that there was no chance to take advantage of the longer morning and evening shadows to bring out the relief of ditches and other partly levelled features. The blue Douglas army plane as a rule flew at a height of ten thousand feet, at which the photographer would shoot 'with clock-like precision' reams of vertical pictures through a hole in the floor. Thus, the Salt and Gila basins were given nearly complete coverage. Since the military personnel employed the routine techniques for aerial mapping, the scale as much as the season was far from ideal. Nevertheless, the seven-hundred-odd photographs disclosed prehistoric canals in an unmistakable web of streaks, from which the irrigation system could be charted. Judd left no doubt that he understood the how and why of aerial observation:

Silt deposited in those old ditches shows dark brown against the drab desert soil; pale yellow lines remain where embankments have been smoothed away. Slight differences in vegetation, imperceptible when close at hand, take on colour variations that enable one at a considerable height to retrace works which otherwise have been wholly effaced.

Despite its technical shortcomings, Judd's survey of the Hohokam canals was no shot in the dark and must rank as a milestone in American archaeological reconnaissance from the air. Later on, we shall return to other aerial discoveries in the United States.

Probably the most important airborne undertaking in the Americas at the time was centred in Peru. This country, with its exaggerated contrasts of terrain and commensurate obstacles to land communication, was made for aviation. Not surprisingly, it had been in the forefront of the development of air transportation. Some of its people became accustomed to the sound of whirling propellers and to the moving shadows of overhead planes before they ever saw wheeled vehicles on land. Its military establishment energetically began to organize the air force in the early 1920s, while the government invited commercial companies such as the Faucett Aviation Company and Pan American Grace Airways to set up regular services. All these agencies early took a hand in photographic surveying in order to aid varied civic projects, from railroad and highway construction to irrigation of the deserts and location of damsites. Mapping with air cameras, particularly of the elongated Pacific littoral, was initiated by the air service of the Peruvian navy, which in 1928 appointed a young United States officer, Lieutenant George R. Johnson, its chief photographer. Johnson, who had already had considerable experience at home with aerial photography, also acted as instructor at the naval air base at Ancón, on the Pacific not far from Lima.

During his three-year stint in Peru, Johnson produced a remarkable array of photographs whose technical excellence remains unsurpassed. A selection of these was published in 1930 by the American Geographical Society and drew the attention of geographers and historians. Johnson's photographic record ranged all over Peru: over oilfields, port installations, arid coastal valleys, desolate altiplanos, snow-crested Andean massifs, conic volcanoes, and the lush tropical banks of Amazon headstreams. It was mainly concerned with presenting a profile of the topography and modern human geography of the southern republic, but could not help registering almost everywhere remains of the land's pervasive antiquities. Indeed, on some pictures, the crumbling, pre-colonial ruins of forts, cities, pyramids, shrines, and burials tended to impress themselves more prominently than signs of present life.

Back in New York, scholars fastened their interest on air pictures of the Colca Valley some seventy miles north of Arequipa, a two-mile-deep canyon (twice as deep as the Grand Canyon) surrounded by majestic Andean crests. Johnson had come across it by accident at the end of a flight through the southern Peruvian Andes, just when his pilot was swinging westward so that he might photograph the towering peaks of Ampato and Chachani. Instead, in one spectacular snapshot he caught the magnificent gorge with its orderly Spanish-style villages at the narrowing valley floor and myriads of the step-like curved green terraces of pre-Columbian farms climbing the slopes. The valley and its history had been 'lost', even though its rectangularly laid-out settlements must have dated from after the Conquest. Neither in Arequipa nor Lima could Johnson find anyone who was informed about it. Later it came out that contacts with the outside had virtually ceased when the once prospering population had been reduced in colonial days by earthquakes, famines, plague, and conscription to the mines.

To fathom the Colca Valley and its forgotten villages required a special effort, which soon grew into a call for an ambitious survey of ancient Peru. The prime mover behind it was a wealthy young pilot, Robert Shippee, who, like Johnson, was a native of New Jersey. The older man had frequently discussed with him the valuable work aerial reconnaissance could accomplish in the Andean lands. Shippee scented adventure and was able to obtain funds. The result was the Shippee-Johnson Peruvian Expedition, led by the two men, Johnson acting, of course, as chief photographer. Altogether there were five permanent members, none of them over thirty (Shippee was barely twenty) and all but one from New Jersey.

The expedition left by boat in December 1930 from Brooklyn. Floating with them were two Bellanca monoplanes, christened the *Washington* and *Lima*. During the eight and a half months the young fliers spent in Peru, they remained in the air for 455 hours, taking some three thousand air pictures and miles of films. Aside from canvassing answers to a questionnaire on the Colca Valley, which the American Geographical

Society had drawn up, all the work was essentially photographic. In the true mould of muscular adventurers, the explorers met with a chain of adversities, none, however, disastrous. They lost one plane in a crash but escaped unscathed. Outbreak of a revolution kept them grounded for several weeks, but twice they were pressed into flying missions for the rebels. On another occasion – whether as a voluntary service or not they fail to tell – they transported by air a shipment of tear bombs to a strike-bound oilfield. Weather in the coastal area, notorious for fogs caused by the cold waters of the Humboldt Current, presented its share of problems, most of all in the last few weeks, which were winter in the Southern Hemisphere.

Shippee, who functioned as both pilot and historian, frankly declared that his expedition had not expected to make any fundamentally new discoveries. Nor did it especially plan for such eventualities. After all, Peru's pre-Columbian ruins had been repeatedly explored for close to a century by a whole cavalcade of renowned scholars, several of whom spent a lifetime there in active research. If anything, the airborne expedition's objective was set as a continuation of Johnson's previous camera work, only with a greater emphasis on antiquities. In other words, archaeological surveying was conceived (and here Shippee invokes Crawford's authority) as response to increasing demands for 'more maps and more air photographs' of known sites. Hence, the goal was set to photograph from above the more or less familiar ruins of Peru, both along the coast and sky high in the Andes. According to specific needs, remains were to be recorded by oblique or vertical photographs and, on occasion, by aerial mosaics to encompass large and complex features.

Foremost among the ancient places to be covered in their entirety by mosaics was the famous Chimú capital of Chan-Chan, in the Moche Valley, an enormous, eleven-mile-square compound of criss-crossing adobe walls which, according to some estimates, may have counted more than two hundred thousand inhabitants and was perhaps the largest pre-Columbian metropolis in the Americas. Johnson's photographic maps brought out all the city's major subdivisions: self-contained, walled complexes with palaces, temples, streets, plazas, gardens, and reservoirs, believed to have been occupied by separate clans and, as the photographs proved, constructed at different times.

During the flights over Chan-Chan, the expedition was quartered at near-by Trujillo, a city founded by Pizarro and named for his birthplace in Spain. Photographs, however, were rushed to Lima to be developed at a laboratory specially set up there. While still engaged in the Chan-Chan survey, the young men undertook several forays into the interior from their Trujillo base. One such side journey transported them to the Marañón River, a major Amazon tributary. They returned to the coast in a wide swing around majestic Mount Huascarán and then followed the Santa River, one of the dozens of 'little Niles' like the Moche which cut across the desert strip along the Pacific. The Santa Valley had been one of the thriving, artificially irrigated oasis focuses of pre-Inca civilizations and was by no means unexplored. What happened on this last leg of their flight is best told in Shippee's own words.

Our course [he reported to the American Geographical Society] was over the edge of the foothills bordering the narrow upper valley of the river on the north. Johnson, co-leader and photographer of the expedition, watching for photographic subjects, noticed what appeared to be a wall flowing up and down over the ridges beneath the plane, wondered for a moment as to the purpose of such a structure, decided that it was worth recording, and made a number of photographs of it. We hoped to be able to return later to make a more complete record of the wall but were not certain that we should have time to do so. The photographs, printed a few weeks later in our Lima laboratory, led to so much discussion, however, that before our departure we arranged to make a special trip to relocate and examine the wall from both the air and the ground.

The episode signalled one of the momentous discoveries in South American archaeology, that of the so-called 'Great Wall of Peru', a writhing rampart that from the river delta onward traversed the stark foothills along the bank of the Santa for many miles into the Andes. It climbed adjacent ridges, for a while trailed mountain crests in a nearly straight line, then fell down to cross dry riverbeds, approached the Santa, only to ascend again, here and there blending indistinguishably into the dun eroded slopes, and then standing out once more like a scar slashed across a withered epidermis.

On their second, more extensive examination of the wall, Shippee and his associates were able to follow it by plane for thirty or more miles (the distance was difficult to gauge because bad flying weather made a straight course impossible). They then noticed that the wall, at some distance and within irregular intervals, was paralleled on both sides by a number of rectangular and circular forts. The more formidable of these structures cropped up on the southern flank along the other side of the Santa River. One large rectangular fort, raised from stone, measured approximately two hundred by three hundred feet, with a height of fifteen feet. Other forts were probably built from adobe only.

Ground examination also revealed the wall's mode of construction which was that of large stone blocks chinked by pebbles and, at least partly, 'cemented' by adobe. Its average base was some fifteen feet, from which it may have once risen from ten to fifteen feet. Like Roman defence points along the desert frontier of North Africa and the Near East, the forts were so placed that they were virtually invisible to approaching enemy invaders.

The explorers at first could not get over the surprise that so prominent a feature as the Great Wall had never been described before. Julio C. Tello, the leading Peruvian archaeologist, declared that he had not the slightest knowledge of it, and, according to his inquiry, neither had the people living on the large sugar plantation of the Santa Valley. However, Tello and others now recalled that they had previously come across sections of ancient walls in several coastal valleys from the vicinity of Lima to the Ecuador border. But none of these could in dimension and design compare with the Santa wall, which inevitably conjured up its counterpart in China. Like Shippee and his companions, we may indeed wonder how the Wall of Peru could have been missed for so long. Yet thirty years later, St Joseph wrote of his own land, surely one of the most accessible and archaeologically and otherwise most thoroughly investigated countries on earth, that 'there exist monuments several hundred feet across, comprising a bank 20 to 30 feet

wide still standing a few feet high, that have remained unrecorded till now ... There are many areas of Britain that
remain archaeologically unexplored'. Here is a retort to those
who may think that, thanks to intensive air surveys or other

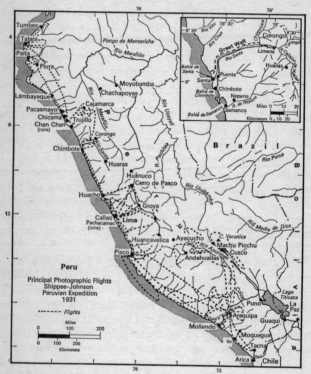

Figure 29. Map of Peru. The dotted lines mark the Shippee-Johnson
flights in 1931. On the insert appears the Santa River valley with the
'Great Wall'

modern techniques, all major discoveries have been made or
are about to be made. In South America, as elsewhere, the
greatest finds are probably still to come.

Various hypotheses were advanced as to the wall's function
and origin. Was it defensive or was it only meant to stake out a

tribal or political boundary? Its adjoining forts, assuming that they are contemporary, certainly imply a military-strategic nature. No unanimity has been yet reached concerning its historical associations. The wall has been connected with Inca expansion and the Chimú's counter-move to stem the mountaineers' advance. One specific purpose may have been the protection of their vital water supply. Several scholars, on the other hand, have thought it marks the Chimú's own imperialist push southward, either as an advance base or, during times of consolidation, a second line of defence. But evidence produced by the more recent researches of an American archaeologist, Gene Savoy, and hinted at already by Tello, who briefly examined the wall in 1934 with Cornelius Roosevelt, points to pre-Chimú people, probably their Moche predecessors, as the builders. Savoy's investigations have also added to the number of forts (some fifty are now known) and to details of construction. At the same time he was able to trace the wall for forty miles inland to its terminus at a height of fifteen hundred feet at the present Hacienda Suchimancillo, where imposing ruins of rock-built fortresses (*pucaras*) dot the site.

A quarter of a century earlier, Shippee and his crew were only partially successful in their ground exploration of the Santa Valley. Eventually they had to break it off, because of their imminent return to the United States. Nevertheless, the land operations taught them a valuable object lesson: they now realized that there were indeed good reasons why the wall had so far been totally missed. While in the air they had made a rough sketch of the wall and its vicinity, thinking that it would easily guide them when afoot. But after five hours of search they almost despaired of even finding the beginning of the wall at a ruined village that clearly stood out from above. On the ground, Shippee wrote, they saw 'nothing but a few ridges, made where crumbled adobe walls were covered by centuries of drifted sand'. The 'great' wall was indistinguishable from a number of shrivelled embankments. One such blind lead they followed to its abrupt end in the middle of the desert. 'Only when one looks down upon the wall from the air,' Shippee is led to conclude after this demonstration, 'and thus able to see long sections of it can one realize that it is a feature quite distinct from the short sections of wall characteristic of the Santa delta. This broad view presented to an observer and camera is what makes the airplane so important an instrument in modern exploration. The aerial observer is afforded, and the aerial camera records frequently in a single exposure, a synthesis of details whose relationships might otherwise never be discovered.' From a twenty-one-year-old neophyte explorer, this is an extraordinarily succinct statement of the unique merits of aerial perspective.

The Shippee-Johnson Peruvian Expedition made quite a few other stunning observations that were as unanticipated and novel as the Great Wall with its accompaniment of fortresses. Among them were a long, wide strip weaving atop a rocky range near the Pisco Valley in southern coastal Peru. From the air the curious ribbon formed by countless hollows looks as if a giant tank or tractor had rolled over the escarpment. Shippee likened it to 'pockmarks'. No landing could be made here to search the ground for answers. Later search through the literature dealing with the region's antiquities failed to come up with any clue. Archaeologists were dumbfounded. The standard explanation that the depressions represent plundered graves remains inconclusive and unconvincing. Sir W. M. Flinders Petrie, the aged pioneer of scientific archaeology in Egypt, who saw the Johnson photograph, proposed (in a communication to *Antiquity*) that the holes stemmed from surface digging for copper ore by pre-Columbian miners.

Another unsolved mystery related to photographs taken of a high Andean plateau some fifteen miles south-west of the Cuzco, the fertile Maras Pampa. There the explorers observed a strange group of almost circular, terraced bowls that immediately evoked the *stadia*, or amphitheatres, of ancient Greece and Rome. That the Peruvians of old built any open-air arenas of the classical type had never been adumbrated. Despite some vague traditions, attributed by Shippee to 'Cuzco priests', that the newly discovered structures had been used during religious festivities, the evidence is slim and as yet unconfirmed. One cannot rule out the prosaic possibility, freely conceded by Shippee, that the odd amphitheatres were 'nothing more than agricultural terraces'.

Unusual data like the Pisco 'pockmarks' and the Maras Pampa 'amphitheatres' furnish further proof of the element of surprise in aerial exploration, but they also disclose a disappointing lag between aerial discoveries and their archaeological analysis. There is no telling how many more unknown features, though caught by the aerial camera and filed away in private or institutional collections, remain for all purposes lost to science. Even those that have been extensively written up will require thorough ground study for proper verification to become part of a body of common cumulative knowledge.

Regrettably, the many first-rate photographs taken by the Shippee-Johnson team soon fell into oblivion. The majority were never published. Victor W. von Hagen, the peripatetic student of Inca and pre-Inca roads, noted that in years to come 'little use was made of this photographic material, since there was neither sufficient ground identification of the ruins nor any archaeologist to interest himself in it'. Luckily, von Hagen, who had befriended Shippee, utilized these pictures two decades later in his own Peruvian researches. He rescued 'the vast archive', as he called it, from its basement burial, published several of the photographs for the first time, and, after acquiring the collection, had it transferred to the Wenner-Gren (Viking Fund) Foundation for Anthropological Research in New York City to make it fully available to scholarship. (It is now deposited at the American Museum of Natural History.) Von Hagen is of the opinion that the Shippee-Johnson discoveries from the air helped to kindle the interest of archaeologists in the desert kingdoms of coastal Peru, so that, as his own 1964 book on the subject testifies, 'the literature has been wonderfully enriched'.

11. Wings over Ancient America: II

Even if the Shippee-Johnson aerial campaign had no far-reaching archaeological consequences at the time, Johnson's photographic work for the Peruvian navy bore fruit, for it was systematically continued by the Servicio Aerofotográfico Nacional in Lima, organized as the mapping department of the Ministry of Aeronautics. Throughout the years this agency has been able to accumulate a stupendous canvas of the land. Relatively little has escaped its winged cameramen. Several of the coastal valleys have been captured in mosaics. Though here again, as in comparable governmental enterprises elsewhere, the objective was non-archaeological, much of the record turned out to be immensely useful to students of Peruvian antiquities. So much so, in fact, that since the Second World War it has become almost a matter of routine for Peruvian and foreign scholars to check the available aerial coverage and, if possible, base a map on it, if not a full-scale excavation plan. When in the small Virú Valley, just north of the Santa Valley, North American archaeologists and anthropologists carried out an ambitious programme to reconstruct thousands of years of prehistory from the first advent of man, the rise of pre-ceramic cultures, and the introduction of farming to the successive ages of Chavín, Moche, Tiahuanaco, Chimú, and Inca, with their local variants, they relied extensively on air photographs at all phases of their campaigns. Likewise, Dr Richard P. Schaedel, who for some time directed the newly established Anthropological Institute of the University of Trujillo, used air photographs from the Servicio extensively in his important work among the lost ceremonial centres of northern Peru.

No one, however, would extract as much information from the photographic archives as another United States scholar, the late Paul Kosok of Long Island University. He had come to Peru first in 1940 to study the ancient 'irrigation societies' of the coast and their transition from theocracies to secular states. After the war he resumed this research. In the course of it, he was to investigate a profusion of ancient temples, pyramids, canals, aqueducts, highways, walls, towns, fortresses, and the like. His ambitious programme called for the mapping of all remains of the coastal irrigation systems and for determining the maximal cultivated area of each valley in the pre-Columbian times.

Already during his stay in 1940–41 he had begun to collect hydrological data at Lima. In addition, he had taken up field work. At the time he felt sorely handicapped by the lack of means of transportation, and still more by being deprived of guidance from aerial surveys of regions he set out to chart. Both handicaps were happily alleviated when, as he later wrote,

the Peruvian Ministerio de Fomento, which was then in the process of building the Pan American Highway ... placed its trucks at our disposal whenever possible. Various *hacendados* along the Coast also kindly loaned us cars, trucks and horses for our work. We were given additional assistance by Señor Pardo y Miguel of Hacienda Pátapo in the Lambayeque Valley. He took us on several flights in his private aeroplane over the many ancient sites in this and neighbouring valleys. Mr Faucett, the director of the Faucett Line, the local Peruvian aviation company, also generously came to our assistance by giving us a pass for planes of the company flying along the Coast. We made full use of this valuable privilege and were thus able to locate additional ancient canals and archaeological sites. Moreover, the Peruvian Government gave us permission to take photographs from these planes. Thus we were able to obtain numerous low-elevation photographs of important ancient canals and sites.

Kosok set aside a good part of the summer of 1946 in Washington to wade through photographs from an aerial survey made of Peru during the war by the United States Army. There were no fewer than twenty thousand negatives. Most had been taken during midday at a high altitude but yielded some novel information nevertheless, especially on areas not covered by other agencies. Of far greater usefulness were the resources of the Servicio Aerofotográfico, at whose headquarters in a Lima suburb Kosok spent weeks on end (altogether more than three months) of his 1947–8 stay in Peru. Before and between his various field trips he would always check the pictorial files in order to pinpoint, confirm, and extend his data. Generally, Kosok laboured at the Servicio's laboratory until ten o'clock at night, Saturdays and Sundays included. The great bulk of the material had never previously been tapped for archaeological research. To facilitate his chores he had enlargements made, which he later deposited with Long Island University in Brooklyn, New York.

In the posthumous volume *Life, Land and Water in Ancient Peru* (1965) that reproduces well over a hundred unpublished aerial photographs, many of hitherto unreported sites and several taken by himself, Kosok reminisced on the 'excitements' of preliminary work at the Servicio which turned out to be

a real treasure hunt. As we studied photograph after photograph we were actually carrying on an intellectual quest for the dead but unburied treasures of the past. There was always tremendous satisfaction discovering new pyramids, settlements, fortifications, walls, courts and canals on a photograph. Indeed, it was even exciting to find such ruins on photographs after we had seen them in the field. For here they looked quite different! We would often exclaim: Why didn't we see that there was another ruin right near by when we were in the field? Why didn't we see that this wall extended all the way up the hill? Why didn't we follow the 'end' of this canal for another half mile and find its continuation? Sometimes it was difficult to decide whether a certain mark on a photograph was a section of a road or of a canal – or perhaps just a scratch on the negative! But even if a set of pictures yielded no 'pay dirt', the beauty of some photographs was often reward in itself!

Extensive as the collection Kosok examined was, not all the thirty-odd valleys had been photographed by the Servicio, and some missing areas Kosok considered vital to his study. A pleasant surprise was in the offing when, just before his scheduled departure, the Servicio made a low aerial survey of two of those valleys. The resulting pictures proved to be of excellent quality and threw so much new light on his researches that Kosok decided to stay on another month.

Despite his enthusiasm, Kosok had no illusions about the shortcomings of the pictures at his disposal, both in the area covered and in their underlying technique. Such deficiencies were to be expected from photographs that had not specifically focused on archaeological objects. Because of inevitable gaps he had to locate a good many ruins and canals by ground reconnaissance alone. Several badly decayed structures were not satisfactorily recorded from the air. Only inspection on foot could determine whether a feature hazily depicted on a photograph was natural or man-made. Kosok found himself therefore in agreement with most pioneers of aerial archaeology, when he insisted that field work remained a basic requirement. 'As in the military field,' he wrote, 'aviation, while important, is, after all, chiefly an accessory to ground action!' (One might argue that Kosok's view, at least of warfare, threatens to become outdated.)

Kosok's exhaustive survey of the irrigation system of coastal northern Peru, which owed so much to aerial photography and could have never hoped to reach a modicum of completeness and detail without it, has so far not been issued in book form. But we have been given a foretaste in his 'memoir'. That work has also a lavishly illustrated chapter on Kosok's related researches in southern Peru. They concern one of the great mysteries of ancient America: the fantastic network of markings on top of the desert plateaus near Nazca.

Our knowledge of this prodigious apparition is also a direct result of the air age. For once it is impossible to name any single explorer or cameraman who saw it first. Rather, it seems that when the region came to be regularly traversed by planes of the Faucett Line, passengers and crew were wont to notice a bewildering maze of designs covering the barren mesa-like uplands at some distance from the Pacific. Most of them proliferated on the cliffs along the Río Grande and its tributaries, in an exceedingly arid zone between the Ica and Nazca valleys. The intricate, ghostlike delineations were roughly 250 miles south from Lima and extended for about sixty miles into the interior at a width of from five to ten miles. Within this area, hardly any plateaus remained free of such 'tattoos'. On occasion the lines would continue down adjoining slopes.

That such a gigantic 'picture book' had been disregarded so long was, of course, amazing, but it is precisely *because* of the tremendous scale of most of the figures that they were not discovered earlier. Travellers walking across the drab lonely hills are likely to see only small sections at a time, and hence remain unimpressed. We need the air view to distinguish extensive geometric figures in their entirety and colour contrast; to be startled by the straightness of these lines which do not deviate an inch from their projectile-like course; and to take in a total picture of the complexity and quantity of this fantastic conglomerate of figures. If any prehistoric feature ever cried for the aerial approach, it was the desert pictographs of southern Peru.

For a number of years the Nazca 'sand drawings', though by then a fairly familiar landmark, were looked upon as little but an odd curiosity. Facetiously they were dubbed 'prehistoric landing fields', or invited comparisons with the canals of Mars. Indeed, a Martian aura clung to them for quite a while. Few serious attempts were made to offer a rational explanation for the odd signs, which undoubtedly had been etched into the soil by some vanished Indian race. Unfortunately no reference to them appeared in the chronicles of the early Spanish period. Of the aboriginal valley people who might have retained certain traditions that could elucidate the jigsaw puzzle, none had survived the massacres in the civil wars between rival Conquistadores whose chattels they had become. The region's present inhabitants, if at all aware of them, alluded to them as 'Inca roads', even though an arm of the actual Inca highway cut right across them and was obviously of a much later date.

During his 1940–41 stay in Peru, Kosok heard of the mysterious carvings on the southern tablelands. In the belief that, if not by themselves waterworks, they might still bear on his subject, he resolved to investigate them further. From then dates the first systematic analysis of the phenomenon, which was to lead to a persuasive hypothesis. To a quite unanticipated degree it was also to shed light on Kosok's main study.

How was one to make any sense of the mad jumble of interwoven, at times overlapping, lines, rectangles, triangles, and trapezoids? The lines or 'roads' ran off in all directions, extended for a few yards or as much as five miles, only to end quite suddenly. As common as single lines and as clearly delineated were lanes of parallel lines, their usually lighter, yellowish inner strips bounded by higher dark edges. An idea of the size of the many elongated rectilinear figures is given by an aerial photograph in Kosok's book. In one corner of a trapezoid we perceive a relatively small, whitish oval blotch. This minor blemish is a good-sized modern football field!

A close examination of the ground leaves no doubt about the manner in which all these figures were produced. The method was as simple as could be. All that was needed was to remove a thin layer of dark weathered pebbles from the lighter subsurface underneath. The removed stones were then piled along the edges where, particularly from above, they stood out like black filaments. In the rainless dry climate where erosion is minimal, the outlines will retain their sharpness for centuries, if not millennia, even though gradual darkening of the scraped-away interstices may eventually blunt the colour contrast caused by oxidation ('desert varnish') of the iron-rich gravel. The pace or rate of the darkening process is not known; otherwise it would be easy to establish the approximate age of the human handiwork.

To Kosok it was clear from the beginning that none of the so-called roads could have served as ordinary means of communication, since they did not lead to any ancient sites – settlements, temples, or burials – and only occasionally connected at one end with other routes. Likewise they did not fit another frequent ascription as furrows. Agriculture was an impossibility on most of the parched ridges, where not a single blade grew, unless irrigation rendered them fertile. But that some of the isolated eminences had once been linked to a watering system (of which there was no evidence whatever) in the valley below outraged the laws of physics. And this did away also with the complementary theory that they were themselves remnants of irrigation canals. A thesis proposed by a Peruvian scholar that the 'roads' played a part in religious ceremonies sounded somewhat more credible.

On a brief sojourn with his wife in 1941, Kosok had the sudden intuition that the lines had an astronomical significance. He and his wife had followed one large 'road', cut by the Pan American Highway, up a small mesa, where they found more figures, including a series of short parallel bars that they guessed might have been a kind of counting scheme. While still immersed in thoughts about the riddles at their feet they unintentionally returned to the centre of the large artery that had guided them to the top. From there radiated a number of single lines. The sun was just then setting; to their amazement it touched the horizon precisely over one of the lines at whose base they stood. Immediately they realized that it was 22 June, the day of the winter solstice in the southern hemisphere. Surely this line was a solstice line!

Thus, Kosok had come up with the first clue which led him to conclude that the desert markings were nothing less than the 'Largest Astronomy Book in the World'. They must have served primarily as calendrical devices to register the change of seasons and, above all, the onset of the life-giving flow of water. Like other primitive civilizations depending on agriculture as their mainstay, these pre-Columbian people of southern Peru had evidently developed astronomical calculations to considerable refinement in order to gain a sympathetic understanding of the productive cycle which linked them to the universe. As in other parts of the Old and New Worlds, such scientific lore was probably wielded by an élite class of priests who encased it in a cocoon of ritual and religion to assure their ascendancy over illiterate believers. Further, these astronomical and calendrical notations of the uninhabited desert could not have existed in isolation but were without doubt intimately connected with the life of the irrigation societies or pre-historic farmers in the valleys below.

Kosok's identification of a solstice line was only a starting point. The great book still had to be read. To test his intuition, he would have to establish the direction of many more lines and make a thorough study of all the features etched into the desert. However, from the ground he perceived only fragments from which one could never hope to gauge the gigantic concept. The drawings owed their original discovery to observation from the air; so, logically, the aerial perspective had to be enlisted if one wanted to progress. Since few satisfactory aerial photographs were then available of this unproductive inland region, Kosok once again relied on the Faucett Aviation Company to let him undertake flying missions in one of their planes. As he wrote,

I was soon able to get a general picture of the whole layout, with the result that I succeeded in locating at least a dozen radiating centres in various parts of the pampas. Then I ascertained the direction of many of the lines radiating from some of these centres, by means of a good compass, the readings from which were corrected by data furnished by the Huancaya Magnetic Observatory. A number of the lines and 'roads' were found to have a solstitial direction; a few with equinoctial direction could also be identified.

No longer were the drawings a chaotic mess. Already Kosok thought he could see at least spatial connections between the lines and the rectilinear shapes. In addition, he became aware of another set of non-geometric designs: outlines of strange figures measuring 150 yards or more, which were drawn like some children's sketches in one continuous line. They depicted a bestiary of demoniacal creatures – spiders, monkeys, birds, fishes, serpents – and closely resembled figures appearing on early Nazca ceramics and tapestry. Archaeologists associate the Nazca people with one of the prominent coastal cultures of southern Peru, roughly contemporary with the Moche of the north. Unlike the northern people, however, they did not build monumentally, a fact that strengthened Kosok's belief that they never advanced to a secular militarist state. Remaining under the thumb of astronomer-priests, much of their energies apparently went into the enormous desert canvas.

Kosok was unable to continue his preliminary work in the Nazca region, because of his commitments in the north. But he had the good fortune to make the acquaintance at Lima of a German-born woman scientist, Dr Maria Reiche, who had been trained in both mathematics and astronomy. From that moment on, Miss Reiche has been something of an apostle of the Nazca desert, where she has lived in a humble adobe hut while measuring and charting, besides adding an immense number of unknown details to the catalogue of figures. It is she who has substantiated Kosok's hypothesis with impressive new material that not only enlarges on lines determining solstices and equinoxes, but relates the Nazca 'calendar' to positions of the sun during other days of the year, as well as to data on the moon, planets, and prominent celestial bodies such as the

Figure 30. These Nazca desert drawings depict bird and monkey effigies as well as geometric patterns that may have had ceremonial and astronomical uses

Pleiades known to have played a significant part in the pantheon of ancient Peruvians.

Less well established, however, remains the meaning of the other figures. Conceivably the rectangular fields, which are reminiscent of the cursuses of prehistoric England, functioned as a kind of outdoor temples where kinship groups assembled, while the zoomorphic figures may represent constellations of stars or totem symbols or, in line with primitive lore elsewhere, both.

Miss Reiche has also fought a winning battle that reached the chambers of the Peruvian parliament with unscrupulous entrepreneurs who threatened to destroy a major part of her 'painted' desert for the sake of their land-development ventures. In 1948–9 when Kosok again took up his Peruvian researches, she joined hands with him. At that time both scholars had at their disposal numerous new air pictures of the Servicio which helped them immeasurably in their field work. Together they then wrote a number of popular articles that brought the Nazca markings before an international audience and, incidentally, helped to elicit financial grants from learned societies for further research.

Since Kosok's untimely death in 1959, Miss Reiche has carried on alone. When the occasion demanded, she has repeatedly called on airborne photographers to present her with panoramic records. Like other archaeologists in recent years, she has come to value the slow-flying helicopter as an ideal vehicle for taking aerial pictures, but she outdid her male colleagues by having herself strapped to the outside, so that she could get her photographs from the best possible angle. One such acrobatic shot angled a giant whale that she was the first to spot and for which she developed a special affection.

From astronomical computations, based on the known annual rate of deviation at which certain 'fixed' stars rise and set, Miss Reiche established a date of approximately A.D. 500. This date was later confirmed by radiocarbon analysis of a wooden post taken from an intersection of two lines. Nevertheless, one has to think of the markings, many of which were scratched over each other, in terms of a sequence evolving through a considerable period of time. Thus they might one day be found to parallel and mirror the development of Nazca culture.

One of the mysteries and glories of the Nazca gravel drawings lies in the fact that their creators could never see them properly. Even if they used scaled models and calibrated ropes (Miss Reiche actually determined some of their basic units of measurement), it strains one's imagination to see how they could have laid out their designs with such precision over such extensive terrain. There may be some truth in the opinion of several students that the figures were planned as messages to the gods residing in the empyrean. If so, the signs and symbols may well flatter the winged men of our day, who have recovered the images, even if they cannot yet claim to fully understand their messages.

It is doubtful whether anywhere else in the world one can find so fantastic and profuse an assemblage of giant prehistoric drawings. Nevertheless, the Nazca figures have their counterparts, particularly in the Western Hemisphere, into which, despite considerable divergencies between the higher and fairly recent civilizations of Middle America and Peru, percolated kindred cultural traditions from Alaska to Patagonia. Kosok himself has sighted roads similar to those of Nazca in the Zana and Lambayeque valleys of northern Peru. Miss Reiche discovered a few just ten miles outside of the Lima city limits. Others have been reported from northern Chile. Possibly the enormous 602-foot-high candelabra-like figure carved deep into a cliff above the Pacific near Pisco, not far from Nazca, and pointing exactly north to south like some of the Nazca effigies, has close affinities, as the related styles of the art of the Paracas-Pisco and Nazca regions suggest. Perhaps the Nazca picture book is, as Kosok proposed, a survival from a calendrical-religious ordering of farming societies that was once prevalent along all the coast of Peru, north and south. The greater advance of the north may then have wiped out most of the pictorial record, after astronomical predictions ceased to be tied to the priest's monopoly of power. There is still a good chance that aerial photographs and a thorough search through existent films may detect further fragments of gravel drawings from the hills above the northern valleys.

Both Kosok and Reiche were impressed by the close resemblance between the representations of demons, snakes, birds, and the like in southern Peru and the famous effigy mounds in the Midwest of the United States. What distinguishes the two groups is not so much their shape and imagery but their mode of construction, which may well be superficial and due rather to material and climatic conditions than the 'spirit' behind them.

However, if one is to stress material make-up and technique, then the Nazca drawings have amazingly close parallels in another section of the United States – California. Pictographs there have been produced by exactly the same process on sun-parched mesas above the lower Colorado River. Here, too, native Indians had cleared the surface of brown-black gravel (its iron-manganese is believed to have been oxidized through the catalytic action of lichens) to free lighter patches. Likewise, the contours were stressed by heaping the darker pebbles alongside. The odd silhouettes, carved by what has been called an 'intaglio' process, were also so over-dimensioned that they could not have been meant for human perception and had therefore frequently escaped detection, even though the region was by no means remote or unexplored; in fact it had frequently been crossed by aeroplanes before the figures were noticed.

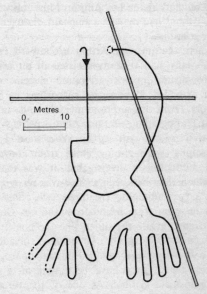

Figure 31. A Nazca ground figure near the Pan American Highway of a pair of hands, notable for its nine fingers. As elsewhere in the ancient world, the number nine seems to have had a sacred meaning in pre-Columbian Peru.

On a hot summer day in 1932, a local aviator, George Palmer, was flying from Las Vegas to Blythe in California. He was in no great hurry and freely cruised around, scanning the drab landscape and, as used to be the hobby of seasoned pilots, looking around for emergency landing fields.

Some eighteen miles from Blythe, flying at an altitude of five thousand feet, he suddenly saw a huge human figure lying spread-eagled on the desert flats as if basking in the sun. Palmer swung his plane over, took a closer look, and a four-legged creature beside the giant swam into his view. Both figures appeared to him about one hundred feet long. But he was not sure whether they were 'painted' on the desert or made from mounds of earth. Soon afterward he returned with his box camera and took a few snapshops. These photographs he presented to officials at the Los Angeles Museum, who realized at once that Palmer had made a significant discovery that warranted closer scrutiny.

The curator of the museum, Arthur Woodward, remembered that the US Army had recently assisted in an aerial survey of the not-too-distant ancient irrigation system in southern Arizona and managed to persuade authorities to render him similar support. From this airborne mission, undertaken by the Twenty-third Photographic Section, Air Corps, US Army, and the consecutive ground visit led by Woodward, Palmer's 'intaglio pictographs' were photographed from above, properly located, and meticulously investigated. It was then that the manner in which they had been shaped was recognized. Apart from Palmer's two adjoining creatures, two additional pictographic sites near by were found from the air. One of them was a single figure, while the other, like the one first seen by Palmer, was, in fact, a 'trinity'. It included, in addition to a human and a four-legged, long-tailed animal image, a smaller, coil-like figure, which may have been that of a snake, the ubiquitous prehistoric symbol. At one of the three sites the scraped human effigy was partly surrounded by a wide circle that evidently had been made by treading human feet. Quite possibly it was a dance ring, thus strengthening the belief that the desert drawings were somehow connected with Indian rituals.

Woodward was unable to give definite answers concerning the age, significance, and makers of the pictographs. He found no allusion to them in the legends of native Indians, the Mohave and Chemehuevi. However, search in the literature led him to a tentative clue at the same Gila Valley in Arizona which Judd had explored for its hydraulic works. There, on a Pima Indian reservation, an outline of another fearsome humanoid had been reported early in the century. Furthermore, that creature was definitely enshrined in Pima mythology and commemorated the slaying by an Indian Theseus of a cannibalistic female monster called Hâ-âk.

Sudden spectacular discoveries will often draw out little-known and half-forgotten and disconnected facts and bring them into a meaningful relationship. Another piece of information Woodward came by gave further proof that the scraped mesa figures near Blythe were by no means as unprecedented and isolated as they had first seemed. Beyond Blythe, some one hundred miles upstream on the Colorado, there had long ago been noted, as Woodward reports,

a mysterious rock 'maze', consisting of many acres of ground covered with a patchwork of parallel rows of small stones, scraped together in ridges, corresponding exactly in technique to the odd figures. This is termed the 'Mohave Maze', but the Mohave deny having built it, nor do they know the builder. At one time, as late as 1888–92, it was learned that there were two gigantic human figures incorporated with this maze. However railroad contractors, building a new line through the desert, found it necessary to lay out the right of way through a portion of this aboriginal creation, and the human figures were destroyed.

To us the most interesting passage of this quotation refers to the 'maze' of rows which, more than the human effigies, tantalizingly recalls the Nazca markings of Peru. Could they also have possessed an astronomical orientation?

However, it was the crudely drawn representations that were to claim all the attention.

A decade after Palmer's discovery, in 1943, General Henry H. Arnold, Commander of the US Army Air Force during the Second World War, was flying General George C. Marshall, the Chief of Staff of the US Army, on an inspection trip across the lower Colorado. Arnold asked his passenger whether he had ever seen the great effigies near Blythe? When Marshall answered in the negative and declared that, in fact, he had never even heard of them but would very much like to see them, Arnold changed course and headed for the bluffs near Blythe.

'Then we saw them,' wrote Marshall years later, 'gravel

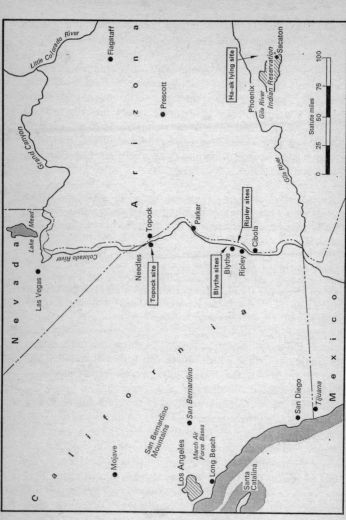

Figure 32. The principal effigy sites along and near the Colorado River in the south-western United States

sculptures such as few men had ever laid eyes on – simple in outline, childish in form, and yet so grandiose in scale as to take one's breath away.'

After the war, when General Marshall joined in a conference of the National Geographic Society as one of their trustees, he remembered the effigies and suggested that they deserved further study. He was perplexed by the same questions Woodward had raised: Who made them? What was their purpose? Were there more like them in the vicinity? The result was a 1951 National Geographic-Smithsonian Institution expedition into the lower Colorado River basin to attack anew the mystery of the desert figures. The leader was Frank M. Setzler, head curator of the Department of Anthropology of the US National Museum in Washington, who had made a special study of the Stone Age cultures of northern Australia. In due respect to the monstrous pictographs, the campaign was largely conducted by air. This time the US Air Force generously lent a whole air rescue team, including a helicopter which could be used as a flying platform. Main flights, however, were undertaken in a Catalina amphibian flying boat based at March Air Force Base outside Los Angeles.

The expedition, whose logistic planning and equipment in themselves spelled a novel phase in aerial archaeology, was a complete success, most notably perhaps for its first-rate colour pictures taken by a staff photographer of the National Geographic Society. As General Marshall had hoped, a number of new effigy sites were now added to the Blythe catalogue, among them a group fifteen miles south-east of Blythe near Ripley and another close to the town of Topock not far from the 'Mohave Maze' mentioned by Woodward.

Above all, it was Setzler's ambition to get to the 'when' and 'why' of the figures. One step forward, a hypothesis rather than established fact, was his tracing of the Gila River monster and the legend pertaining to it to Yuman-speaking people once living in the area, who may have passed the myth on to the Pima. Now Yumans were also living on the Colorado and had common roots with their kinsmen along the Gila. Hence the identity of Colorado and Gila figures. Setzler thus accepted Woodward's theory of the monsters as effigies of Hâ-âk, only he thought they were originated by the Yumans. He also argued for the relative lateness of the figures, mainly on account of the drawings of quadrupeds, apparently horses, which, as everybody knows, were introduced by the Spanish. (The native American horse had died out in the Pleistocene some ten thousand years before.) In sum, Setzler stated his belief that 'the giant effigies we found at Blythe and at Ripley were made by Yuman-speaking Indians; that they served in some fashion as shrines to the memory of Hâ-âk and her destroyer, Elder Brother; and that they were fashioned sometime between 1540 and the middle of the 19th century.'

At about the same time as Setzler's army-supported expedition to the gravel images of California, another major find was made in the United States that was quite certainly of far greater antiquity but had as much relevance to widely distributed pre-Columbian culture traits. It also touched on effigies. Though pertaining to a place in the deep South in the lower Mississippi flood plain – Poverty Point in north-eastern Louisiana – it hinted at close ties with ancient Indian earthworks of the upper Mississippi and Ohio valleys, a thousand miles away. John Bradford did not hesitate to call it 'the most remarkable instance of US air archaeology in recent years'.

Poverty Point, a mound of seventy feet high, situated in a rich farming area, had attracted archaeologists for many years and was first described in 1872. Time and again it had been combed for its profuse artefacts, from which several antiquarians assembled impressive collections. The great bulk of this refuse had come from the cultivated land between Poverty Point mound and a loop of the Bayou Maçon. James A. Ford, a curator of North American Archaeology at the Museum of Natural History in New York and, from 1963 until his death in 1968, a professor at the University of Florida, worked at the site in 1952 and 1953. Ford had participated in campaigns at the Virú Valley of northern Peru, where the value of aerial survey photographs was driven home to him, and in Alaska and Columbia. He was especially intrigued by the two strange mounds (Poverty Point and Motley) in the vicinity. These he established as being definitely man-made. Furthermore, they

were oriented north to south and east to west respectively and
appeared to display in their high platforms and side ridges the
shape of large birds with spreading wings.

While these important observations were made in the field,
Ford consulted the cartographic laboratory of the Mississippi
River Commission at Vicksburg, evidently in order to aid his
mapping chore. A perusal of the air photographs commissioned
by that agency led him to one unmistakably depicting the

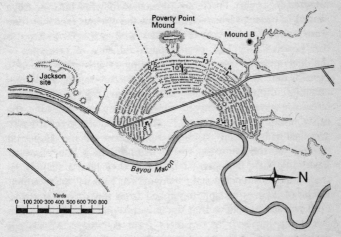

Figure 33. Sketch plan of Poverty Point site in Louisiana showing
remains of octagonally arranged parallel earth ridges first noted on
an air survey photograph of the Mississippi River Commission

Poverty Point area! In the fields where so many 'Poverty Point
objects' of flint had been gathered for decades, without anyone's noticing anything else unusual, he now saw a stunning,
perfectly arranged geometric pattern. It consisted of an earthwork of six concentric ridges, the better part of an octagon, of
which river erosion of the bordering bayou had carried roughly
one third away. Its diameter measured no less than three-
quarters of a mile, and the total length of the ridges amounted
to 11·2 miles. To the inevitable question of how such a feature
could have been missed by all the antiquarians and fieldhands
who had trodden and ploughed it, Ford was forced to the

chastening, but to us by now familiar, admission that for discovery on the ground it was simply 'on too large a scale'.

Of course, the over-dimensioned earthwork had been greatly reduced, and the aerial photograph brought it out through colour differentials in the cultivated fields, with the ridges appearing as light rows between the much darker swales. Nevertheless, further investigation found that the rounded elevations still rose from four to six feet. They were about one hundred feet apart. Ford sank three trial trenches into the ridge system in order to learn – aside from the obvious fact that they were artificial – whether they had served as dwelling sites. He was positive they had, even though evidence of postholes or building material was not forthcoming at this stage. He was certain that the whole complex had been raised by a pre-ceramic culture. A carbon-14 date obtained from a near-by related site gave a reading of approximately 400 B.C. Like the other prominent features of Poverty Point, the geometrically arranged ridges were strongly reminiscent of the Hopewell mounds of the Midwest, which belonged to a late phase of Eastern Archaic (800–600 B.C.). In fact they bore a striking resemblance to the octagonal earthworks at Newark, Ohio, which Dache M. Reeves had photographed from the air in the 1930s. Ford was led to believe that the Poverty Point earthworks were raised (or inspired) by invaders from the upper Mississippi drainage basin.

Poverty Point also immediately came to mind when a system of orderly arranged ridges, only on a much vaster scale, was reported in 1966 from far away in the South American country of Colombia. A professor of geography at Berkeley, James J. Parsons, had identified them in much the same manner as Ford: on routine aerial photographs that were taken without the slightest attention to actual or potential archaeological remains.

But the identification was not a pure accident. Parsons had been carrying out studies in Colombia for close to twenty years, travelling here and there. On his flights as passenger on commercial planes he had occasionally seen odd patterns in the extensive flood plains of the San Jorge and Cauca rivers, main tributaries of the Magdalena in the country's north-west. When he asked his Colombian friends about them, he was told that they were most likely caused by gold-dredging operations. That intelligence put his mind at rest; at least for a while. But one day a student at the University of California, William M. Denevan, brought Parsons a draft of his doctoral thesis dealing with pre-Spanish agriculture in the northern Bolivian lowlands, which described earth ridges looking precisely like the ones that had once aroused the professor's fancy in Colombia. Leafing through the dissertation, he all at once realized a possible connection between the Bolivian and Colombian earthworks, though they were two thousand miles apart. There was no holding him. He had to go back to Colombia.

So in the spring of 1963 he took his son along on a visit to rancher friends in the back country near the San Jorge River. What followed was the usual tale of frustrations. Father and son looked all over, rode on horseback days on end – and could not locate a single ridge. Discouraged, Parsons was about to depart from Bogotá, when it occurred to him to make one last attempt. He knew of a collection of aerial photographs at the headquarters of a geographical society, the Instituto Geográfico Agustín Codazzi, in the capital, and there he went. No sooner had he sorted out the photographs of the San Jorge area than he beheld all the ridged patterns he had pined for, even though the pictures had been taken (as recently as July 1954) from an altitude of forty thousand feet.

What Parsons saw was a veritable cyclopean enterprise of prehistoric engineering, lines on lines of parallel mounds placed at right angles to various river arms. With their intervening, apparently waterlogged furrows, some of the elevations looked for all the world like some immense corrugated washboards. Others were reminiscent of iron filings clinging to a magnet. Had he not just faced an abortive experience of his own when trying to find the ridges without aerial aid, Parsons would have wondered even more why none of the Conquistadores had bothered to notice them, while gorging themselves with looted gold from burial mounds in this very area. More surprising still, the regular air routes from Bogotá and the country's commercial metropolis, Medellín, to the coastal cities on the Caribbean flew right across the zone. Yet, except for his own hazy observations and the passing comments of a Colombian archaeologist of Austrian extraction, Gerardo Reichel-Dolmatoff, the mammoth earthworks had until now been totally ignored by both travellers and scholars.

Parsons's task had just begun. Now he had to explore the ridges more closely, plot them, and try to solve the archaeological problems they posed. Hence, in the summer of 1965 he set out once more for Colombia, this time accompanied by a graduate student of his department, William A. Bowen, who proved himself a first-rate photographer. Having now a far better knowledge of where to look, the two men negotiated the flooded water arms of the San Jorge basin in a dugout canoe. But once again all was in vain. Only after the renewed failure did they decide to continue their search in a flying boat, a De Havilland Beaver, and their luck changed at once. At last they had found precise locations and could proceed to them on land.

There were ridges everywhere. In their authoritative article in the *Geographical Review* of July 1966 announcing their discoveries, they wrote:

When the San Jorge old fields are partly inundated by floodwater, modest relief contrasts can be clearly distinguished, and our reconnaissance visit in mid-June, 1965, was especially well timed in this respect. At that time, in the first days of the rainy season, the humped backs of the ridges were still accentuated by parched grass, while the depressions between them, not yet inundated, remained green. From the ground, however, they are not always easy to detect and may sometimes be unrecognized by a person who is not familiar with them; from a dugout canoe, the commonest means of travel in the area, they are rarely visible. Moreover, these old fields (*lomillas*) are not always recognized by the local inhabitants as manmade. It has remained for air photography and low-level air reconnaissance to make known their extent and nature.

The main zone they perceived from the air was not far from where the San Jorge and Cauca joined the Magdalena, at about 150 miles from the coast. Its area of about one hundred and sixty thousand acres amounted to a length of roughly seventy miles and a width of twenty miles of the regularly flooded mesopotamian plain. However, they thought that the original extent must have been considerably larger. Additional traces, not evident on high-altitude verticals, could be discerned from a low-flying plane. Some of the typical ridges were no less than one mile long, with a relief of three to five feet and a width of four feet.

By and by they came to distinguish several arrangements of ridges. Apart from the parallel system first discovered on the Bogotá photographs, they found ridges in a chequerboard pattern, more or less at right angles to each other, which when flooded gave an appearance not unlike Far Eastern rice paddies. Large areas of slightly undulating parallels looked as if they had been 'swept by a giant comb', while other ridges were grouped in herringbone fashion, or in still more intricate patterns. On a good many ridges, better drained than the swales, grew trees resembling a neatly planted orchard. The explorers had evidence that much of the terrain was once overgrown by dense forests, which have been cleared since the nineteenth century. Only thus did the 'old fields' become once more exposed. Deforestation, by the way, has played a similar part for abandoned medieval fields and villages in England, which were eventually revealed by aerial archaeology. Quite likely, the Colombian aboriginal ridge systems were largely covered by forest when the first Spaniards arrived, which may help to account for their long-delayed discovery. By the same token one may assume that the San Jorge civilization of an unknown Indian people had disappeared from the scene before the Conquest.

Parsons and his associate were convinced that these stupendous earthworks had been laid out for agriculture, in all likelihood for the cultivation of yuca (the starchy staple of the Indians in the region, according to Spanish chroniclers) rather than maize. In a plain seasonally drowned under the water flow gushing down from the Andes, the ridges and troughs must have been built for drainage, rather than irrigation. Yet irrigation was an alternative or complementary possibility; the more so if one allows for the region having sunk in recent centuries, as Parsons persuasively argues. Besides, at one time, perhaps during the first millennium, the riverine basin of the Magdalena and its branches may have been much drier. However, at other humid periods, the swales could conceivably have been put to use for the growing of various swamp plants and even for fish drives.

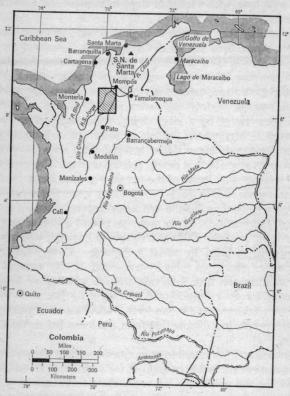

Figure 34. Outline map of Colombia. The main area of pre-Columbian ridged fields is centred in the shaded rectangle along the San Jorge and Cauca rivers of the country's north

Though granting all such beneficial functions, the two scholars rightly asked: Why such an extravagant effort? Were the practical advantages gained from constructing these immense earthworks without metal tools and beasts sufficient to justify the expenditure of human toil? Without offering a satisfactory answer, they allow that these aboriginal structures 'may have had some nonutilitarian purpose but there seems to be no systematic regularity or alignment to the earthworks of the sort that one would expect from a religiously motivated society'. Yet, whatever aboriginal Americans undertook, whether primarily utilitarian or not, was at the same time 'religiously motivated' and ran completely counter to the creed of cost accountants and efficiency experts. Also, when seized by building fever pre-Columbians, like the priest-rulers of the ancient Near East, were utterly disrespectful of the life and comfort of the common man.

The two California scholars estimated that the agricultural ridges in the San Jorge area could have fed some eight thousand people. This substantial figure illustrates the capacity of tropical lowlands in South America for supporting a much larger population than had hitherto been assumed for the pre-Spanish era. No doubt with modern technology it could be greatly exceeded, and the labour needed today for controlling the waterways, freeing the land of malaria, and reclaiming it for rice culture and animal husbandry would be infinitely less than that extracted centuries ago from aboriginals to shape the endless ridges and swales with little but their bare hands.

Raised fields quite similar to the ones in Colombia have been found, outside Bolivia, in other far-flung places of South America, especially the llanos along the Orinoco in Venezuela's interior, and the coast of Surinam on the Atlantic. 'Such a remarkably disjunct distribution', Parsons and Bowen commented, 'of what would appear to be a rather sophisticated way of utilizing an environment subject to high flood risk, and certainly one requiring a high degree of social organization and work-force co-ordination, opens a Pandora's box of questions relating to cultural origins and the process of dispersal.'

As we have seen in previous glimpses of discoveries throughout the Americas, aerial archaeology has played a prominent part in opening the Pandora's box, which is, after all, an eminently scientific and creative role. Yet thanks to its panoramic view from on high, while releasing new mysteries and new problems, it has spread glimmers of light that shine over the two continents and their lost yesterdays.

12. Between Past and Future

Startled as airborne archaeologists often were by the novelty of their own discoveries, they were no less surprised to find that, at ground level, the clear and distinct outlines of ancient foundations were likely to melt away to nothing. A good many conclusions can be drawn from these experiences, all pointing up the vital role aerial archaeology and photography have yet to play in the exploration of the human past. They demonstrate graphically that exploration from above has opened up possibilities of expanding the horizon beyond the most sanguine expectations of 'dirt' archaeologists. Not even the men who had longed for an aerial view dreamt of its almost magic properties. As it happened, investigators met with some of the most astonishing windfalls in terrains long turned over by the spade; and, as Dr St Joseph once observed, more often than not they hit upon the least known aspects of prehistory.

Moreover, thanks to their unique perspective, observers and cameras in flight not only depicted a great many sites of which they had not had the slightest hint, but registered familiar as well as lost remains in an entirely new light. Suddenly they beheld a Mediterranean scene they never knew, an England they had not imagined. Ancient American farming societies lost to history were seen in their stupendous effort to subdue a hostile environment. Under the millennial shroud of desert sand and northern bogs emerged the once throbbing provincial frontiers of the Roman Empire, paradigms of the engineering skill and military drive of their departed masters. Sprawling cities dwarfing all the ancient centres of Europe, as quickly erected as abandoned by the naked will and whim of Asiatic potentates, filed before the aerial viewer in neat battalions of endless walls, broad avenues, temples, palaces, and blocks of houses.

Quite often the airborne observer was likely to record not just one phase in history or prehistory, but a whole chain of transformations wrought by man upon a physical environment Photographs would thus mirror human efforts from a remote dawn to the present in a succession that differed from the static exhumations of conventional archaeology. And into this dynamic study all epochs could be drawn. Even the Old Stone Age, when man's mastery over nature was almost nil and left no material evidence of any building activity, has yielded information. A careful reading of geographical and geological conditions displayed in air photographs enabled French scholars to locate natural shelters and camping grounds visited by early man in Indo-China and Provence. Old shorelines of rivers, lakes, and oceans, determined from above, proved particularly bountiful in deposits of Palaeolithic and Neolithic industries, some of them piled in shell middens. The French archaeologist Roger Agache, adept in analysing air photographs for geomorphic changes, thus discovered Stone Age flints on beaches and low terraces in north-western France. At Abbeville, where some of the revolutionary discoveries of the last century were made about Palaeolithic man, air photographs helped Agache to select pieces of land which had not yet been excavated or built on, and which warranted further ground investigation. Likewise, a South African scientist, Clarence van Riet Lowe, flying over the northern Transvaal in 1937, noticed 'a dirty creamy coloured area undergoing surface erosion', which he knew was characteristic for African sites where Mesolithic implements occurred. He made a sketch, and, on reaching the locality on foot a few months later, could report that he 'reaped a rich reward'.

No doubt, past accomplishments are only a prologue. In time to come the technique of aerial surveying and photography, if properly applied and provided that it avails itself of the various new aids at its command, will continue to immensely increase the range of archaeology. And staggering as their numbers may be, those additions will not run to a matter of sheer quantity – miles on miles of abandoned canals, hundreds of levelled mounds, dozens of Roman frontier camps – they will turn out to disclose facets of the past in overall patterns, distributions, and cultural and topographical relationships rarely, if ever, evident to the field worker glued to the ground. In sum, as an instrument of locating and plotting buried features aerial archaeology will probably remain without peer.

There is, of course, the danger of unintentionally exaggerating the importance of a subject in a volume devoted solely to it; but this book never claims that aerial archaeology is the one and only royal road to the fallen mansions of antiquity, nor that it is without limitations.

For example, in the absence of prominent landmarks one faces the excruciating, and often insoluble, dilemma of establishing correspondence between an air photograph and the actual site. A ruin whose location has not been fixed and verified literally remains a castle in the air. Also, air photography will prove to be far more effective in tracing disturbances in the soil caused by major geometric or linear structures than in showing up scattered postholes, pits, kilns, and so on. At a certain depth below the surface, underground features will fall outside its margin of sensitivity. Cities buried deep under layers of windswept soil or alluvial silt leave no surface traces that can readily be picked up from above. In agricultural areas which have been divided for centuries into thin strips, as in much of Central Europe, subterranean walls and ditches are not likely to produce coherent marks. Success or failure hinges invariably on climate, season, time of day, intensity and direction of light, composition of soil, nature of plant growth, the plane's altitude and camera angle for obliques, not to speak of optic equipment and the photographer's dexterity. Every so often it is an accidental and unpredictable combination of these factors that, for a brief period, conjures up the ghostlike imprints of prehistory.

At times, other methods may be in order. Based on the knowledge that prolonged human occupation will change the chemistry of the ground (particularly by adding phosphates), soil analysis, as first applied by the Swedish scientist Arrhenius, has become a valuable aid in unmasking former settlements. At a threshold where air photographs ceased to give sufficient precision, Lerici and his co-workers in the Etruscan cemeteries resorted to electronic apparatus (e.g. proton-magnetometer, resistivity probes) to gauge the exact placement, shape, and dimensions of burial chambers. In their persistent search for famed Sybaris, the pleasure-loving Greek colony in Calabria near Italy's instep, all aerial search over the approximate area had to be abandoned by the joint Italo-American team in favour of geophysical methods, which at last announced in the early 1960s the presence of walls and buildings at a considerable depth probably belonging to the lost city's port. Then, in the autumn of 1968, the city itself was located by a caesium-magnetometer within an area of roughly six miles in circumference and buried underneath some twenty feet of water-logged alluvial silt. Postholes, by the way, which seldom appear on air photographs if less than two or three feet in diameter, can be registered fairly easily by a magnetic device.

In our age of atomic and space science the archaeologist has an ever-growing arsenal of instruments at his disposal, from the by-products of nuclear physics to the high-speed drill designed for exploration on the moon. The bearded nineteenth-century romantic, digging for the gold of Troy or braving the hazards of the Near East to turn the soil for Biblical truths, has become as outdated as his objectives. Progress in unveiling the past depends more and more on an application of methods and processes developed by engineers, physicists, geologists, botanists, and other scientists. Aerial archaeology is itself the product of the technological reorientation of all branches of antiquarian research. By applying the scientific advances of the age it ensures its vitality and growth. At its own peril will it slight methods that complement it or that are, on occasion, more effective.

Aerial photography is then, needless to say, one technique of many. (But it is also much more.) It does not claim to render others obsolete or to go it alone. Crawford never tired of insisting that it should not be looked upon as 'a substitute of excavation, but a valuable preliminary'. Most workers who followed in his footsteps have re-echoed his sentiment. This, however, may be overstating the case. After all, to some features spotted from the air, such as road sections or canals, excavation will add little, particularly if their standard mode of construction is already known. When it comes to establishing the plan of a ruin, one picture may be far more satisfactory than laboriously honeycombing the ground with ditches to trace all its walls. If the goal is to record the frequency of a prehistoric 'type' structure in a certain region, the aerial survey may gather all the information that is needed.

In reviewing Bradford's exploration of Neolithic Apulia, the American classical archaeologist Rhys Carpenter has admirably summarized the importance of this avenue of research, which

lies in its transcendence of traditional spade-and-shovel work by substituting for laborious and time-consuming piecemeal excavation of restricted extent a comprehensive countrywide survey. Such a survey, by establishing the distribution, size, and formal type of hundreds of contiguous settlements, would permit an analysis of the ecological adaptation to physical environment of an entire cultural area during periods on which written history is silent. Success in such an undertaking would raise the status of archaeological study as a branch of reconstructive cultural history.

A better case is made by the majority of authorities when they affirm that any extensive dig of the least scientific pretension should not get under way before securing air coverage. Indeed, this has become increasingly the practice and should be even more so in the future. In the ambitious onslaught on the Judaean mountain fortress of Masada, air photographs were put to good use prior to launching actual operations. (More were taken throughout the eleven-month campaign.) These photographs, though their main purpose was to furnish excavators with reliable maps of the sites to be uncovered – often already betraying their material make-up, age, purpose, and history – also helped the leader, who incidentally was a military man, to plan his campaign. When the expedition was cut off from the outside world by floods, supplies were flown in by helicopter. Even if the latter, quite valuable application to archaeology of 'air power' is beyond the scope of this book, it may be worth while to recall that Lindbergh, too, was greatly concerned with the auxiliary function of air transport in carrying out research in more or less remote areas. His then novel ideas have by now become almost commonplace. Thus, Matthew Stirling, the excavator of the great 'Olmec' centres in

Southern Mexico, hopped around by helicopter in order to investigate antiquities in the Panamanian lowlands in the late 1940s. Helicopters now convey bulky artefacts from their locale for shipment to far-away learned institutions where they can be restored, displayed, and studied. A recent (1968–9) exhibit of Maya art at New York's Metropolitan Museum had as its prize piece an inscribed seven-foot stela air-lifted bodily from a ruined site (Machaquila) in the Petén jungle of Guatemala.

Over areas of rough or relatively inaccessible terrain, aerial reconnaissance recommends itself because of its simplicity rather than by virtue of being the only or best method of sighting remains. This was perhaps the case with some of the semi-desert searched by Poidebard in Syria, where ground exploration, provided that funds, loss of time, and physical hardship were of no account, could have been just as productive. Today, airplanes guard the supply lines of expeditions to far-away ruins. They, and other modern conveyances, have largely replaced the inevitable mule trains known to readers of the colourful nineteenth-century accounts.

All the major achievements of aerial archaeology since the First World War have been linked with airplanes. The alliance has been so close that one is tempted to take it for granted. But this is to forget that photographs were taken from above long before the airplane was ever invented. Nadar over Paris in 1858, S. A. King and J. W. Black over Boston in 1860–61, a Union Army balloon-borne photographer hoisted above the Confederate line near Arlington, Virginia – all produced pictures that displayed the characteristic bird's-eye view that is the very essence of air photography. When Wilbur Wright, on a flight in Italy in 1909, came up with some of the first pictures from a heavier-than-air flying machine he did not really add anything new to the image obtained. Subsequently, however, military missions in wartime were to prove the superiority of aeroplanes for reconnaissance. Planes, thanks to their manoeuvrability and speed, could search out their targets and cover considerable ground. They could experiment with light angles, and change altitude at will in order to get the most dramatic or revealing shot. At length, airmen were able to produce pictures that plotted a whole area in successive striplike photographs thereby making stereoscopic viewing possible, which greatly enhances perception in depth. Such advantages could hardly be claimed for balloons, whether captive or free, manned or passengerless.

But balloons also have their advantages. They are quite cheap and can be kept in a more or less steady position over a specific location. While they will probably never do for screening a large territory, they have their uses for taking a pictorial inventory of a dig and its strata. Now and then balloons have been called back to duty as, for example, in the early 1930s during the Megiddo (Palestine) expedition of the Oriental Institute of the University of Chicago or to obtain a vertical imprint of the pre-Second World War excavations at Biskupin, a large prehistoric wood-constructed settlement in Poland. (The Poles, by the way, also adopted the helicopter which, just because of its ability to slow down and remain almost motionless above the target, is becoming more and more a favourite of air surveyors.)

Even box kites, equipped with ground-controlled cameras, like those so ingeniously operated by Sir Henry Wellcome in the Sudan, came into their own again. A Belgian used them from 1932 on over the region of Tournai, as did another project under the aegis of the Oriental Institute of the University of Chicago set up in the 1950s in the Near East to determine the ancient irrigation system of southern Mesopotamia and the part it may have played there throughout 7,000 years of human history. In rare instances, dirigibles were also sent on photographic missions. The Italian archaeologist Guido Calza inspected his own excavation of Ostia from a height of one thousand feet in an Italian military airship shortly after the First World War and thence used the photographs for reconstructing the ancient port city as a whole.

Certainly, none of these undertakings actually challenged the airplane; they simply made it clear that aerial photography and archaeology did not depend exclusively on it. What mattered was the lofty perspective rather than the type of carrier. A cartoon on display in the Copenhagen National Museum illustrates the point with a humorous drawing of a giraffe which straddles an excavation site with a camera suspended from its ears. 'Aerial' observation or photography without airborne agents has been successfully practised from natural elevations or from extensible ladders. Agache, on occasion, operated from a step ladder on a moving motor car, and Poidebard, choosing a more traditional means of transportation on his field trips, remarked that vision notably improved on camel-back.

Whether the future of the science will be as closely wedded to the airplane as it has been during the past few decades is difficult to predict. Non-archaeological aerial photography has already stepped out into space. Pictures from man-made satellites depicting entire continents have become a common feature of our daily papers. Meanwhile space crafts have been charged with detecting mineral and oil deposits, finding fishing grounds, or investigating plant disease. Perhaps it is only a question of time till artificial stars will be made to screen the past and relay to us from far away its long-muted messages.

Among the many blessings bestowed by the air age, archaeologists can count the photographic surveys that have been executed over vast areas of the globe. Dr Glyn Daniel has made the valid point that the Second World War not only widened the range of air photography by its global scale but changed the stress from oblique and vertical shots of selected sites to a photography of 'total vertical cover of extremely large areas' for which stereoscopic examination has become common practice. This development Daniel considers a new phase in archaeological air photography.

According to a 1950s estimate more than one half of the land surface has been photographed at least once. Today there are probably few territories left that have not been recorded. In these undertakings, military establishments, administrative authorities, mining, commercial, or industrial interests, and a host of other various agencies, have taken the initiative. The implications to archaeology are manifold.

First, these enterprises, thanks to their well-endowed sponsorship and expertise, pioneered advanced photographic methods well ahead of any archaeologists and archaeologically minded airmen, hence aerial archaeology is of military paternity, with Mars as godfather. To date, air photography teams have engaged in such varied schemes as pinpointing one of the world's largest iron deposits in Venezuela; computing the annual crop of grapes in California; finding suitable locations for airports and new cities (e.g. the new capital of Brazil at Brasília); or divining fresh water and oil resources under the ground or at the bottom of the sea. Missions of this kind have brought the art to a technical perfection from which archaeologists have much to learn and with which they have not yet completely caught up.

All these military, scientific, and commercial programmes in the air are backed by extensive research. *Barron's*, the American business weekly, carried a special article in its 23 October 1967 issue which reviewed, for the benefit of eager investors, aerial photography as one of the nation's zooming growth industries. The article, appropriately titled 'Eagle in the Sky', goes a long way to explain how aerial photography is being revolutionized. It estimates that the US Defense Department alone has been spending 'upwards of $1 billion a year' to get the best equipment. Little need be said of the stake military establishments have in this field. It is common knowledge that aerial reconnaissance has become a chief source of intelligence. In fact, two major international crises in recent years can be directly attributed to its 'nosiness': the U-2 incident over Russia and the Cuban missile showdown.

While the military provided the main stimulus, the innovations were bound to alert other groups, who in turn contributed to further growth. The result is an explosion in knowledge and technology. To quote *Barron's*:

Today's films are three to four times faster than twenty years ago. High-speed computers, moreover, enable optical designers to bring lenses up to the capability offered by faster materials. All told, aerial photographic equipment today is said to provide anywhere from four to 15 times greater capacity than the best available devices of World War II. Yet the military is demanding (and civilians would like) even more; in consequence, the state of the art has been developing at a faster clip than ever.

Now, these developments do not apply just to traditional photography, but concern a battery of other means of airborne detection apart from material sensitive to ultra-violet and infra-red rays: sonar beams, magnetic waves, radars and lasers, all of which can be employed to produce some forms of images, and all of which expand 'vision' into realms which the human eye by itself could never hope to penetrate.

So far, little of the new optic technology has been employed for strictly archaeological purposes, though measured by some of its successes in other fields its benefits to the search for the buried yesterdays might well be fantastic. By freeing the airborne observer from the bondage of sunlight alone, it may one day render the principles and practices evolved by Crawford and his successors obsolete. Entirely new perspectives open for the scouting of shorelines and water bodies.

No one can begin to count the body of photographs produced throughout the world in the last thirty or forty years, by both the newer and the more conventional processes. Any attempt to catalogue these pictorial resources even within one nation has been doomed to failure. A large part of the collections, of course, is 'classified' and safely kept away from taxpaying citizens and alien curiosity seekers. To students of antiquity enamoured of the sky view this is a great pity indeed. There is no way of telling how many vistas of unknown sites are frustratingly locked away to be eventually lost. Yet, discounting all the secret governmental or industrial files, there remains more than enough, the great majority no doubt never examined for possible archaeological data. Here, as so often at the crossroads of science, progress is handicapped not so much by the lack of evidence, but by the failure to take notice of it and assimilate it to the existent body of knowledge. The call may well be not so much for new experiments, but for co-ordination of available facts. Hence, aerial archaeology in the future will have to meet one of its challenges in the systematic study of untapped photographic archives.

What aerial photographs taken for non-archaeological purposes can be made to yield in terms of antiquities we have seen in several notable instances: in Etruscan Italy, Indian Louisiana, or pre-Columbian Colombia. It is easy to underrate these resources and stress their inadequacies. Yet to overlook such 'ready-mades' would be folly, particularly while means and skills are lacking to undertake strictly archaeological projects of comparable magnitude.

Naturally, routine air photographs should not be accepted as the last word (or rather, picture) of any ancient landscape. This was the opinion of Kenneth Steer of the Scottish Ancient Monuments Commission who, nevertheless, did not hesitate to examine photographs of the National Air Survey of the British Isles initiated by the Royal Air Force in post-war 1945. He was well aware of the small scale (1/10,000 or about six inches to the mile), which was not likely to register a plethora of smaller monuments. Because no attention had been paid to season, Steer did not expect many crop-marks to appear either. However, as he soberly stated: 'If it did nothing more, it seemed possible that the Survey would at lest mend the more obvious holes in our field-work.' In 1950, he and his colleagues, though quite aware that the Scottish Lowlands south of the Clyde and Tay had been thoroughly combed, decided to crosscheck known remains against the survey photographs, which, by the way, could be stereoscopically examined in pairs. In a short time they came up with no fewer than four hundred newly dis- covered sites, including native hill forts, henges, and medieval moated homesteads. Two of the native forts turned out to be the largest of their respective counties. More surprising, the one of the two in Dumbartonshire – totally unnoticed till then – was positioned above a teeming valley. It extended for no less than six acres and had massive walls still standing! Another completely levelled Roman fort near Glasgow by a happy acci- dent betrayed its ditches by crop-marks.

Faced with the formidable techniques and complex, expen- sive apparatus applied more and more in aerial surveys, one may expect air photography to become restricted to specially trained experts in the employ of affluent agencies. But just as there is always room in the modern natural sciences and engineering for the resourceful loner and improviser who, tinkering in his garage with penny equipment, will produce epochal inventions, so aerial archaeology is likely to be tied for a long time to come to the inspired researcher in his shaky monoplane rather than exclusively to robot technicians and their sophisticated gadgetry. As we have seen, high-altitude vertical photographs, ideal as they are for mapping and general surveying, cannot offer all the answers, even if examined stereoscopically. A great number of potential sites will remain invisible. Air pictures taken from an oblique angle and at relatively low heights will still be needed in intensive investigation of the surface. They will require ingenuity and patience, a feeling for the terrain, and a sensitive understanding of light and shadows during the course of day and seasons. Only then can one hope to bring out most of the inconspicuous relief of low earthworks and the colour differentials associated with fleeting vegetation-marks. It is safe to predict that in this pursuit individual initiative and ability will, at least in the foreseeable future, remain prime prerequisites. In the words of one of the most prominent and scientific-minded aerial archaeologists of recent years, Dr Irwin Scollar of Bonn, 'Even the most thorough examination of available air photographs will fail to produce the same results as taking one's own pictures on one's own flights'.

Aerial archaeology – we need hardly dwell upon this point – owes some of its finest accomplishments to outsiders or amateurs, men who were driven by enthusiasm instead of professional or academic pressures. Their competence in archaeology was self-acquired rather than university-fed. Since aerial archaeology demands a smattering in several disciplines, it is attractive to men of many talents and interests, who are not committed to a narrow specialty. Of course, much of archaeology itself has long been the precinct of so-called amateurs, and this tradition has been passed on to its offshoots. Sportsman pilots like Major Allen and air force officers like Wing-Commander Insall and Colonel Baradez have made outstanding discoveries. Both Crawford and Bradford, who were trained to archaeology – though not strictly to aerial archaeology – have repeatedly paid tribute to such men and invited their cooperation. 'The amateur', wrote Crawford in an *Antiquity* editorial discussing aerial archaeologists, 'can always somehow familiarize himself with the facts of archaeology, or history, or geology, or whatever subject it is that interests him.' Bradford, even more emphatically, asserted that

on occasion, the skilled amateur can be unsurpassed in this field ... There is a wide range of objectives within the scope of individual enterprise which could make contributions of real weight – as, e.g., to piece together the field system that surrounded a Romano-British farm, ... or, to look abroad, the discovery of an Iron Age farmstead in north-western France that could advance the study of the period as much as that at Little Woodbury has done in England.

Here is indeed a scientific frontier that is wide open. In circumscribed terrains, where a maximum of significant detail can be elicited by repeated flights under changing conditions, the indefatigable, experiment-minded 'amateur' may well reign supreme, particularly if he takes pains to become fully conversant with the methods of taking aerial pictures and interpreting them. What challenges await adventurous fliers and photography buffs who want to prove their mettle by hunting down vanished cultures. In North America alone they might conceivably find long-lost English colonies wiped out by Indian raids, Viking settlements on the Canadian and New England coast, the small fort Sir Francis Drake presumably built near his landing place in Northern California, and thousands upon thousands of effaced Indian sites across the continent.

There is no reason aerial archaeology should not be as ardently embraced by amateur fliers as underwater archaeology has already been by amateur divers. The rewards are bound to be at least as exciting. In England the opportunities facing all kinds of airmen have long been recognized. Undeterred by the official vertical survey and the multiple efforts made by 'professionals' or 'amateurs' in former years, private pilots and, on occasion, members of flying clubs have joined in the chase. Such fliers as K. Jopp and W. A. Baker, in their planes, have added valuable material on the Thames Valley, even in terrain that had been thoroughly combed by Major Allen. Baker, who wrote knowledgeably on his hobby, was gratified to find that his activities were appreciated by archaeological societies. To fellow airmen he recommended archaeological pursuits also as 'good exercise in pilot navigation, map-reading and recording observations accurately'. In the hope of recruiting others he stated his conviction that 'although this country has been well photographed there is still much work to be done, and flying clubs can make interesting discoveries in their own areas, and provide valuable assistance in solving specific problems'.

If discoveries remain to be made in England, where aerial archaeology has been practised for nearly half a century, the potential in other countries is much greater. Bradford purposely alluded to France in the above-quoted passage. And before him Crawford never tired of arousing – indeed, needling – French colleagues. It was a source of constant bewilderment to him that the methods so successfully pioneered by Frenchmen in Syria, North Africa, and Indo-China were almost completely ignored in metropolitan France. In one of his cantankerous editorials he castigated the backwardness of French archaeology and admonished it that 'the days of "cheremaîtrism" are past, and a fresh approach is needed'. When the awakening came at last, it came with a vengeance.

Active participants in the conquest of the French prehistory written large across the land were air-minded amateurs and local archaeologists now progressing at an impressive pace. Flying clubs played a significant part in supporting their work. However, within barely a decade aerial archaeology has become a full-fledged discipline in France. Creditable research is done in all parts of the country. Schemes are backed by the Institut Géographique National (IGN), the Institut Français de Pétrol (IFP), and a number of other organizations. Colloquiums and exhibitions are frequently held. Publications are proliferating. In advance even of England, energies are being pooled, and work in progress is co-ordinated on a national and international basis. Because of French awareness of the necessity to train specialists, the subject has been taught since 1961 at the École Pratique des Hautes Études of the Sorbonne by Raymond Chevallier, a former member of the French School in Rome who had been associated with Italian aerial enterprises before becoming the leading spokesman, bibliographer, and theoretician in France. The true awakening of the French to the possibilities of aerial archaeology can probably be dated from 1953, when the Institut Géographique National published an entire atlas of the Roman centuriation systems in Tunisia (Chevallier signed as one of the editors), based on some fifteen thousand aerial photographs. This magnificent work showed the incomparable way in which air photography could be made to illuminate historical geography, and thus turned attention to similar remains engraved in the soil of the French mother country, which cried for airborne reconnaissance. Chevallier, by the way, owes his first interest in air photography to his student days, when his teacher, the Etruscologist R. Bloch, mentioned the technique in one of his lectures.

So far, most of the important research in France has been carried out on a local or regional basis by renowed antiquarians intimately steeped in the past of their respective regions. Among them we may name Daniel Jalmain in the Paris area and farther along the Seine, Robert Ertlé in the Ardennes, Roger Chevallier in the Aisne Valley, Pierre Parruzot and Roger Kapps in central France, Joël Le Gall in the Bourgogne, Bernard Edeine in Normandy, and, above all, Roger Agache in his native Picardy. All these men, starting out in the mid-1950s or later, have been operating on a shoestring, with hand-held cameras, and from diminutive sports planes put at their disposal by local *aéro-clubs*. Their concentration on relatively small territories, coupled with a determination to bring back oblique pictures (in black and white as well as in colour) of high quality and repeat shots if need be, has met with striking success. A wealth of buried features from the Palaeolithic to the Middle Ages are being added to the archaeological map of the country. These discoveries have also aroused passionate interest among laymen. Members of the French Touring Club in particular have helped to follow up observations made from above. Meanwhile, ambitious projects, guided by the Service de la Documentation Technique of the IGN, are under way to synthesize the isolated data gathered and to produce comprehensive archaeological maps of all of France. Quite sensibly the recovery of ancient roadnets has been conceived as fundamental to the reconstruction of ancient landscapes in their multi-faceted details and territorial continuity and contiguity. Thanks in the main to aerial surveying, to give just one instance, the pre-Roman history of the Rhône Valley has now become an open book. There have also been rumours of finding new princely tombs comparable to the fabulous levelled tumulus at Vix, which yielded one of France's greatest archaeological bonanzas.

Northern France probably leads the country in the number and variety of buried remains sighted. Though it had been surveyed from the air for military ends as early as 1938 and 1939, no one bothered to examine the small-scale but excellent vertical photographs for archaeological vestiges. The first person to identify crop-marks was John Bradford, who can also claim priority in reporting signs of Roman centuriation in southern France. He made a special study of the Second World War photographs of the Somme Valley, where he thought that the chalk and gravel subsoil would be conducive to results closely resembling those obtained in the upper Thames basin. His expectations – which had, by the way, been shared by Crawford – were fully borne out. He spotted evidence of several razed mounds and felt justified in proclaiming that 'north west France is full of crop-sites'.

In the few years that Roger Agache, a prehistorian of Picardy, now antiquities director of five northern departments, has been scanning the region from planes based at the *aéro-club* of Abbeville, more than one thousand lost structures have been spotted in the Department of the Somme alone. They include funerary barrows and ritual circles from the Neolithic and Bronze Age, Iron Age enclosures, Gallo-Roman settlements, extensive Roman villae (some more than four hundred yards long), Celtic temples, and a variety of medieval structures, as well as the siegeworks raised by Henri IV around Amiens in 1598, of which no one had had an inkling. In a brief nine-day reconnaissance in the summer of 1961, Dr J. K. S. St Joseph also noted in northern France some one hundred ploughed-out barrows, besides Roman roads, great hill forts, tribal *oppida*, Roman camps and villae, well-preserved lynchets, and castle mottes of the early Middle Ages.

Aerial archaeology, which Bradford on one occasion called, perhaps whimsically, 'an almost veteran aspect of archaeological method', is certainly anything but ancient in France, even though some Frenchmen, presumably on account of Léon Rey and Père Poidebard, will label it a French invention. It is difficult to realize that Agache, the most productive worker in the field and already a peer of Allen and St Joseph, has only been active since 1960. And the returns from other parts of France, though as recent, are almost as abundant. At last, by giving the beautiful French countryside a new depth in time and making its soil speak with the tongues of many ages, French archaeology, which had been lagging behind the scientific methods of the Germans and British, has been propelled into the twentieth century. Considering the splendid support aerial research is now receiving, there is little doubt that our discipline has barely passed its threshold in France.

This observation holds *mutatis mutandis* for a number of nations whose adoption of sophisticated archaeological techniques cannot be detailed within the modest compass of our story. At the International Colloquium on Aerial Archaeology in Paris in 1963, an exhibition was assembled in which Germany, Belgium, Italy, Poland, the Netherlands, and Switzerland participated. At least occasional use of the aerial approach has been made in many more countries. Thus, for example, the Soviet Russian scientists Tolstoff and Orloff studied from the air a civilization in the Khorezm, in the steppes south-east of the Aral Sea, which was destroyed by Genghis Khan in the thirteenth century. From Palestine (now Israel) we have photographs illustrating the remarkable irrigation works of early farmers in the Negev desert, published by Nelson Glueck. Utilizing photographs taken by the RAF in 1924 and 1928, the British archaeologist Christopher Hawkes published in 1929 an article in *Antiquity* on the various Roman camps and siegeworks around Masada. (Fairly detailed plans of that cliff-fortress, based in the main on air photographs were already available before Yigael Yadin launched his expedition in 1963.) And a soil scientist from Hebrew University of Jerusalem, the late A. Reifenberg, who in the Second World War served with the British Army as an interpreter of aerial photographs, has announced interesting results from his study of Royal Air Force and Israel Air Force photographs of such Biblical and

Hellenistic-Roman-Byzantine places as Tell Dothan, Kurrub, dune-encroached Caesarea with its harbour and ancient theatres and hippodrome, the Samaritan sanctuary on Mount Garizim, the Jewish stronghold against the Romans at Beth-Ter near Jerusalem, where two Roman camps were detected, and the hitherto unknown Philistine harbour of Ashdod.

Switzerland cannot be said to offer specially favoured ground for aerial investigation, but it has produced a few photographic observations of merit, notably by the prehistorian Hans-Georg Bandi. Jean-Jacques Pittard of the University of Geneva has gathered highly original aerial documents from his study of pile-dwellers in Lake Geneva. Before taking to the air he marked the tip of each water-logged post. On the air photograph the whole complex then stood out in a pattern of dots that gave him a precise chart.

To round off this brief and random catalogue, we may mention one of the most unlikely places, New Zealand. There an English doctor, G. Blake Palmer, discovered several striking prehistoric Maori earthworks. One strange feature of a coastal lagoon Dr Palmer could identify as a canal constructed by the natives 'to facilitate the fixing of eel weirs and the driving of moulting wild-duck'.

Germany, though it helped to found aerial archaeology, had for years lagged far behind the British. It had, nevertheless, made occasional efforts in the inter-war years, as for instance in the tidewater area (*Wattenmeer*) off the Holstein North Sea coast, where receding floods would bring out in remarkable relief drowned villages with their drainage canals, piers, building fundaments, and farmlands. Some of these, stirring up memories of the famed city of Rungholt, had been swallowed by the sea in the fourteenth century.

Crawford was invited to Berlin in March 1938 to a special session of the Lilienthal Society devoted to the use of air photographs in the study of prehistory. His lecture, published in the same year with illustrative material by Hansa-Luftbild, gave the first theoretical exposition of the new technique available in German. Under its impact German workers were now quite eager to follow up Crawford's suggestions. However, the approaching war cut their plans short.

During the Second World War German military fliers reportedly photographed the major Roman road from Boulogne to Cologne in the west, as well as Gaulish *oppida*, but the negatives appear to have been lost in the chaotic aftermath. Extensive use of airborne research, however, began with the appearance on the scene of an unusual American, Dr Irwin Scollar, who had started his professional career in 1948 as a sound technician for NBC television in New York. Taking up archaeology first as a hobby, he went to Europe in 1953 on a scholarship and enrolled at Edinburgh University. It was then that he met English pioneers of aerial archaeology, including Dr St Joseph, and made up his mind to specialize in that subject. Thereafter he worked in Belgium and Denmark, and in 1959, at an archaeological congress, he made the acquaintance of a German museum director to whom he expounded the possibilities of air photography in archaeological research. The director was so intrigued that he recruited Scollar for his museum at Bonn. The rest is archaeological history in the making. In the beginning Scollar had to brave the customary continental bureaucratic and military obstacles to the execution of air observations. He learned to subscribe to the rule of thumb of German pilots that the amount of paper needed to secure a flight permit equals approximately the weight of the fuel consumed on that mission. Once he overcame the red-tape barrier Scollar almost committed suicide by flying right into the hidden precincts of an American rocket station. Since then he has literally populated the Rhineland with newly discovered sites. During his first hour of flight he found no fewer than four Roman villae. To this were soon added Roman roads, prehistoric mounds, and a number of Roman marching camps. Some of the earthworks he found resemble the cursuses of Bronze Age England.

Flying at quite low altitudes, usually no more than three hundred to nine hundred feet, Scollar has mastered the technique of taking oblique photographs – preferably in colour – with a simple hand-held Fairchild camera. Practically all his finds are crop-marks, which as a rule appear in the fields of West Germany for barely two weeks of the year. Engineer-archaeologist Scollar is, by the way, also an ardent experimenter with geophysical methods and has devised complicated machinery of his own.

French aerial archaeologists are inclined to look for inspiration to Italy rather than perfidious Albion, yet significant developments in the Latin sister state date only a few years further back than France's own and were, as we have noted, largely initiated by British experts during and after the Second World War. True, several of the first balloon pictures of archaeological features were taken in Italy almost as early as those of Stonehenge. A resolute attempt to launch airborne reconnaissance was made in 1938 by Professor Giuseppe Lugli of the Istituto di Studi Romani in Rome, but the outbreak of the war made it impossible to implement the ambitious programme he had laid out for four different zones in the central and southern peninsula; only a few photographs were garnered.

Prior to Lugli's effort (and probably the main impetus for it), the long-time director of the venerable British School in Rome, Dr Thomas Ashby, impressed by the discoveries reported in England from the twenties on, had again and again urged Italian archaeologists to take to the air, but, as Crawford relates, 'Every sort of excuse was made for doing nothing; the soil was unsuitable because under cultivation; or archaeologists moaned that they could do nothing because they were forbidden to fly and take their own air photos'. Italy, we now know, is, of course, like most Mediterranean lands, supremely responsive to aerial detection. And the man who did most to bring about the reversal was John Bradford. His finding of a cavalcade of prehistoric and historic sites on RAF war photographs (and during his own reconnaissance) remains a high-water mark in the annals of aerial exploration. Moreover, against the ill-advised disclaimers of Italian savants – direct descendants of Galileo's foes who refused to look through the telescope – they were largely recorded by crop-marks. The irony did not escape Crawford, prompting him to remark: 'The cultivation of the soil, so far from being (as alleged) an obstacle to discovery, was in fact its cause. Without cultivation many of these sites would not be visible.'

After the end of hostilities Bradford co-operated with several of his Italian colleagues. Within a few years Italy probably had more airborne explorations under way than any other land. One of the leaders to emerge was Guido Schmiedt, head of the section of photographic interpretation at the Istituto Geografico Militare in Florence. Teaming up with men more familiar with antiquities and ancient topography (among them Raymond Chevallier and the Italian Ferdinando Castagnoli) he started a fertile research programme that restored the lost town plans, and on occasion the very sites, of the centre of Magna Graecia in Southern Italy and Sicily such as Selinunte, Eraclea Minoa, Agrigentum, Metapontum, and Caulonia. Upon his initiative, work was also begun on an atlas of human settlements in Italy, comprising urban and rural features since the dawn of pre-history. Italian scholars, superb technicians as they are, have become particularly adept in applying photogrammetric methods to the construction of archaeological relief maps, which are the best conceivable guides for excavators. Studies concerning ancient roads and agricultural systems are legion.

Both Italian and foreign scientists have shared in these explorations. Etruscan researches, which we have discussed at length, form only a small part of the ground now being covered from above, and here too, though much has been accomplished, more has yet to be done. Meanwhile, the historical geography of Sicily, Sardinia, Latium, the Campania with the Bay of Naples is constantly being enriched. Some of the most remarkable new insights of aerial photography concern the great battles of the Punic Wars and the reconstruction of ancient harbours like Ravenna. Through the studies embarked upon by the Lerici Foundation, aerial archaeology is also developed in close contact with a variety of new geophysical methods. In these ramifications, Italian archaeology is now at the forefront. The catalogue could be continued in order to show how Italy is forging a leading role in the discipline. Her astonishing contributions, erupting so suddenly on the post-war scene, recall Italy's contemporary vitality in the arts, architecture, literature, and cinematography.

That aerial archaeology in Italy has reached a high level is perhaps best manifested by the establishment of its Aerofototeca Archeologica (at EUR, the modern satellite city of Rome), which acts not only as a unique national archive for photographic records of the entire country, but has become a centre and initiator of research, launching exploratory flights of its own, preferably by helicopter. The institution, which is attached to the Ministry of Public Education, has from its start in 1959 been directed by another pioneer in aerial archaeology, Professor Dinu Adamesteanu, a Rumanian exile who had settled in Italy. The Aerofototeca supervises as well the teaching of special courses in aerial archaeology to antiquity officials, cartographers, and to archaeology students of the University of Rome. It so happens that several first-rate discoveries were made during the practical course work at Tarquinia, Vulci, Portus Iulius, and elsewhere. Italian aerial archaeologists are now also engaged in exploration outside their country, notably in Iran and Afghanistan, and have trained their eyes on South America.

The entrance of Italy and France into the field, no matter how belated, is in itself a momentous development in the growth of aerial archaeology that bodes well for the future, and, it is to be hoped, will be an incentive to other countries. Bradford was particularly enthusiastic about the potential of Greece, Turkey, and Spain. But it would be idle to speculate where findings will soar in years to come. Possibilities lurk almost everywhere. Most of the land areas of the globe that have seen the passing of man, and in one form or another are indelibly marked by him, qualify. To invoke the authority of Crawford once more: 'It is evident that we are merely at the beginning of discoveries ... If one were to attempt to indicate where the most abundant harvest of crop-sites was likely to be gathered, one would find it difficult to exclude any country in the world outside the Polar Regions and the tropical forests and deserts.' Crawford continues then, by flitting through his atlas, to name some of the regions of considerable promise where far too little has yet been done: 'China, Indo-China and Siam, northern India, western Turkey, Thessaly and Thrace, central Europe from the Russian steppes (which must abound in crop-sites) to Hungary (where I have seen them myself), Nigeria, the corn-lands of North and South America.' Vast as these territories are, Crawford limits them, at least in this quotation, to presently cultivated areas. Jungles and deserts, as well as specific lands, such as Australia and Central Asia, he definitely excludes. But future discoveries need not depend on crop-sites alone.

Instances, even if only briefy alluded to in this book, show that detection from above can be effective in the arid and forested zones of the topics. Large parts of Central Asia, where Sir Aurel Stein uncovered buried civilizations fed by a network of silted-up and now sand-swept irrigation channels, would perhaps make a fine target. That the nomadic aborigines of Australia can be brought into the aerial orbit was brilliantly proved in 1947 by Williams-Hunt, who located abandoned camp-sites on beach lines near Melbourne. In near-Arctic latitudes of northern Alaska, explorers on foot were able to trace a large prehistoric settlement from the grass-marks appearing during the brief summer.

Singling out the huge regions that have barely been brought within the compass of our science indicates vast opportunities. But the new frontiers need not be defined by geography alone, or land masses, for that matter. Aerial archaeology, as Père Poidebard was the first to demonstrate systematically, can be harnessed to pick up ancient remains sunk beneath the seas and inland water bodies. One of his excellent photographs depicts a drowned village at the bottom of Lake Homs in Syria. In his three-year campaign Poidebard accomplished the extraordinary feat of recovering the virtually complete plan of the two ancient harbours of the Phoenician city of Tyre with their ingenious installations. His operations combined aerial photography with underwater diving (including submarine photography) and some digging on adjacent, formerly flooded, land. Though the earliest achievement of their kind, the Tyre explorations exemplify with how great a profit the aerial approach can be joined with other archaeological avenues. In later years, Poidebard employed similar amphibian, or rather tri-phibian, techniques at the port of Sidon and elsewhere in Syria and North Africa. Other scholars were to follow him. The Italian archaeologist Lugli, in his short-lived enterprises, came up with a revealing shot of Anzio's old Roman harbour. A frequent plea was then made for an aerial view of Baiae, the ancient luxury resort favoured by Hadrian, which had been largely submerged in the shallow waters along the subsiding shoreline of the Bay of Naples. Thus, even before the invention of the aqualung and the post-war boom in underwater exploration, the two archaeological disciplines of the airy and watery elements were already forming a partnership.

That the camera poised from above might, under favourable circumstances, pierce the water surface had been known since the First World War, when this method was used to spot enemy submarines. But what improved techniques could accomplish in penetrating seemingly opaque waters was suggested during the Second World War. It was then that the military requested information on potential landing points and intervening coastal hazards. As a result of many photographic experiments off such far-flung places as Cornwall and Ceylon, and points in between, techniques were worked out, in which colour filters played a decisive part. John Bradford, who during the war had a chance to tinker with aerial exploration of the seascape, mainly in Northern Africa, analyses this kind of photographic work at length and testifies that, at times, underwater features – natural or man-made – can be brought out 'as clearly as the print on a page'. In some instances, underwater detail appeared 'down to fifty feet'.

Needless to say, after the Second World War further technical improvements were added. Yet, while we hear now and then of aerial observers sighting cities buried under the waves from Lake Titicaca to the Aegean, and while aerial photography is increasingly employed to study totally or partly submerged ports such as Caesarea in Israel, surprisingly little use seems to have been made of this type of photography in the presently most popular branch of underwater archaeology which deals with sunken ships. But a turnabout is perhaps in the making, *vide* newspaper reports of a Colombian diplomat-aviator, who, in 1963, traced by air Columbus's voyages and later helped to locate off Jamaica two caravels which may have been abandoned by the great admiral.

The reasons why most shipwrecks and many cities fallen

into the sea will not readily appear to observer or camera from above are not far to seek. In the first place they may have settled too deep in the water to be rendered visible, and, secondly, they are often covered with a thick layer of sand or silt so that only direct physical contact is likely to betray their presence, unless it be a near-by detached artefact. This is also why George Bass in his first-rate *Archaeology Under Water* stated that of all the notable classical wrecks (which form the body of his discussions) not one was found 'as the result of a scientific search ... all were chance discoveries of fishermen, sports divers, and spongers'.

If the objects of a science are in the great majority only found haphazardly, that science itself is seriously limited. However, it is conceivable that aerial archaeologists may come to the rescue of their harassed underwater brethren. Perhaps it is only a matter of time until what can be termed metaphotographic techniques, producing eventually as clear pictures as the camera lens by means of airborne sonar, proton-magnetic radar, or like devices, will chart the bottom of the sea in precise and minute detail. In fact, the ocean floor may become eventually as susceptible to aerial surveying as dry land surfaces. Once this is feasible, then another of Bass's problems should be at least partly overcome: 'The sea', as he says, 'is simply far too large to be surveyed for ancient wrecks by divers swimming beneath the waves.' But in time we will have as comprehensive maps of the sea floors as of the land masses. At such a perhaps utopian stage aerial archaeology of land and sea will be one, though the ways of identifying and 'excavating' discovered sites are bound to vary. Spatially the scope of aerial archaeology as of aerial 'photography' will be immensely enlarged. There will loom sunken cities, fabulous art-laden triremes, and, more important, evidence on unknown cultures and on transoceanic contacts and migration routes. As to the inevitable 'lost' continents of Mu and Atlantis, no, they will never rise from the waves, but they will undoubtedly continue to quicken the heartbeat of muddle-headed romantics.

One may get a foretaste of things to come from an announcement made in 1967. Not surprisingly George Bass and the University Museum of the University of Pennsylvania, which has long taken a lead in the promotion of new technological methods in archaeology, were involved. The Philadelphia team, alerted by sponge fishers finding a bronze statue of a Negro boy, had successfully employed sonar equipment to detect the wreck of a Roman ship in the Aegean Sea off the coast of Turkey. A sonar scanner, which can emit and receive sound waves within a range of six hundred feet, had recorded five suspicious 'bumps' at the bottom of the sea. Their identity was quickly established once they were scrutinized by the museum's own midget submarine.

A magnetometer, this time operated from a helicopter, was instrumental in 1969 in the discovery of the guns James Cook reputedly threw overboard. The incident occurred in 1768 when HMS *Endeavour*, heavily armed and with a complement of thirty men, ran aground on a coral bank (later baptized Endeavour Reef) of the Great Barrier Reef off north-eastern Australia. To free his ship, Captain Cook decided to sacrifice her six heavy iron cannons. For two hundred years all search for them had been in vain. But members of an expedition sent out by the Academy of Science of Philadelphia to collect rare fish had made a sideline of seeking out the water-buried artillery. Sure enough, the airborne device, passing over the reef, produced vigorous impulses. These were sufficiently strong and accurate to mark the location, and the iron weapons were soon after found by divers. According to a newspaper release by the academy's director, 'It is no wonder that nobody found them before. They were so encrusted by marine growth that you could not see them from above.'

The dependence of aerial archaeology on the physical sciences is basic to its principles and objectives. However, as a branch of archaeology it has even closer affinities with the social sciences (and humanities) and can only flourish in a constant give and take with those disciplines that define the role and career of man on this planet.

That the study of archaeology stands to gain from an exchange of data and methods with anthropology, which deals with contemporary native rather than dead communities, has by now become a truism. 'Living' artefacts, both mental and physical, are known to persist among present, not necessarily backward, people, even though the likelihood for a significant number of such survivals to crop up is much greater among primitive or arrested cultures. In indigenous parts of the Americas and elsewhere, where the continuity with the remote past is almost unbroken and relatively few inroads have been made by modern civilization, archaeology can be studied, so to speak, *in vivo*. No wonder that Americanists are usually trained in both pre-Columbian antiquity and Indian ethnology and a line is rarely drawn between the two. Whether we accept the equation between the two sciences or not, we can make a good case that the aerial approach can prove as productive in an examination of contemporary tribal cultures as in one of their defunct predecessors. There is the advantage that the aerial camera registers and catalogues the living scene without any irritating interference which may prejudice the work of the field worker. By photographing housing or a complex of habitations, forms of farming and arrangement fields, communal compounds, defence posts, burial sites, and road systems, as well as their placement within and adaptation to a wider natural setting, an incomparably vivid concept of a way of life and material culture can be obtained. How a survey of this kind will tend to speed up and enrich anthropological research is obvious. Some of the data collected are precisely those that the earthbound anthropologist, preoccupied with interviewing and consequently, a psychological, if not subjective, approach, is likely to overlook. Furthermore, some of the very features and customs captured from above will help to dress the fragmented, decayed bones of archaeological investigations with flesh. Hence the considerable importance of such aerial research to archaeology. In discussing crop-mark patterns pertaining to the first farmers of the Italian peninsula, we have seen that comparable structures built in recent years by African natives can throw light on them. Such parallels also hold for the fortified earthworks still built in the African highlands, which have their close counterpart in the ancient hill forts of prehistoric England.

Despite the fruitfulness of this approach, it has never been as widely practised as it deserves to be. Among the first to adopt it systematically were an American couple, Richard and Mary Upjohn Light, who took photographs on flights over native African settlements between Cape Town and Cairo. An illustrated report of their work was published in the *Geographical Review* (New York) of October 1938. A few years earlier, French scholars incorporated available air photographs into their studies of the cultural geography of Indo-China. After the war, French ethnologists continued to use aerial pictures effectively to gauge primitive villages and their economy in North Africa, Cameroons, and South-East Asia, while Williams-Hunt employed them imaginatively in Malaya. John Howland Rowe, an American anthropologist, who supplemented his 1948 ethnographic studies in Colombia by aerial photographs, considers the airview 'an incomparable and perhaps indispensable tool in studying the patterns of settlement and land use in a modern community, because it shows in a very vivid fashion transient human activities that would not find a place on a topographic map'. In America's own backyard, Stanley A. Stubbs examined by air the still occupied pueblos of Arizona and New Mexico. Their ground plans had never been charted. And it was high time that each of them should be recorded before they disappeared completely. The villages, Stubbs argued, are as much an expression of the people as their customs, ceremonies, and beliefs. 'Inasmuch as they reflect the history, social structure, and religious system of the people, they are themselves worthy of thorough study.' Since it was impractical for various reasons, not the least being the reluctance of the Indians, to do the mapping on the ground, vertical aerial photographs offered an expeditious solution. As a result, Stubbs's *Bird's-Eye View of the Pueblos* (1950) came to furnish comprehensive blueprints from which archaeologists as much as anthropologists stood to profit.

On a more ambitious plan, a Harvard-directed project under Professor Evon Vogt set out in the 1960s to explore the behaviour and settlement patterns of present-day Maya-descended Indians in the Chiapas Highlands of Southern Mexico. A contract was signed with a California optical firm to take pictures with a special multilens camera. The novel apparatus made it possible to come up with detailed photographs from some twenty thousand feet above. Thanks to the high altitude, the local Indians were not alarmed and faithful data on their activities could be collected.

To travel in such a manner from the knowable present, alive and articulate, toward the little-known past is, despite certain methodological pitfalls, a most promising line of aerial investigation. However, the call for its wider application in the future rings with tantalizing urgency, if one realizes the pace with which residues of ancient and primitive human societies are steadily being extinguished.

Critics of aerial archaeology have on occasion deplored the quantity rather than scarcity of sites that have been located on photographs: because of their seemingly great number, they point out that archaeologists can never hope to keep up with and duly excavate them all. The argument is fallacious on many grounds, not the least being that it is against the very spirit of knowledge to call for a moratorium on its perpetual quest. But there are more realistic arguments against this view. First of all, despite the growing wealth of material, enormous gaps persist in our roster of the past that cry out to be filled. Indeed it is impossible to foresee how we can ever have too many pictures. Aerial photography supplies us with incomparable records, which, aside from and beyond written documents, are primary sources for the reconstruction of history and prehistory. Like historical manuscripts, stored away and unexamined for years or centuries, their value will only increase. The more such photographs have been taken and the greater experience men have gained in interpreting their marks of ancient features, the more intelligible they will become even without immediate follow-up on land. Paramount, however, is the need to rescue vestiges of antiquity like those of surviving primitive cultures, before they are wiped from the face of the earth. The astonishing progress of aerial archaeology after the Second World War in Italy and France can be directly related to the growing awareness in these countries of the threat to their buried national legacy. The International Colloquium on Aerial Archaeology which met in Paris in 1963 constantly invoked that spectre and proclaimed as its *raison d'être* the 'sauvegarde du patrimoine historique' (the safeguarding of the historical patrimony).

In the face of urban spread and sprawl, public enterprises, jet airports, motorways, canals, quarries, deep ploughing of farmlands by tractors, and other advance forces of modern civilization bulldozing their way through the countryside today, one cannot afford to wait for plodding, costly field work to do the job alone. Besides, there are simply not enough trained excavators available. Air photography's ability to rapidly take stock offers by far the best answer. Its drastic intervention happens to be not only swift, but relatively inexpensive and complete.

A whole branch of 'salvage archaeology' has shot up in recent years to secure at least a fraction of the threatened archaeological treasury. Not surprisingly, one of its most dependable weapons is forged in the air. 'Only so', St Joseph once noted, 'can the limited resources of archaeology be directed where they are most effective, and a delicate choice has to be made of what to salvage and what not. No means other than air photography exists for assessing the archaeological potentialities of an area where there are no visible remains.' St Joseph's own photographs of the gravel beds in England are notable examples of such salvage action. In the United States, federal and state governments are backing archaeological salvage programmes to precede such major construction works as dams and highways. If need be, enlightened authorities will delay building to permit completion of a dig or survey. Occasionally, plans may be altered or a road rerouted to save valuable features that cannot be removed.

As is well known, the problem has also aroused the international conscience. In connection with the various rescue campaigns on behalf of monuments menaced by the new Aswan Dam, particularly notable was an aerial mission over the Nubian Sudan prior to its inundation. In this non-Egyptian section along the upper Nile beyond Wadi Halfa and the Second Cataract, no proper survey – on land or by air – had ever been previously carried out. No detailed map was available. Notions about the actual wealth of antiquities were vague. No doubt, a great many of its sites remained unidentified. Others, though located, had never been properly explored or mapped. Thus, the potential loss was far graver than that of the much-touted Egyptian temples and statuary which had been repeatedly studied since the nineteenth century and which had hardly anything new to tell. Worse still, little had transpired of the history of this section of Africa, a vital link between the heart of the continent and the Mediterranean since the dawn of man and probably a fountainhead of pre-dynastic and Pharaonic Egypt. Paradoxically, just when the new independent Africa was beginning to take an interest in its ancestry, it was to be deprived of crucial testimony.

The then director of the Commission for Archaeology of the Sudan Antiquities Service, Professor Jean Vercoutter, took up the challenge as soon as the building of the High Dam was announced in 1955. Limited in personnel and other resources, he had to move fast. A preliminary examination of a small section only convinced him of the multitude of sites, far more than could be entered on the area map at his disposal. An intensive programme had to be somehow improvised. In 1956 he decided on a change of strategy. Prior to systematic groundwork, he called for an air survey, at first of the territory near the Egyptian frontier. When this material proved too complex to handle, he turned to UNESCO for assistance. The international body then dispatched an expert, Dr William Y. Adams, to take charge of the interpretation of air photographs.

With the technical assistance provided by UNESCO the programme could now be expanded. A new aerial coverage was launched for the entire area to be flooded. This was executed by Adams together with P. E. T. Allen of the Sudan Survey Department in November and December 1959. An interesting adjustment to local conditions was the need to fly at comparatively low elevation beneath an omnipresent layer of suspended dust. Actually three different series of photographs were produced in separate operations. One extended over the whole zone with the principal purpose of supplying adequate topographic maps, mandatory for consecutive field work. The second set of photographs, on a larger scale, pertained to the region between the Second Cataract and the Egyptian boundary, which would be the first to be inundated. It gave greater archaeological detail, including remains previously unsuspected. In addition the team took a number of low-level, large-scale photographs of selected already known sites to aid in their further excavation.

After the photographs had been carefully catalogued, interpreted, and made available for easy use, ground parties could once more proceed. Some ninety archaeological sites had been singled out on the Nile west bank alone for excavation by UNESCO archaeologists attached to the Sudan Antiquities Service. Their labours were complemented by a Scandinavian team on the east bank. American prehistorians, following the UNESCO appeal, searched for Palaeolithic clues. Crash programmes at the most important historic places in the north such as Buhen, Faras, Serra, and Debeira were handled by experts from France, the United States, Britain, Poland, Spain, Argentina, and Ghana. Though the definitive report of all these operations has not yet been released, announcements of first-rate discoveries – among them Christian churches, frescoes, sepulchres, ancient manuscripts, stone tools, camp-sites, etc. – have reached the world press. Even now the Sudan enterprise, though overshadowed in popular appeal by the removal of Abu Simbel, exemplifies 'salvage archaeology' at its most effective and may stand as a model of international scientific co-operation.

Certainly, without aerial reconnaissance the salvage action would have remained grounded, in every sense. It has always been archaeology's task to rescue and preserve the past for the future. Today, in Africa, in Western Europe, in the United States, and wherever human imprints are etched into the land, the airborne arm of archaeology strives to live up to this aspiration.

Acknowledgements

The author and publishers wish to thank the following:

For Permission to Reproduce Drawings

Figure 1 Museum of Fine Arts, Boston. Bequest of William G. Russell Allen

Figure 2 *Antiquity*, March 1935

Figure 3 British Crown Copyright; reproduced with the permission of the Controller of Her Britannic Majesty's Stationery Office from *Stonehenge and Avebury*, London, 1959

Figure 4 O. G. S. Crawford, 'The Stonehenge Avenue', *Observer*, 23 September 1923

Figure 5 British Crown Copyright; reproduced with the permission of the Controller of Her Britannic Majesty's Stationery Office from *What is Stonehenge?*, London, 1962

Figure 6 D. N. Riley, 'The Technique of Air-Archaeology', *Archaeological Journal*, 1944; reproduced by permission of the Royal Archaeological Institute, London

Figures 7–9 Reproduced by permission of the Royal Archaeological Institute, London

Figure 10 British Crown Copyright; reproduced with permission of the Controller of Her Britannic Majesty's Stationery Office from *Stonehenge and Avebury*, London, 1959

Figures 11–13 I. A. Richmond, *Roman Britain*, Harmondsworth, Middlesex, Penguin Books, 2nd edition 1963

Figure 14 A. Poidebard, 'Sur les traces de Rome', *L'Illustration*, 19 December 1931

Figure 15 S.E.V.P.E.N., *Archéologie aérienne*, Paris, 1965

Figure 16 Henri-Paul Eydoux, *Réalités et énigmes de l'archéologie*, Paris, Librairie Plon, 1962

Figure 17 John Bradford, 'The First Farmers in Southern Italy', *Illustrated London News*, 29 April 1950

Figure 18 J. Bradford, '"Buried Landscapes" in Southern Italy', *Antiquity*, June 1949

Figures 19–20   J. Bradford, *Ancient Landscapes*, London, G. Bell & Sons, Ltd, 1957

Figure 21   *Archaeological Prospecting*, Milan–Rome, Fondazione Lerici, 1955

Figure 22   J. Bradford, 'Getting the "Inside Information" ', *Illustrated London News*, 30 March 1957

Figure 23   Drawn by Earle Goodwin

Figure 24   J. B. Ward Perkins, 'Early Roman Towns in Italy', *Town Planning Review*, October 1955, Liverpool University Press

Figure 25   Henri-Paul Eydoux, *L'Histoire arrachée de la terre*, Paris, Librairie Arthème Fayard, 1962

Figure 26   *Art and Archaeology*, December 1929, New York, Archaeological Institute of America

Figure 27   Oliver Ricketson, Jr, and A. V. Kidder, 'An Archaeological Reconnaissance by Air in Central America', *Geographical Review*, April 1930

Figure 28   The Carnegie Institution, Washington, D.C.

Figure 29   Robert Shippee, 'The Great Wall of Peru', *Geographical Review*, January 1932

Figure 30   George Kubler, *The Art and Architecture of Ancient America*, Harmondsworth, Middlesex, Penguin Books, 1962

Figure 31   Paul Kosok, *Life, Land and Water in Ancient Peru*, New York, Long Island University Press, 1965

Figure 32   Drawing by Earle Goodwin

Figure 33   James A. Ford and Clarence H. Webb, *Poverty Point*, New York, The American Museum of Natural History, Anthropological Papers, Volume 46, part 1, 1956

Figure 34   James J. Parsons and William A. Bowen, 'Ancient Ridged Fields of the San Jorge River Floodplain, Colombia', *Geographical Review*, July 1966

For Photographs

Major G. W. G. Allen for photographs 6, 7, 9, 10, and 11
Dr Junius Bird for photograph 28

For Permission to Reproduce Photographs

Aerofilms Limited, London, for photograph 5
R. Agache, Direction générale des Antiquités, Abbeville, for photographs 8 and 30
American Museum of Natural History, New York, for photographs 24, 25, and 28

Ashmolean Museum for photographs 6, 7, 9, 10, and 11

W. A. Bowen for photograph 29

Mrs P. Bradford for photograph 17

Fairchild Aerial Survey, courtesy University Museum, Philadelphia, for photographs 22 and 23

Fondazione Lerici, Rome, for photographs 19 and 20

Institut Géographique National, Paris, for photograph 16

Library of Congress, Washington, D.C., for photograph 1

Long Island University Press, Brooklyn, New York, for photograph 27

Oriental Institute, University of Chicago, for photographs 2, 3 and 4

RAF, Crown copyright, for photograph 18

Dr J. K. St Joseph, Cambridge University, for photographs 12, 13, 14, and 15

I. Scollar, Labor für Feldarchäologie, Landesmuseum, Bonn, for photograph 31

US Air Force for photograph 26

Professor V. Valvassori, Ravenna, for photograph 21

Selected Bibliography

Note: in the *Sources of Quoted Passages* and *Selected Bibliography*, where specific page numbers are given they refer to the American editions of the books.

Ackerman, James S., and Rhys Carpenter: *Art and Archaeology*, Prentice-Hall, Englewood Cliffs, N.J., 1963

Adams, William Y., and P. E. T. Allen: 'The Aerial Survey of Sudanese Nubia', *Kush*, 1961, pp. 11–14

Agache, Roger: 'Aerial Reconnaissance in Picardy', *Antiquity*, June 1964, pp. 113–18

> *Vues aériennes de la Somme et recherche du passé*, Société de Préhistoire du Nord, Amiens, 1962

'Airborne Surveyors', *Fortune*, June 1952, pp. 119–23, 144–50

Alfieri, Nereo: 'The Etruscans of the Po and the Discovery of Spina', *Italy's Life*, 1957, pp. 92–104

> 'Spina e le nuove scoperte: Problemi archeologici e urbanistici', *Studi Etruschi*, Vol. 25, suppl., 1959, pp. 25–44

> (and Paolo Enrico Arias): *Spina; Guida al Museo archaeologico in Ferrara*, Sansoni, Florence, 1961

> *Spina. Die neuentdeckte Etruskerstadt und die griechischen Vasen ihrer Gräber*, Max Hirmer, Munich, 1958

Arias, P. E.: 'Archaeology as a By-Product of Land Reclamation: Magnificent Greco-Etruscan Remains of 2,400 Years Ago Recovered from the Mud of Lake Comacchio', *Illustrated London News*, 4 December 1954, pp. 1013–15

Ashmolean Museum, Oxford: *Guide to an Exhibition of Air-Photographs of Archaeological Sites*, Preface by D. B. Harden, Oxford, 1948

Atkinson, R. J. C.: *Field Archaeology*, Methuen, London, 2nd revised edition 1953

> *Stonehenge*, Hamish Hamilton, London, 1956; Penguin Books, Harmondsworth, Middlesex, 1960

Bailloud, G., and P. Chombart de Lauwe: 'La photographie aérienne' in Laming, Annette (ed.), *La Découverte du passé. Progrès récents et techniques nouvelles en préhistoire et en archéologie*, A. et J. Piccard, Paris, 1952, pp. 45–57

Baker, W. A.: 'Archaeology from the Air; a rewarding pursuit for the private pilot', *Flight; and Aircraft Engineering*, 19 February 1954, pp. 200–201

Bandi, Hans-Georg: 'Luftbild und Urgeschichte', 33ᵉ *Annuaire, Société Suisse de Préhistoire*, Frauenfeld, 1942, pp. 145–53

Bandini, Franco: 'Un fotografo dal cielo ha scoperto una città', *L'Europeo*, 9 December 1956, pp. 28–31

Baradez, Jean: *Fossatum Africae: recherches aériennes sur l'organisation des confins sahariens à l'époque romaine*, Arts et métiers graphiques, Paris, 1949

Bass, George F.: *Archaeology Under Water*, Thames and Hudson, London, Frederick A. Praeger, New York, 1966; Penguin Books, Harmondsworth, Middlesex, 1970

Beazeley, Lieut.-Col. G. A.: 'Air Photography in Archaeology', *Geographical Journal*, May 1919, pp. 331–5

'Surveys in Mesopotamia during the War', *Geographical Journal*, February 1920, pp. 109–27

Bennett, R. R.: 'Cobá by Land and Air', *Art and Archaeology*, April 1931, pp. 194–205

Beresford, Maurice W.: 'The Lost Villages of Medieval England', *Geographical Journal*, June 1951, pp. 129–47

(and J. K. S. St Joseph): *Medieval England: an aerial survey*, Cambridge Air Survey, Vol. 2, Cambridge University Press, Cambridge, 1958

Black, Glenn A.: 'Angel Site, Vandenburgh County, Indiana', *Indiana Historical Society, Prehistory Research Series*, December 1944, pp. 445–54

Bloch, Raymond: *The Etruscans*, Thames and Hudson, London, Frederick A. Praeger, New York, 1958

Bowen, H. C.: *Ancient Fields*, British Association for the Advancement of Science, London, 1961

Bradford, John S. P.: 'The Ancient City of Arpi in Apulia', *Antiquity*, September 1957, pp. 167–9

Ancient Landscapes. Studies in field archaeology, G. Bell & Sons, London, 1957

'The Apulia Expedition: An interim report', *Antiquity*, June 1950, pp. 84–95

' "Buried Landscapes" in Southern Italy', *Antiquity*, June 1949, pp. 58–72

'An Early Iron Age Site at Allen's Pit, Dorchester', *Oxoniensia*, 1942, pp. 36–60

'Etruria from the Air', *Antiquity*, June 1947, pp. 74–83

'Fieldwork on Aerial Discoveries in Attica and Rhodes', *Antiquaries Journal*, January–April 1956, pp. 57–69; July–October 1956, pp. 172–80

'The First Farmers in South Italy: Village Life 4000 Years Ago', *Illustrated London News*, 29 April 1950, p. 674

'Getting the "Inside Information" of an Unopened Tomb: Exploring an Etruscan Necropolis without Excavation by means of "Periscope Photography"', *Illustrated London News*, 30 March 1957, pp. 506–7

'Humanity from the Air', *Archaeological News Letter*, July 1948, pp. 1–5

'Mapping Two Thousand Tombs from the Air: How Aerial Photography Plays its Part in Solving the Riddle of the Etruscans', *Illustrated London News*, 16 June 1956, pp. 736–8

'Progress in Air Archaeology', *Discovery*, June 1952, pp. 177–81

'A Technique for the Study of Centuriation', *Antiquity*, December 1947, pp. 197–204

(and P. R. Williams-Hunt): 'Siticulosa Apulia', *Antiquity*, December 1946, pp. 191–200

Bruce-Mitford, R. L. S. (ed.): *Recent Archaeological Excavations in Britain*, Routledge & Kegan Paul, London, 1956

' "Buried" Italian Landscapes. History Revealed by Air Photographs', *The Times* (London), 28 August 1958, p. 5

Bushnell, T. M.: 'Aerial Photography for Indiana', *Proceedings of the Indiana Academy of Science*, 1927, pp. 63–73; 1929, pp. 229–30

Caillemer, A., and E. R. Chevallier: *Atlas des centuriations romaines de Tunisie*, I.G.N., Paris, 1953

'Caistor next Norwich: A Roman Camp Charted from the Air. Archaeology by Air Photographs', *The Times* (London), 4 March 1929, p. 20

Calza, Guido: 'Aviation and Archaeology', *Art and Archaeology*, October 1920, pp. 149–50

Capper, Col. J. E.: 'Photographs of Stonehenge as Seen from a War Balloon', *Archaeologia*, 1907, p. 571, figs. 69, 70

Carpenter, Rhys: 'Discovery from the Air' in Ackerman, James S., and Rhys Carpenter, *Art and Archaeology*, Prentice-Hall, Englewood Cliffs, N.J., 1963, pp. 22–31

Casson, Stanley: 'Archaeology from the Air', *Scientific American*, September 1936, pp. 130–32

Caton-Thompson, Gertrude, and E. W. Gardner: *The Desert Fayum*, Royal Anthropological Institute, London, 1934

Chart, D. A.: 'Air-Photography in Northern Ireland', *Antiquity*, December 1930, pp. 453–9

Chevallier, Raymond: *L'Archéologie aérienne en France*, Fondazione Lerici, Milan–Rome, 1962

   L'Avion à la découverte du passé, Arthème Fayard, Paris, 1964

   Bibliographie des applications archéologiques de la photographie aérienne, Fondazione Lerici, Milan–Rome, 1957; revised edition *Bulletin de l'archéologie marocaine*, II, suppl., 1957

Chombart de Lauwe, Paul: *Photographies aériennes, méthodes et procédés d'interprétation*, Armand Colin, Paris, 1951

   (*et al.*): *La Découverte aérienne du monde*, Horizons de France, Paris, 1948

Clark, Grahame: *Archaeology and Society*, Methuen, London, 3rd revised edition 1957; University Paperbacks, 1960

Colloque international d'archéologie aérienne, 31 August–3 September 1963, S.E.V.P.E.N., Paris, 1964

Courbin, Paul (ed.): *Études archéologiques*, S.E.V.P.E.N., Paris, 1963

Crawford, O. G. S.: 'Air Photographs of the Middle East', *Geographical Journal*, June 1929, pp. 497–512

   Air Photography for Archaeologists, Ordnance Survey Professional Papers, n.s., no. 12, H.M.S.O., London, 1929

   'Air Photography; Past and Future' (Presidential Address), *Proceedings of the Prehistoric Society for 1938*, pp. 233–9

   'Air Photos Show Celtic Fields on Palimpsest of English Soil', *Christian Science Monitor*, 14 December 1923, p. 11

   'Air Reconnaissance of Roman Scotland', *Antiquity*, September 1939, pp. 280–92

   'Air Survey and Archaeology', *Geographical Journal*, May 1923, pp. 342–66; revised edition Ordnance Survey Professional Papers, n.s., no. 7, H.M.S.O., London, 1924, 2nd edition 1928

   'Archaeology from the Air' in Wheeler, Mary (ed.), *A Book of Archaeology*, Cassell, London, 1957, pp. 83–9

   'Archaeology from the Air. More Wessex Discoveries', *Observer*, 24 August 1924, p. 3

   Archaeology in the Field, Phoenix House, London, 1953

   'Celtic Britain from the Air. Ghosts of Ancient Fields', *Observer*, 8 July 1923, p. 9

   'A Century of Air-Photography', *Antiquity*, December 1954, pp. 206–10

   'Luftbildaufnahmen von archäologischen Bodendenkmälern in England' in Crawford *et al.*, *Luftbild und Vorgeschichte* (*Luftbild und Luftbildmessung*, no. 16), Lilienthal-Gesellschaft für Luftfahrtforschung, Hansa-Luftbild, Berlin, 1938, pp. 9–18

'Lyonesse', *Antiquity*, March 1927, pp. 5–14

'The Past Revealed from the Air', *Listener*, 1 November 1956, pp. 699–701

'Revelations of the Past', *Listener*, 31 October 1957, p. 706

'Rhodesian Cultivation Terraces', *Antiquity*, June 1950, pp. 96–8

Said and Done. The autobiography of an archaeologist, Weidenfeld & Nicolson, Phoenix House, London, 1955

'Some Linear Earthworks in the Danube Basin', *Geographical Journal*, December 1950, pp. 218–20

'Some Recent Air Discoveries', *Antiquity*, September 1933, pp. 290–97

'Stonehenge from the Air. Course and Meaning of "the Avenue"', *Observer*, 22 July 1923, p. 13

'The Stonehenge Avenue', *Antiquaries Journal*, 1924, pp. 57–9

'The Stonehenge Avenue. Missing Branch Found', *Observer*, 23 September 1923, p. 16

'What Air Photography Means to the Future of Archaeology', *Christian Science Monitor*, 21 December 1923, p. 9

'Woodbury. Two Marvellous Air Photographs', *Antiquity*, December 1929, pp. 452–5

(and Alexander Keiller): *Wessex from the Air*, Clarendon Press, Oxford, 1928

(and Erich Ewald and Werner Buttler): *Luftbild und Vorgeschichte* (*Luftbild und Luftblidmessung*, no. 16), Lilienthal-Gesellschaft für Luftfahrtforschung, Hansa-Luftbild, Berlin, 1938

Cunnington, M. E.: 'Prehistoric Timber Circles', *Antiquity*, March 1937, pp. 92–4

Woodhenge, G. Simpson, Devizes, 1929

Daniel, Glyn E.: *A Hundred Years of Archaeology*, Gerald Duckworth, London, 1950

Davis, Kenneth S.: *The Hero. Charles A. Lindbergh and the American Dream*, Doubleday & Co., Garden City, N.Y., 1959

Dawley, T. R., Jr: 'Yucatan before Lindbergh', *Commonweal*, 11 December 1929, pp. 167–9

Decker, K. V., and Irwin Scollar: 'Iron Age Square Enclosures in Rhineland', *Antiquity*, September 1962, pp. 175–8

Deuel, Leo: *Conquistadors Without Swords: Archaeologists in the Americas*, St Martin's Press, New York, Macmillan, London, 1967

Eardley, Armand John: *Aerial Photographs: Their Use and Interpretation*, Harper & Brothers, New York, 1942

Eastman Kodak Company: *Kodak Data for Aerial Photography*, Rochester, N.Y., 1961

Engelbach, R.: 'The Aeroplane and Egyptian Archaeology', *Antiquity*, December 1929, pp. 470–71

Eydoux, Henri-Paul: *The Buried Past. A Survey of Great Archaeological Discoveries*, Frederick A. Praeger, New York, Weidenfeld & Nicolson, London, 1966
  Réalités et énigmes de l'archéologie, Plon, Paris, 1964
  Les Terrassiers de l'histoire, Plon, Paris, 1966

Fagan, B. M.: 'Cropmarks in Antiquity', *Antiquity*, December 1959, pp. 279–81

Field Archaeology, Ordnance Survey Professional Papers, n.s., no. 13, H.M.S.O., London, 4th edition 1963

Ford, James A.: 'Additional Notes on the Poverty Point Site in Northern Louisiana', *American Antiquity*, May 1954, pp. 282–5
  (and Clarence H. Webb): *Poverty Point: A Late Archaic Site in Louisiana*, American Museum of Natural History, Anthropological Papers, Vol. 46, pt 1, New York, 1956

Glory, A.: 'L'Aviation et l'archéologie', *La Nature*, 1938, pp. 225–8

Goodchild, R. G.: 'The Limes Tripolitanus II', *Journal of Roman Studies*, 1950, pp. 30–38

Gova, Sabine: 'Spina Rediviva', *Archaeology*, September 1960, pp. 208–14

Grimes, William Francis (ed.): *Aspects of Archaeology in Britain and Beyond; essays presented to O. G. S. Crawford*, H. W. Edwards, London, 1951

Guy, P. L. O.: 'Balloon Photography and Archaeological Excavation', *Antiquity*, June 1932, pp. 148–55

Harden, D. B.: 'Air Photography and Archaeology', *Transactions of the Lancashire and Cheshire Antiquarian Society*, 1956, pp. 22–8

Hawkes, Christopher F. C.: 'The Roman Siege of Masada', *Antiquity*, June 1929, pp. 195–213

Hawkes, Jacquetta and Christopher: *Prehistoric Britain*, Chatto & Windus, London, revised edition 1962

Heizer, Robert F. (ed.): *The Archaeologist at Work*, Harper & Brothers, New York, 1959

Heurgon, Jacques: *Daily Life of the Etruscans*, The Macmillan Company, New York, 1954; Weidenfeld & Nicolson, London, 1964

Hopkins, Clark: 'A Bird's-Eye View of Opis and Seleucia', *Antiquity*, December 1939, pp. 440–48

Insall, Squadron-Leader G. S. M.: excerpt from letter in 'Notes and News', *Antiquity*, March 1927, pp. 99–100

International Institute of Intellectual Co-operation: *Manual on the Technique of Archaeological Excavations*, International Museums Office, Paris, 1940

Jessup, Ronald Frederick: *The Story of Archaeology in Britain*, Michael Joseph, London, 1964

Johnson, Lieut. George R.: *Peru from the Air*, American Geographical Society Publications, no. 12, New York, 1930

Johnson, Jotham: 'The Dura Air Photographs', *Archaeology*, September 1950, pp. 158–9

Judd, Neil M.: 'Arizona Sacrifices Her Prehistoric Canals', Smithsonian Institution, *Explorations and Fieldwork 1929*, pp. 177–82

'Arizona's Prehistoric Canals, from the Air', Smithsonian Institution, *Exploration and Fieldwork 1930*, pp. 157–66

Kidder, Alfred V.: 'Air Exploration of the Maya Country', *Bulletin of the Pan American Union*, December 1929, pp. 1200–1205

'Colonel and Mrs Lindbergh Aid Maya Archaeologists', *The Masterkey*, January 1930, pp. 5–17

'Five Days over the Maya Country', *Scientific Monthly*, March 1930, pp. 193–205

Kirkpatrick, P. and Y.: 'American Antiquity, aerial photographs and Indian pictographs', *Flying*, March 1955, pp. 42–3

Knowles, David, and J. K. St Joseph: *Monastic Sites from the Air*, Cambridge Air Survey, Vol. I, Cambridge University Press, Cambridge, 1952

Kosok, Paul: 'Desert Puzzle of Peru', *Science Illustrated*, September 1947, pp. 60–61

Life, Land and Water in Ancient Peru, Long Island University Press, New York, 1965

(and Maria Reiche): 'Ancient Drawings on the Desert of Peru', *Archaeology*, December 1949, pp. 206–15

'The Mysterious Markings of Nazca', *Natural History*, May 1947, pp. 200–207, 237–8

Kruse, Harvey: 'A Remarkable Aerial Photograph of a Mandan Village Site', *Minnesota Archaeologist*, July 1942, pp. 80–81

Laet, Siegfried J. de: *Archaeology and Its Problems*, Phoenix House, London, 1957

Laming, Annette (ed.): *La Découverte du passé. Progrès récents et techniques nouvelles en préhistoire et en archéologie*, A. et J. Piccard, Paris, 1952

Lerici, Carlo Maurilio: *A Great Adventure of Italian Archaeology. 1955/65 – Ten years of archaeological prospecting*, Lerici Editori, Milan, 1965

'Periscope on the Etruscan Past', *National Geographic Magazine*, September 1959, pp. 336–50

'Periscope Sighting and Photography to the Archaeologist's Aid', *Illustrated London News*, 10 May 1958, pp. 774–5

'La photographie et la recherche archéologique', *Camera* (Lucerne), June 1959, pp. 42–5

Light, Richard Upjohn and Mary: 'Contrasts in African Farming; aerial views from Cape to Cairo', *Geographical Review*, October 1938, pp. 529–55

Lilienthal-Gesellschaft für Luftfahrtforschung (Crawford *et al.*): *Luftbild und Vorgeschichte*, Hansa-Luftbild, Berlin, 1938

Lindbergh, Charles A.: 'Air Transport', *Saturday Evening Post*, 1 February 1930, pp. 7, 50

Linton, David: 'Aerial Aid to Archaeology', *Natural History*, December 1961, pp. 16–26

Macdonald, Sir George: 'Rome in the Middle East', *Antiquity*, December 1934, pp. 373–80

MacKendrick, Paul: *The Mute Stones Speak: The Story of Archaeology in Italy*, St Martin's Press, New York, Methuen, London, 1960; New American Library-Mentor Books, 1966

MacLean, R. A.: 'The Aeroplane and Archaeology', *American Journal of Archaeology* (summary of a paper read 29 December 1922), January–March 1923, pp. 68–9

Madeira, Percy C., Jr: 'An Aerial Expedition to Central America', *Museum Journal*, March 1931, pp. 95–147

Maitland, Flight-Lieut. P.: 'The "Works of the Old Men" in Arabia', *Antiquity*, June 1927, pp. 197–203

Marshall, Gen. George C.: 'Giant Effigies of the Southwest', *National Geographic Magazine*, September 1952, p. 389

Mason, Gregory: *South of Yesterday*, Henry Holt & Co., New York, 1940

Mason, J. Alden: *The Ancient Civilizations of Peru*, Penguin Books, Harmondsworth, Middlesex, 1957

Matheny, Ray T.: 'Value of Aerial Photography in Surveying Archaeological Sites in Coastal Jungle Regions', *American Antiquity*, October 1962, pp. 226–30

Meggers, B. J., and C. Evans: 'Archaeological Investigations at the Mouth of the Amazon', Smithsonian Institution, Bureau of American Ethnology, *Bulletin 167*, Washington, 1957, pp. 6–11

Miller, William C.: 'Use of Aerial Photographs in Archaeological Field Work', *American Antiquity*, July 1957, pp. 46–62

Morris, Ann Axtell: *Digging in the Southwest*, Doubleday, Doran Company, New York, 1940

Mouterde, René, and A. Poidebard: *Le Limes de Chalcis, organisation de la steppe en haute Syrie romaine. Documents aériens et épigraphiques*, 2 vols., Paul Geuthner, Paris, 1945

Parsons, James J., and William A. Bowen: 'Ancient Ridged Fields of the San Jorge River Floodplain, Colombia', *Geographical Review*, July 1966, pp. 317–43

Payne, A. W.: 'Flying over the Past. Archaeological exploration by air in Middle America', *Pan-American Magazine*, November 1929, pp. 201–7

'Photographing the Romans', *Life*, 25 June 1951, pp. 101–2, 105

Piggott, Stuart: *Approach to Archaeology*, Harvard University Press, Cambridge, Mass., A. & C. Black, London, 1959; McGraw-Hill Paperback, New York, 1965; Penguin Books, Harmondsworth, Middlesex, 1966

Pittard, Jean-Jacques: 'Une nouvelle station lacustre dans le lac de Genève (Léman) (station de la Vorze) – technique des recherches', *Archives suisses d'anthropologie générale*, 1938, pp. 16–30

Poidebard, Antoine: 'L'ancien port de Tyr', *L'Illustration*, 3 June 1937, pp. 326–8

    Un grand port disparu, Tyr. Recherches aériennes et sous-marines, 1934–6, Paul Geuthner, Paris, 1939

    'La photographie aérienne dans la lumière éblouissante du désert', *L'Illustration*, 12 August 1933, pp. 312–14

    'La recherche des civilisations anciennes', *Comptes rendus du premier congrès de géographie aérienne*, Paris, 1938, pp. 258–62

    'Les révélations archéologiques de la photographie aérienne – une nouvelle méthode de recherches et d'observations en région de steppe', *L'Illustration*, 25 May 1929, pp. 660–62

    'Sur les traces de Rome – exploration archéologique aérienne en Syrie', *L'Illustration*, 19 December 1931, pp. 560–63

    La Trace de Rome dans le désert de Syrie. Le limes de Trajan á la conquête arabe. Recherches aériennes 1925–1932, 2 vols., Introduction by Franz Cumont, Paul Geuthner, Paris, 1934

    (and Jean Lauffray): *Sidon. Aménagements antiques du port de Saida. Étude aérienne, au sol et sous-marine*, Public. du Gouvernement Libanais, Beirut, 1951

Randall, H. J.: 'History in the Open Air', *Antiquity*, March 1934, pp. 5–23

Rees, L. W. B.: 'The Transjordan Desert', *Antiquity*, December 1929, pp. 389–407

Reeves, Dache M.: 'Aerial Photography and Archaeology', *American Antiquity*, October 1936, pp. 102–7

Reiche, Maria: *Mystery of the Desert*, Médica Peruana, Lima, 1949

Reifenberg, A.: 'Archaeological Discoveries by Air-Photography in Israel', *Archaeology*, March 1950, pp. 40–46

    'Palaestina: Aufstieg, Verfall und Wiederaufbau der Landwirtschaft', *Atlantis* (Zürich), September 1947, pp. 371–85

Richmond, I. A.: 'Recent Discoveries in Roman Britain from the Air and in the Field', *Journal of Roman Studies*, 1943, pp. 45–54
  Roman Britain, Penguin Books, Harmondsworth, Middlesex, revised edition 1963

Ricketson, Oliver, Jr, and A. V. Kidder: 'An Archaeological Reconnaissance by Air in Central America', *Geographical Review*, April 1930, pp. 177–206

Riley, F./Lt D. N.: 'Aerial Reconnaissance of the Fen Basin', *Antiquity*, September 1945, pp. 145–53
  'The Technique of Air-Archaeology', *Archaeological Journal for 1944* (1946), pp. 1–16

Rowe, John Howland: 'Technical Aids in Anthropology: A Historical Survey' in Kroeber, A. L. (ed.), *Anthropology Today*, University of Chicago Press, Chicago, 1953, pp. 895–940

Royal Commission on Historical Monuments (England): *A Matter of Time. An archaeological survey of the river gravels of England*, H.M.S.O., London, 1960

St Joseph, J. K. S.: 'Aerial Reconnaissance in Wales', *Antiquity*, December 1961, pp. 263–75
  'Airborne Archaeology. Recent Revelation of Early Britain by Camera', *The Times* (London), 8 April 1950, p. 5
  'Air Photographs and Archaeology', introduction to catalogue of Kodak Exhibition of aerial photographs at Kodak Gallery, London, July 1948
  'Air Photography and Archaeology', *Geographical Journal*, January 1945, pp. 47–61
  'Air Reconnaissance and Archaeological Discovery', *Nature*, 4 November 1950, pp. 749–50
  'Air Reconnaissance in Britain, 1951–55', *Journal of Roman Studies*, 1955, pp. 82–91
  'Air Reconnaissance in Britain, 1958–60', *Journal of Roman Studies*, 1961, pp. 119–35
  'Air Reconnaissance in Britain: Some Recent Results' in Bruce-Mitford, R. L. S. (ed.), *Recent Archaeological Excavations in Britain*, Routledge & Kegan Paul, London, 1956, pp. 275–96
  'Air Reconnaissance of North Britain', *Journal of Roman Studies*, 1951, pp. 12–65
  'Air Reconnaissance in Northern France', *Antiquity*, December 1962, pp. 279–86
  'Air Reconnaissance: Recent Results', *Antiquity*, September 1964, pp. 217–18, 290–91; June 1965, pp. 60–61, 143–5
  'Air Reconnaissance of Southern Britain', *Journal of Roman Studies*, 1953, pp. 81–97

'Antiquity from the Air', *Geographical Magazine*, March 1949, pp. 401–7

'A Survey of Pioneering in Air Photography' in Grimes, W. F. (ed.), *Aspects of Archaeology in Britain and Beyond; Essays Presented to O. G. S. Crawford*, H. W. Edwards, London, 1951, pp. 303–15

(ed.): *The Uses of Air Photography. Nature and man in a new perspective*, John Baker, London, John Day, New York, 1966

Saville, Marshall H.: 'The Ancient Maya Causeways of Yucatan', *Antiquity*, March 1935, pp. 67–73

Schaedel, Richard P.: 'The Lost Cities of Peru', *Scientific American*, August 1951, pp. 18–23

Schmidt, Erich Friedrich: *Flights over Ancient Cities of Iran*, Chicago University Press, Chicago, 1940

Schmiedt, Col. Giulio: *La prospezione aerea nella ricerca archaeologica*, Fondazione Lerici, Milan–Rome, 1962

Scollar, Irwin: *Archäologie aus der Luft. Arbeitsergebnisse der Flugjahre 1960 un 1961 im Rheinland*, Rheinland-Verlag, Düsseldorf, 1965

'International Colloquium on Air Archaeology', *Antiquity*, December 1963, pp. 296–7

Setzler, Frank M.: 'Seeking the Secret of the Giants', *National Geographic Magazine*, September 1952, pp. 390–404

Shippee, Robert: 'Air Adventures in Peru', *National Geographic Magazine*, January 1933, pp. 80–120

'Forgotten Valley of Peru: Colca Valley', *National Geographic Magazine*, January 1934, pp. 100–134

'The Great Wall of Peru and other aerial photographic studies by the Shippee-Johnson Peruvian Expedition', *Geographical Review*, January 1932, pp. 1–29

'Lost Valleys of Peru. Results of the Shippee-Johnson Peruvian Expedition', *Geographical Review*, October 1932, pp. 562–81

Smith, Harold Theodore Uhr: *Aerial Photographs and their Applications*, Appleton-Century-Crofts, New York, 1943

Smith, Robert A.: 'Temple Hunting', *The Sportsman Pilot*, February 1931, pp. 13–16, 55

Solecki, Ralph S.: 'Practical Aerial Photography for Archaeologists', *American Antiquity*, April 1957, pp. 337–51

'Spina Discovered – From the Air', *Illustrated London News*, 8 December 1956, p. 998

'Spotting Ancient Relics with Mr and Mrs Lindy', *Literary Digest*, 28 December 1929, pp. 33–5

Steer, Kenneth: 'Archaeology and the National Air-Photography Survey', *Antiquity*, March 1947, pp. 50–53

'The Past from the Air', *Listener*, 26 April 1956, pp. 492–3

Stone, K. H.: 'World Air Coverage', *Photogrammetric Engineering*, September 1954, pp. 605–10

Strohl, Erle: 'Eye in the Sky', *Barron's*, 23 October 1967, pp. 11, 20, 21, 25

Stubbs, Stanley A.: *Bird's Eye View of the Pueblos*, University of Oklahoma Press, Norman, 1950

Van Dusen, William I.: 'Exploring the Maya with Lindbergh', *Saturday Evening Post*, 11 January 1930, pp. 40, 43, 154, 157, 158; and 1 February 1930, pp. 6, 91, 92, 97, 98

Vercoutter, Jean: 'La Nubie soudanaise et le nouveau barrage d'Assouan' in Courbin, Paul (ed.), *Études archéologiques*, S.E.V.P.E.N., Paris, 1963, pp. 23–32

'Sudan Archaeology Endangered – an S.O.S.', *Archaeology*, September 1959, pp. 206–8

von Hagen, Victor W.: *The Desert Kingdoms of Peru*, New American Library-Mentor Books, New York, New English Library, London, 1968

Highway of the Sun, Duell, Sloan and Pearce, New York, Little, Brown and Company, Boston, 1955

World of the Maya, New American Library-Mentor Books, New York, 1960; New English Library, London, 1965

Ward Perkins, J. B.: 'Recording the Face of Ancient Etruria before Modern Agricultural Methods Destroy the Traces', *Illustrated London News*, 11 May 1957, pp. 774–5

Watzinger, Carl: *Theodor Wiegand, ein Deutscher Archaeologe, 1864–1936*, C. H. Beck, Munich, 1944

Weyer, Edward Moffat, Jr: 'Exploring Cliff Dwellings with the Lindberghs', *World's Week*, December 1929, pp. 52–7

Wheeler, R. E. M. (Sir Mortimer): 'Caistor, a Comment', *Antiquity*, June 1929, pp. 182–7

Wiegand, Theodor: *Sinai*, Wissenschaftliche Veröffentlichungen des Deutch-Türkischen Denkmalschutzkommandos, Heft 1, W. de Gruyter, Berlin, 1920

Willey, Gordon R.: 'Aerial Photographic Maps as Survey Aids in Virú Valley' in Heizer, Robert F. (ed.), *The Archaeologist at Work*, Harper & Brothers, New York, 1959, pp. 203–7

Williams-Hunt, P. R.: 'Anthropology from the Air', *Man*, May 1949, pp. 49–51

'Archaeology and Topographical Interpretation of Air-Photography', *Antiquity*, June 1948, pp. 103–5

'Irregular Earthworks in Eastern Siam: an air survey', *Antiquity*, March 1950, pp. 30–36

Woodward, Arthur: 'Gigantic Intaglio Pictographs in the Californian Desert', *Illustrated London News*, 10 September 1932, pp. 378–80

Woolley, Sir Leonard: *Digging Up the Past*, Penguin Books, Harmondsworth, Middlesex, 1937

Young, Rodney S.: 'The Excavations at Yassihuyuk – Gordion', *Archaeology*, December 1950, pp. 196–201

'Making History at Gordion', *Archaeology*, September 1953, pp. 159–66

Sources of Quoted Passages

FOREWORD

16. Bradford, John S. P.: 'Progress in Air Archaeology', *Discovery*, June 1952, p. 177

CHAPTER I: ARCHAEOLOGY IN THE AIR

25. Bass, George F.: *Archaeology Under Water*, Thames and Hudson, London, Frederick A. Praeger, New York, 1966, pp. 15–16
35–6. Beazeley, Lieut.-Col. G. A.: 'Air Photography in Archaeology', *Geographical Journal*, May 1919, p. 330
36. Beazeley: 'Survey in Mesopotamia during the War', *Geographical Journal*, February 1920, pp. 118–19
36. Beazeley: 'Air Photography in Archaeology', p. 334

CHAPTER 2: GHOSTS OF WESSEX

39. Crawford, O. G. S.: *Said and Done*, Weidenfeld & Nicolson, Phoenix House, London, 1955, p. 19
40. Crawford: quoted by Huntingford, G. W. B., 'Osbert Guy Stanhope Crawford: 1886–1957', *Man*, February 1958, p. 28
40. Crawford: *Said and Done*, p. 44
40. Williams-Freeman, J. P.: in 'Discussion' following Crawford's 'Air Survey and Archaeology', *Geographical Journal*, May 1923, p. 361
41. Crawford: 'Archaeology from the Air' in Wheeler, Mary (ed.), *A Book of Archaeology*, Cassell, London, 1957, p. 85
41. Crawford and Alexander Keiller: *Wessex from the Air*, Clarendon Press, Oxford, 1928, p. 5
41. Crawford: 'The Past Revealed from the Air', *Listener*, 1 November 1956, p. 700
43. Crawford: 'Air Survey and Archaeology', *Geographical Journal*, May 1923, p. 346
43. Crawford: *Air Survey and Archaeology*, Ordnance Survey Professional Papers, n.s., no. 7, London, 1928, p. 10
46. Crawford: 'The Past Revealed from the Air', p. 700
49. Crawford: 'Stonehenge from the Air. Course and Meaning of "the Avenue" ', *Observer*, 22 July 1923, p. 13

49–50. Crawford: 'The Stonehenge Avenue. Missing Branch Found', *Observer*, 23 September 1923, p. 16

50. ibid.

54. Crawford: 'Archaeology from the Air. More Wessex Discoveries', *Observer*, 24 August 1924, p. 3

54. ibid.

54. Crawford: *Said and Done*, p. 172

54. Scollar, Irwin: *Archäologie aus der Luft*, Rheinland-Verlag, Düsseldorf, 1965, p. 12

CHAPTER 3 : CONTOURS OF CULTURE

55–6. Woolley, Sir Leonard: *Digging Up the Past*, Penguin Books, Harmondsworth, Middlesex, 1937, p. 30

56. Close, Sir Charles: in 'Discussion' following Crawford's 'Air Survey and Archaeology', *Geographical Journal*, May 1923, p. 363

56. Kenyon, John: quoted in Bradford, John, *Ancient Landscapes*, G. Bell & Sons, London, 1957, p. 19

58. Crawford: *Wessex from the Air*, p. 6

58. Bourdon, David: 'Down-to-Earth Sculpture', *Life*, 25 April 1969, p. 86

60. Crawford: 'The Past Revealed from the Air', p. 700; and *Wessex from the Air*, p. 7

61. Poidebard, Antoine: *La Trace de Rome dans le désert de Syrie*, Paul Geuthner, Paris 1934, Vol. I, p. 11; also quoted in Brion, Marcel, *The World of Archaeology*, Elek Books, London, Macmillan Company, New York, 1962, Vol. I, p. 34

62. St Joseph, J. K. S.: 'Air Reconnaissance in Britain: Some Recent Results' in Bruce-Mitford, R. L. S. (ed.), *Recent Archaeological Excavations in Britain*, Routledge & Kegan Paul, London, 1956, p. 281

62. St Joseph: 'Airborne Archaeology', *The Times* (London), 8 April 1950, p. 5

68–9. St Joseph: 'Air Reconnaissance in Britain', 1956, p. 276

70. Jessup, Ronald F.: *The Story of Archaeology in Britain*, Michael Joseph, London, 1964, p. 65

CHAPTER 4 : THAT MARVELLOUS PALIMPSEST

72. Chombart de Lauwe, Paul: in Laming, Annette (ed.), *La Découverte du passé*, A. et J. Piccard, Paris, 1952, p. 46

74. Insall, G. S. M.: in 'Notes and News', *Antiquity*, March 1927, pp. 99–100

78. Editorial in *The Times* (London), 4 March 1929, p. 17

78. Wheeler, R. E. M.: 'Caistor, a Comment', *Antiquity*, June 1929, p. 182

81. Crawford: 'Air Photography; Past and Future' (Presidential Address), *Proceedings of the Prehistoric Society for 1938*, n.s., Vol. IV, part 2, no. 9, p. 236

82–3. Anon.: 'The Late Major G. W. G. Allen, M.C., F.S.A.' in 'Notes and News', *Oxoniensia*, 1940, p. 172

82. Crawford: op. cit.

86. Crawford: 'Air Reconnaissance of Roman Scotland', *Antiquity*, September 1939, p. 290

86. St Joseph: 'A Survey of Pioneering in Air Photography' in Grimes, W. F. (ed.), *Aspects of Archaeology in Britain and Beyond; Essays Presented to O. G. S. Crawford*, H. W. Edwards, London, 1951, p. 303

87–8. St Joseph: 'Air Photography and Archaeology' in St Joseph (ed.), *The Uses of Air Photography*, John Baker, London, John Day, New York, 1966, p. 122

90. Salisbury, Marquess of: in Royal Commission on Historical Monuments, *A Matter of Time*, H.M.S.O., London, 1960, p. 4

90–91. St Joseph: *The Uses of Air Photography*, p. 30

91–2. St Joseph: 'Air Reconnaissance and Archaeological Discovery', *Nature*, 4 November 1950, p. 750

CHAPTER 5 : ROMA DESERTA

94–5. Macdonald, Sir George: 'Rome in the Middle East', *Antiquity*, December 1934, p. 69

97. Poidebard: *La Trace de Rome*, p. 4

97. ibid.

98. ibid., p. 5

98. Dumast, Général de: 'Le Père Poidebard, promoteur de la découverte aérienne en archéologie', *Forces Aériennes Françaises*, May 1955, p. 898

98–100. Poidebard: op. cit., p. 15

101. ibid., p. 6

102–3. ibid., p. 11

103. Poidebard: 'Les révélations archéologiques de la photographic aérienne', *L'Illustration*, 25 May 1929, p. 664

104. Poidebard: 'La photographie aérienne dans la lumière éblouissante du désert', *L'Illustration*, 12 August 1933, pp. 312–14

107. Macdonald: op. cit., p. 374

110. Schmidt, Erich F.: *Flights over Ancient Cities of Iran*, Chicago University Press, Chicago 1940, p. 4

111. Crawford: 'Air Photographs of the Middle East', *Geographical Journal*, June 1929, pp. 501–2

114. Leschi, Louis: in Baradez, Jean, *Fossatum Africae*, Arts et métiers graphiques, Paris, 1949, p. vii

CHAPTER 6: ITALIA AETERNA

122. Bradford: 'The Apulia Expedition: An interim report', *Antiquity*, June 1950, p. 84
122. Bradford: *Ancient Landscapes*, G. Bell & Sons, London, 1957, p. 88
125. Bradford: 'The Apulia Expedition', p. 85
126. Bradford: 'Progress in Air Archaeology', *Discovery*, June 1952, p. 181
127–8. Bradford: *Ancient Landscapes*, pp. 89–90
128. ibid., p. 91
131. Bradford and P. R. Williams-Hunt: 'Siticulosa Apulia', *Antiquity*, December 1946, p. 200
132. ibid., p. 199
135. Bradford: 'The Apulia Expedition', p. 86
136. ibid.
136. ibid., p. 87
137. Bradford and Williams-Hunt: op. cit., p. 200
137. Bradford: 'The First Farmers in South Italy: Village Life 4000 Years Ago', *Illustrated London News*, 29 April 1950, p. 674
137. Bradford: ' "Buried Landscapes" in Southern Italy', *Antiquity*, June 1949, p. 59
137. ibid., p. 66

CHAPTER 7: BURIED ETRURIA

141. Bradford: 'Getting the "Inside Information" of an Unopened Tomb: Exploring an Etruscan Necropolis without Excavation by means of "Periscope Photography" ', *Illustrated London News*, 30 March 1957, pp. 506–7
146–7. Lerici, Carlo M.: 'Periscope on the Etruscan Past', *National Geographic Magazine*, September 1959, p. 348
148. Bradford: 'Etruria from the Air', *Antiquity*, June 1947, p. 76
149. ibid., p. 75
154–5. Bradford: *Ancient Landscapes*, p. 122
158–9. Lerici: op. cit., pp. 342, 346
160. Bradford: 'Getting the "Inside Information" ', p. 506
161. ibid., pp. 506–7
162. ibid., p. 506
163. Lerici: op. cit., pp. 342 ff.

CHAPTER 8: SPINA: LOST PEARL OF THE ADRIA

165. Bloch, Raymond: *The Etruscans*, Thames and Hudson, London, Frederick A. Praeger, New York, 1958, p. 45
166–7. Heurgon, Jacques: *Daily Life of the Etruscans*, Macmillan

Company, New York, 1954, p. 135; Weidenfeld & Nicolson, London, 1964

175. Gova, Sabine: 'Spina Rediviva', *Archaeology*, September 1960, pp. 209, 211
177. ibid., p. 208
180. Alfieri, Nereo: 'The Etruscans of the Po and the Discovery of Spina', *Italy's Life*, 1957, p. 103
181. ibid., 104
181. ibid.

CHAPTER 9: LINDBERGH SEARCHES FOR MAYA CITIES

189. Kidder, A. V.: 'Colonel and Mrs Lindbergh Aid Maya Archaeologists', *The Masterkey*, January 1930, p. 15
191. Weyer, Edward Moffat, Jr: quoted in *Literary Digest*, 28 December 1929, p. 32
192. ibid., p. 33
194. Kidder: op. cit., p. 6
195. ibid., p. 8
198. Anon.: 'Huge Ruins Found in Yucatan', *Literary Digest*, 28 May 1932, p. 26
199. Kidder: 'Five Days over the Maya Country', *Scientific Monthly*, March 1930, p. 199
199–200. Van Dusen, William I.: 'Exploring the Maya with Lindbergh', *Saturday Evening Post*, 11 January 1930, p. 157
200. ibid.
201. Van Dusen: op. cit. (second instalment), 1 February 1930, p. 6
202. Kidder: 'Colonel and Mrs Lindbergh Aid Maya Archaeologists', pp. 11–12
204. Peissel, Michel: *The Lost World of Quintana Roo*, E. P. Dutton Company, New York, 1963; p. 257; Hodder, London, 1964
205. Kidder: op. cit., p. 12
205. Van Dusen: op. cit., 1 February 1930, p. 97
206–7. ibid., p. 98

CHAPTER 10: WINGS OVER ANCIENT AMERICA: I

210. Crawford: 'Note', *Antiquity*, March 1935, p. 73
210. Madeira, Percy C. Jr: 'An Aerial Expedition to Central America', *Museum Journal*, March 1931, p. 95
211–12. Smith, Robert A.: 'Temple Hunting', *The Sportsman Pilot*, February 1931, p. 15
212. Mason, Gregory: *South of Yesterday*, Henry Holt & Co., New York, 1940, p. 50
213. Meggers, B. J., and C. Evans: 'Archaeological Investigations at the Mouth of the Amazon', *Bulletin 167* of the Smithsonian Institution, Bureau of American Ethnology, Washington, 1957, p. 11

214. Matheny, Ray T.: 'Value of Aerial Photography in Surveying Archaeological Sites in Coastal Jungle Regions', *American Antiquity*, October 1962, p. 226

215. ibid., pp. 226–7

216. Crawford: *Archaeology in the Field*, Phoenix House, London, 1953, p. 214

217–18. Judd, Neil M., 'Arizona's Prehistoric Canals, from the Air', Smithsonian Institution, *Explorations and Fieldwork 1930*, p. 158

218. ibid., p. 166

221. Sheppee, Robert: 'The Great Wall of Peru and other Aerial Photographic Studies by the Shippee–Johnson Peruvian Expedition', *Geographical Review*, January 1932, p. 1

222. ibid., 1–2

223–4. St Joseph: *The Uses of Air Photography*, p. 118

225. Shippee: 'Air Adventures in Peru', *National Geographic Magazine*, January 1933, p. 118

225–6. Shippee: 'The Great Wall of Peru', p. 14

226. Shippee: 'Air Adventures in Peru', p. 120

227. von Hagen, Victor W.: *The Desert Kingdoms of Peru*, New American Library–Mentor Books, New York, New English Library, London, 1968, p. 29

227. ibid.

CHAPTER II: WINGS OVER ANCIENT AMERICA: II

229. Kosok, Paul: *Life, Land and Water in Ancient Peru*, Long Island University Press, New York, 1965, p. 16

230. ibid., pp. 40, 44

231. ibid., p. 47

234. ibid., p. 49

235. Kosok and Reiche, Maria: 'The Mysterious Markings of Nazca', *Natural History*, May 1947, p. 203

241. Woodward, Arthur: 'Gigantic Intaglio Pictures in the Californian Desert', *Illustrated London News*, 10 September 1932, p. 378

243. Marshall, Gen. George C.: 'Giant Effigies of the Southwest', *National Geographic Magazine*, September 1952, p. 389

244. Setzler, Frank M.: 'Seeking the Secret of the Giants', *National Geographic Magazine*, September 1952, p. 404

244. Bradford: *Ancient Landscapes*, p. 81

245. Ford, James A.: 'Additional Notes on the Poverty Point Site in Northern Louisiana', *American Antiquity*, May 1954, p. 282

248. Parsons, James J., and William A. Bowen: 'Ancient Ridged Fields of the San Jorge River Floodplain, Colombia', *Geographical Review*, July 1966, p. 319

249. Sullivan, Walter: 'Archaeological Finds from High Altitude', *New York Times*, Sunday, 31 July 1966, p. 10E

251. Parsons and Bowen: op. cit., p. 342
251. ibid.

CHAPTER 12 : BETWEEN PAST AND FUTURE

253. van Riet Lowe, Clarence: quoted in Crawford, *Archaeology in the Field*, p. 264
256. Carpenter, Rhys: in Ackerman, James S., and Rhys Carpenter, *Art and Archaeology*, Prentice-Hall, Englewood Cliffs, N.J., 1963, p. 27
259. Daniel, Glyn E.: *A Hundred Years of Archaeology*, Gerald Duckworth, London, 1950, p. 301
260. Strohl, Erle: 'Eye in the Sky', *Barron's*, 23 October 1967, p. 11
260. ibid.
262. Steer, Kenneth: 'The Past from the Air', *Listener*, 26 April 1956, p. 492
263. Scollar, Irwin: *Archäologie aus der Luft*, p. 12
263. Crawford: Editorial note in *Antiquity*, March 1949, p. 1
264. Bradford: *Ancient Landscapes*, p. 84
264. Baker W. A.: 'Archaeology from the Air; a Rewarding Pursuit for the Private Pilot', *Flight; and Aircraft Engineering*, 19 February 1954, p. 201
265. Crawford; in *Antiquity*, June 1946, p. 59
267. Bradford: *Ancient Landscapes*, p. 76
267. ibid., p. 1
269. Review of Palmer, G. Blake, *New Zealand Archaeology and Air Photography*, in *Antiquity*, December 1949, p. 223
271. Crawford: *Archaeology in the Field*, p. 24
271. ibid.
273. ibid., p. 50
273. ibid.
275. Bradford: *Ancient Landscapes*, p. 43
276. Bass, George F.: *Archaeology Under Water*, p. 161
277. ibid.
277. Radclyffe Roberts, H.: quoted by McFadden, Robert D., 'Cannons Identified as Captain Cook's Found off Australia', *New York Times*, Monday, 13 January 1969, p. 10
279. Rowe, J. H.: 'Technical Aids in Anthropology: A Historical Survey' in Kroeber, A. L. (ed.), *Anthropology Today*, University of Chicago Press, Chicago, 1953, p. 909
279. Stubbs, Stanley A.: *Bird's-Eye View of the Pueblos*, University of Oklahoma Press, Norman, 1950, p. xi
281. St Joseph: *Uses of Air Photography*, p. 28

Index

Abbeville, 253, 267

Académie des Inscriptions et Belles-Lettres, Paris, 97, 98, 105

Adria (Atria), Etruscan city, 169, 170

aerial archaeology (selected topics): of agriculture, 42–7; alleged gimmickry, 16; altitude in, 29, 30, 69, 102, 112, 117, 124, 181, 215, 249, 257 (*see also* high-altitude; low-altitude); 'amateurs' active in, 29, 80, 263–5; *avant la lettre*, 56–7; benefiting from physical science and technology, 19, 255, 268, 277; Bradford's concept of, 154; British leadership in, 19, 38–9, 72–4, 95, 265; its dependence on airplanes, 257–9; early history of, 13, 14, 30–37, 38, 41–2; economy and simplicity of, 27, 257–8; errors in, 16, 46, 57, 67, 70; as excavation aid, 27, 46, 231; extended to underwater realm, 17, 109, 274–7; its growth in wartime, 13, 31–2, 33–7, 41, 95, 98–9, 115 (*see also* World War I; World War II); as instrument of discovery, 28–9; limitations of, 127, 133, 157, 254; literature on, 15, 54; magnitude of its discoveries, 16, 90; military associations, 32–4, 111, 115, 122, 124, 128–9, 218, 229, 240, 241, 243, 259, 260; potentials of, 28, 29, 71, 78, 127, 187–9, 152, 253–4, 261, 264–5, 273–4; prerequisites for its success, 127, 262–4; principles and techniques, 16, 25–6, 38–9, 42, 46, 52, 54, 58–71, 81, 95, 103–4, 125, 126, 189,

201, 205–7, 208, 211–12, 213, 260, 267–8; priority over ground work and excavation, 78, 82, 159, 255, 256; its revolutionary role and scope, 26, 89–90, 257; and salvage of threatened antiquities, 90, 147, 155–6, 281–3; and social sciences, 18, 228, 277–80; teaching of, 134, 247, 272; universal application of, 17, 273; unpredictable results of, 252–3, 254–5; variables in, 57, 60, 64–5, 66, 67–8, 69–70, 81, 83, 254; its vision of the past, 17, 25–6, 28–9; without airplanes, 30–33, 258–9

Aerofototeca Archeologica, Rome, 273

Agache, Roger, 13, 63, 253, 259, 266, 268

Agra, 32

agriculture, 24, 37, 42–7, 96, 97, 120, 121, 123, 124, 126, 128, 133, 134, 137, 138, 189, 217–18, 220, 234, 252, 267, 271–2; *see also* field-systems; lynchets

Aguacatal, Campeche, 215, 216

air cameras, 13, 29–30, 31, 33, 226, 227; automatically released, 29–30, 33, 34, 180; ground-controlled, 34, 258–9; hand-held, 29, 85, 126, 214, 266, 270

air colour photographs, 65, 135, 180, 181, 214, 215, 266

Air Ministry, London, 78, 79, 87

air photographs: collections of, 38, 47, 85, 91, 139, 149, 213, 227, 228, 229, 230, 243, 247, 261, 266, 273, 280; as historical records, 17, 34, 92, 280; interpretation of, 28, 70, 128–32,

148, 214; as maps, 29–30; military, 32, 33, 36–7, 38, 41, 52, 219, 228, 260; other non-archaeological uses of, 214, 219, 228, 229, 230, 246, 260–62
air transport, in archaeology, 199–206, 208, 219–20, 256–7
airplanes, 24, 33, 52–3, 81, 87, 110, 117, 125–6, 186, 188, 192, 195, 208, 121, 213, 216, 218–19, 222, 223, 248, 257, 259; advantages of, 33, 257–9
airports, and ancient remains, 206
Alaska, 237, 244, 274
Alesia, France, 56
Alexander's Barrier, Persia, 110
Alfieri, Nereo, 175, 176, 177, 180, 181, 183, 184
Algeria, 102, 112–20
Allen, Major George W. G., 14, 29, 54, 67, 70–71, 80–83, 85, 86, 91, 122, 126, 208, 210, 263
'amateur' aerial archaeologists, 29, 80–81, 263–5
Amazon, river and region, 213, 219, 222
American Geographical Society, New York, 219, 220–21, 222
amphitheatres, pre-Columbian Peru, 227
Andrae, Walter, 111
anthropology, 18, 228, 227–80
Antiquity, journal, 18, 38, 74, 77, 82, 85, 94, 148, 226, 268
Antonine Wall, 88, 106
Anzio, 275
Apulia, 121–9, 130, 133, 134–5, 136, 137, 138, 139, 256
Ararat, Mount, 16
archaeology, 15, 16, 17, 23–4, 25, 165, 252, 263; British characteristics of, 39; its early use of photographs, 30–32; new concepts and methods of, 24, 26, 46, 154, 157–64, 254–5; war and military ties, 33–4, 114–15, 256; *see also* excavation
Arias, P. E., 175, 176, 182
Arnold, Gen. Henry H., 241, 243
Ashmolean Museum, Oxford, 83, 91

Asia Minor, 34, 143, 158
astronomy and astronomical hypotheses, 47, 50, 234, 235, 236, 237, 241
Atkinson, R. J. C., 157
Australia, 130, 274
autogiro plane, 212
Avebury, Wiltshire, 52
Avenue, The, Stonehenge, 47–50, 51–2, 57, 75
Avon River, Wiltshire, 48, 50, 51

Baiae, 275
Baker, W. A., 264
balloons and balloon photography, 30–33, 115, 257, 258, 271
Bandi, Hans-Georg, 269
Banditaccia, Cerveteri necropolis, 143, 151, 155
Baradez, Jean, 13, 54, 112–20, 138, 263
barley, 68, 78
barrows, prehistoric, 55, 59, 60, 74, 77, 82, 90, 145, 267; *see also* burial mounds; tumuli
Bartoccini, R., 166
Bass, George F., 25, 276
Beazeley, Lieut.-Col. G. A., 13, 35–6, 37, 111
Bedouins, 94, 107
Belgium, 37, 258, 268, 270
Berkshire, England, 52, 122
Bersu, Gerhard, 34, 53
Black, J. W., 257
Bloch, Raymond, 165, 168, 266
Blom, Frans, 208
Blythe, California, 239, 241, 243
Bolivia, 247, 251
Bologna (Felsina), 142, 169
Bostra (Bosra), Syria, 94, 106
Bowen, William A., 248, 249, 251
box kites, 33, 258
Bradford, John S. P., 13, 16, 18, 56, 70, 80, 83, 122–40, 141, 148, 149, 150, 152, 153, 154, 155, 158, 159, 161, 162, 165, 244, 263, 267, 271, 275
British Isles, 69, 72–4, 93–5, 170; *see also* Great Britain
British School of Archaeology, Rome, 165, 271

Bronze Age, sites and remains, 29, 44, 54, 61, 75, 82, 90, 137, 267, 270, 283

burial mounds, 57, 67, 76, 248; *see also* barrows; Etruscan necropolises; tumuli

Byzantine ruins, Near East, 34, 105

Caesarea, 275

Cahokia mounds, Illinois, 216

Caistor-by-Norwich (Venta Icenorum), 78–9, 88

California, 239, 244, 264

Calza, Guido, 258

Campania, 127, 168, 272

Campeche, 188, 197, 198, 211, 213, 214

camps, prehistoric, 44–5; *see also* hill camps and forts; Roman camps

canals, 36, 67, 120, 217, 218, 229, 230, 254, 255, 269; *see also* irrigation works

cannons (Capt. Cook's), 277

Canyon de Chelly, Arizona, 170

Canyon del Muerto, Arizona, 170

Capper, Col. J. E., 32

caravels, shipwrecked, 275

carbon-14 dating, 24, 137, 237, 246

Carnegie Institution of Washington, 188, 192, 193, 196, 198, 205–9, 210

Carpenter, Rhys, 256

Castagnoli, Ferdinando, 272

Caton-Thompson, Gertrude, 65

Cauca valley, Colombia, 246–7, 248

causeways, 59, 62, 193, 205, 207, 210, 212–13; *see also* roads

CEDAM (Exploration and Water Sports Club of Mexico), 194

'Celtic' fields : *see* lynchets

Central America, 186–7, 192, 193, 194–5, 209, 210, 213, 214, 238

Central Asia, 274

Central Europe, 132, 254, 273

centuriation (Roman land division), 112, 113, 123, 134, 137–8, 139, 152, 167, 266, 267

cereals, 65; *see also* oats; wheat; *etc.*

Cerveteri (Caere), 142, 143, 145, 147, 148, 150, 151, 153, 155, 165, 168, 179

Chaco Canyon, New Mexico, 190

chalk, 45, 63, 68, 69, 82, 267

Chan-Chan, Peru, 221, 222

Chevallier, Raymond, 13, 15, 265, 266, 272

Chiapas, 188, 211, 213, 279

Chichen Itzá, 192, 199, 205, 206, 213

Chimú culture, Peru, 221

Chombart de Lauwe, Paul, 13, 72

circles and enclosures, prehistoric, 73, 76, 77, 110–11, 267; *see also* henges; Stonehenge; Woodhenge

city plans, restored from air photographs, 272; *see also* town plans

Civil War, US, air photography in, 32, 257

Clark-Hall, Air Commodore, 42, 46

Colca Valley, Peru, 220

Colombia, 244, 246–51, 261, 279

colour differentials, in vegetation, 63, 64–5, 100, 123, 215, 246, 263

Colorado River, US, 238, 241, 243

Comacchio, 173, 174, 176, 184

continuous strip air photographs, 218, 257–8; *see also* stereoscopy

Cook, Capt. James, 277

Cosa, Italy, 167

counterlight, in air photography, 101–2

Cozumel, island, Mexico, 206

Crawford, O. G. S., 13, 14, 18, 26, 38–54, 57, 58, 59, 60, 61, 62, 63, 65, 67, 68, 69, 70, 72, 74, 77, 79, 81, 82, 83, 85, 86, 87, 91, 95, 100, 111, 115, 119, 122, 125, 138, 149, 152, 203, 208, 210, 216, 221, 263, 265, 267, 271, 273, 274

crop-marks and crop-sites, 42, 49, 56, 57, 64, 65–70, 77, 82, 83, 100, 122, 124, 125, 126, 127,

128, 134-5, 203, 210, 262, 267, 270, 271, 273-4; *see also* vegetation-marks
crop-rotation, 66, 123
crops, 123, 135; 'sensitive' and 'sympathetic', 63, 64, 65, 67, 68
cultural geography, 279; *see also* historical geography
Cunetio (Mildenhall), Wiltshire, 80
Cunnington, M. E. and W., 75
cursuses, 29, 50, 77, 82, 90, 270

Dalmatia, 134, 167
damp-marks, 63
Daniel, Glyn, 13-14, 19, 85, 259
danses de fées, 56
Daumier, Honoré, 31
de Terra, Helmut, 158
Denmark, 23, 85, 270
desert drawings (markings), Peru and US, 232-44
deserted villages, medieval England, 29, 91
deserts, 23, 26, 34, 36, 61, 99, 107, 109, 116, 130, 218, 231, 234, 235, 236-7, 238, 239, 239-40, 241, 257, 268, 274
dirigible, 258
distribution patterns of archaeological remains, 39, 77, 79, 123, 126, 130, 132, 254, 256
ditches, 39, 42, 45, 49, 54, 58, 59, 62, 63, 64, 68, 69, 73, 74, 120, 125, 126, 131, 135, 136, 149, 218, 262; *see also* canals; earthworks; *fossatum*
Ditchley 'villa', Oxfordshire, 71, 83, 84, 88
Dobrudja, 34, 106
Dorchester, Oxfordshire, 77, 82, 122
droughts, 65, 69, 79, 88, 90
dust storms, 94, 101-2, 103

'earth sculpture', 58
earthbanks and ridges, 39, 40-41, 45, 47, 54, 59, 60, 62, 63, 64, 77, 245, 246, 247, 248, 249, 251
earthworks, 29, 32, 37, 43, 45, 53, 59, 60, 62, 64, 68, 77, 209, 217, 245, 246, 247, 249, 269

Eastman Kodak Company, 214
ecology, 256; *see also* environment
effigy drawings, pre-Columbian, 235-44
Egypt, 23, 65, 93, 99, 144, 282-3
emulsions, photographic, 101, 180
England, 32, 33, 38-46, 72-92, 122, 130, 134, 224, 264; *see also* Great Britain
environment, 24, 41, 132, 200, 256
equinox lines, Nazca, 235-6
Etruria, 142-3, 144, 147, 150-51, 152, 153, 154, 158, 162, 166-7, 170
Etruscan art and artefacts, 142-4, 146, 153
Etruscan cities, 142, 153, 154, 165-9, 174, 185
Etruscan murals, 141, 162-3
Etruscan necropolises and tombs, 141, 144, 145-65, 173, 174, 175, 177, 178, 179, 254
Etruscan roads, 148, 154, 165, 167, 254
Etruscan and Etruscan civilization, 18, 140, 142-4, 149, 158-9, 162-3, 165-79, 181-2, 184, 185, 261, 272
Euphrates, river and valley, 35, 98, 99, 102, 104, 106, 108, 118
Evans, Clifford, 213
excavation, 23, 25, 26, 27, 39, 40, 46, 49, 50, 56, 70, 71, 78, 79, 82, 86, 104, 105, 118, 125, 129, 132, 134, 135, 136, 141, 145, 149, 152, 154, 155, 156, 158, 160-61, 167, 173, 175, 177, 179, 182-3, 184, 245-6, 255, 256, 258, 280; costliness of, 156; 'primacy' of, 132-3; scientific, 40

Fairchild Aerial Survey Company, 211
farming: *see* agriculture; field-systems; lynchets
Faucett Line and Aviation Company, Peru, 219, 229, 231, 235
Fayum, 65
Fenlands, 68, 73, 88

field archaeology, 13, 39, 40, 55, 72, 78

field-systems: medieval, 138; pre-Columbian, 248, 249–51; prehistoric, 34, 40–46; Roman, 138; *see also* agriculture; centuriation; lynchets

films and plates, photographic, 28, 32, 33, 52–3, 101, 102, 126, 157, 161, 215

filters, 53, 101, 157, 180, 207, 215

Flinders Petrie, Sir W. M., 24, 180, 226

flint tools, prehistoric, 41, 105, 254

flood-marks, 62

floodplains, 248–9

Foggia, 121, 131, 133, 134

fogs, 221

Ford, James A., 244, 245, 246

forests, 210, 212, 215, 274; *see also* jungle

forts, ancient: Syria, 104; Mesopotamia, 36, 104; Palestine, 268; Persia, 109; Peru, 220, 223, 229, 230; *see also* hill camps and forts; *limes;* Roman fortifications

fossatum, North Africa, 115–20

France, 13, 14, 23, 33, 37, 41, 56, 63, 86, 114, 120, 134, 253, 264, 265–8, 271, 273, 280, 283

French air force, 98, 103, 112, 115

frontier walls: Persia, 109; Peru, 222–6; Scotland, 88, 106, 118; *see also limes*

frost cracks, 67

'fungi rings', 67

Gann, Thomas, 203, 208

Geneva, Lake, 269

geometric patterns (marks), in aerial reconnaissance, 27–8, 232, 254

geometric plans, urban, 181, 182; *see also* centuriation; town plans

geophysical methods, in archaeology, 24, 158–64, 254–5, 270–71, 274–5; *see also* magnetic and electronic devices

Germany, 13, 18, 33, 41, 68, 106, 268, 269–71

Gila, river and valley, Arizona, 217, 240, 243

glacial terraces, 68

Goodchild, R. G., 112

Gova, S., 175

grass and grasslands, 60, 65, 121, 123, 126, 127, 152, 215

grass marks, 56, 60, 100, 124, 127, 217, 274; *see also* vegetation-marks

gravel beds, 82, 91, 267, 281

Great Britain, 13, 16, 29, 32, 33, 34, 41, 42–92, 100, 106, 118, 185, 206, 210, 216, 224, 236, 253, 264, 265, 270, 278, 283; *see also* England; Scotland; Wales

'Great Wall of Peru', 222–6

Greece, 23, 132, 273

grids, urban: *see* town plans

ground exploration, archaeological, 27, 28, 43, 46, 52, 63, 83, 86, 97, 103, 104, 105, 117–18, 113, 134, 135, 148, 154, 189–92, 199–200, 211, 252

ground location of sites, from air photographs, 29–31, 103–4, 125, 134–6, 156–7, 197–8, 211–12, 252, 253; *see also* photogrammetry

growth inhibitors, 65

growth-marks: *see* vegetation-marks

Guatemala, 188, 193; *see also* Petén

Gur, Persia, 110

Hadrian's Wall, 106, 118

Hampshire, England, 39, 40, 42, 52, 56, 79

harbours, ports, 61–2, 109, 269, 272, 274

Hatra, upper Mesopotamia, 111

helicopters, 212, 237, 256, 257, 258, 273, 277

henges, prehistoric England, 75–6, 77, 82, 90; *see also* Stonehenge; Woodhenge

Heurgon, J., 166

high altitude air photography and reconnaissance, 36, 37, 91–2, 117, 207, 214, 262, 280

highlights, in air photography, 60, 61

hill camps and forts, prehistoric, 29, 62, 68, 77, 130, 262
historical geography, 115, 175–6, 179, 265, 272
history, early, of aerial archaeology, 13, 14, 15, 30–37, 38
Hohokam Indians, Arizona, 217, 218
Homs, Lake, Syria, 274
humus, 64, 69, 149, 182

Inca roads, 167, 213, 232
Inchtuthil, Perthshire, 88
India, 32, 58, 99, 273
Indo-China, 130, 253, 265, 273, 279
infra-red photography, 101, 215, 261
Insall, Squadron-Leader G.S.M., 54, 74, 75, 78, 86, 111, 263
inscriptions ancient, 102, 105, 118, 174, 184
Institut Géographique National, 266
insulae (city blocks), 29, 79; *see also* town plans
International Colloquium on Aerial Archaeology (1963), Paris, 268, 280
Iran : *see* Persia
Iraq : *see* Mesopotamia
Ireland, 85, 90
Iron Age, sites and artefacts, 24, 45, 54, 61, 123, 170, 217, 263, 267
irrigation works, ancient, 36, 94, 96, 108, 116, 120, 217–18, 222, 229, 231, 234, 240, 249, 258, 269, 274
Israel : *see* Palestine
Italy, 13, 18, 33, 121–85, 206, 255, 257, 258, 261, 265, 268, 273, 280

Jessup, Ronald F., 70
Johnson, Lieut. George R., 219, 220, 221, 222, 226
Jordan, 111, 112, 158
Judd, Neil M., 217, 218, 240
jungle, tropical, 171, 187, 188, 192–3, 197, 198, 200, 201, 203, 207, 208, 210, 212, 213, 214, 215, 274

Keiller, Alexander, 52, 53, 60, 69, 74, 81
Khabour, basin, Mesopotamia, 97, 104
Khmer ruins, 214
Khorezm, USSR, 268
Kidder, Alfred V. (Sr), 188, 189, 194, 195, 197, 198, 202–7, 208
King, S. A., 257
Kosok, Paul, 229–37, 238

ladders, in 'aerial' observation, 259
Ladle Hill, Hampshire, 61
lagoons, 139, 170, 173, 182, 183, 184
Lambayeque Valley, Peru, 230, 235
land reclamation and drainage, 173, 175, 176, 180, 182, 249
Lebanon, 23, 112; *see also* Syria
lenses, photographic, 33, 101, 157, 207
Lerici, Carlo M., 146–7, 158–60, 162, 163, 254
Leschi, Louis, 112, 114
Libya, 112
light conditions, in air photography, 59, 69, 100–103, 127, 206, 254, 263
lime and limestone, 67, 68, 122, 210
limes, Roman : in Europe, 114; Mesopotamia-Jordan, 112; North Africa, 112–20; Syria, 105–9
Lindbergh, Anne Morrow, 186, 191–2, 194, 196, 198, 200, 204
Lindbergh, Charles A., 14, 186–191–2, 194, 196, 198, 200, 204
Lindbergh Cave, Arizona, 191, 192
Little Woodbury, Wiltshire, 53, 134, 264
low-altitude air photography and reconnaissance, 97, 101, 114, 181, 195, 207, 211, 230, 248, 270
Lugli, Giuseppe, 271, 274
lynchets, 'Celtic' and Saxon, 40, 42–6, 54, 60, 61, 62, 63, 267

Macdonald, Sir George, 94, 107
MacIver, D. R., 55, 57
McKinley, Lieut. A. C., 216
Madeira, Percy C., Jr., 210, 212
magnetic and electronic devices, in archaeological detection, 24, 161, 255, 261–2, 276, 277
Maiden Castle, Dorset, 61, 82
Maras Pampa, Peru, 226
Marshall, Gen. George C., 241, 243
Marzabotto, 169, 171, 173
Masada, 256, 268
Mason, Alden J., 211
Mason, Gregory, 203, 211, 212
Matheny, Ray T., 214, 215, 216
Maya causeways, 206, 207, 210–13
Maya sites, 186–8, 194–216, 279–80
Meggers, Betty J., 213
Megiddo, 258
Mesopotamia, 23, 35–7, 112, 258
'metaphotographic' techniques, 276
Mexico, 279
Middle Ages, 29, 43, 90, 122, 125, 138, 139, 179, 266, 267
Midwest, US, 209, 238, 246
military aviation and air photography, 98, 114, 115, 213, 258–9
mine detectors, 24; *see also* magnetic and electronic devices
Mississippi, river and valley, 244, 246
Moche, culture, Peru, 225, 228, 235
Moche Valley, Peru, 221, 222
'Mohave Maze', California, 241, 243
Monte Abbatone (Abetone), Cerveteri, 151, 155
Monterozzi, Tarquinia, 143, 145, 151
Morley, Sylvanus, 193, 198
mosaics, aerial, 111, 212, 222, 228
mounds, 41, 244, 248, 253; *see also* barrows; earthworks; pyramids; tumuli

Nadar (G. F. Tournachon), 30, 31, 257
Naples, Bay of, 272, 275
National Air Survey of the British Isles, 91, 262
navigation, prehistoric, 51, 132
Nazca culture and region, Peru, 232–8
Nazca desert markings, 232–5
Near East, 34–7, 38, 56, 93–120, 136, 208, 223, 251, 255, 258
Negev, 34, 268
Negrioli, A., 173, 174
Neolithic sites and artefacts, 45, 53–4, 61, 75, 77, 82, 90, 122, 125, 128–38, 139, 152, 206, 253, 256, 267
Netherlands, 268
New Zealand, 269
Newark, Ohio, 246
Nile, river and valley, 55, 281–2, 283
Nissibin, upper Mesopotamia, 104
Noah's Ark, Mount Ararat, 16
North Africa, 17, 54, 112–20, 121, 168, 185, 223, 265, 274, 279
Nubia (Egypt-Sudan), 281–3

oats, 54, 65
oblique air view and photographs, 29, 32, 34, 69, 81, 83, 85, 97, 102, 124, 125, 126, 207, 254, 259, 263–4, 266, 270
octagonal earthworks, US, 245, 246
Ohio Valley, 217, 244
Old Samarra, 35, 111
oppida, 267, 270
optical equipment, 101, 126, 207, 260–62, 279–80
Ordnance Survey, Great Britain, 38, 39, 41, 46, 59, 81, 91
Oriental Institute, University of Chicago, 109, 110, 258
Ostia, 33, 62, 258

Paestum, 80
Palaeolithic, 253, 266, 283
Palestine (Israel), 34, 257, 268, 275; *see also* Jordan
'palimpsests', air photographs as, 29, 72, 73

Pallottino, Massimo, 155
Palmer, George, 239
Palmyra, 94, 102, 104, 106, 109
Pan American Airways, 186, 192, 194, 196, 197, 206
parch-marks, 65, 88, 100
Parsons, James J., 247–51
patterns, artificial, seen from above, 27, 28, 58; *see also* geometric patterns
Peissel, Michel, 194, 203–4
Pennsylvania, University of, 25, 158, 210, 211, 213, 276
periscope photography, 261–4
Persia (Iran), 54, 94, 96, 97, 98, 99, 107, 109–10, 116, 273
Peru, 23, 219–38, 239, 241, 244
Petén, Guatemala, 193, 194, 195, 201, 204, 213, 257
photogrammetry, 16, 28, 30, 103, 125, 126, 272
photographic equipment, 33, 207, 214; *see also* air cameras; films; lenses; optical equipment
photographs, early use in archaeology, 30
Picardy, 266, 267
pictographs: *see* desert sand drawings: effigy drawings
Piranesi, G. B., 151
Pittard, Jean-Jacques, 269
Pitt-Rivers, Gen. A. H., 40, 80
plants, and human occupation, 202, 207, 210, 215, 216, 254
ploughing, 43, 56, 58, 62, 67, 78, 150, 156
Po region, 121, 123, 147, 169, 171, 172, 173, 176, 177, 178, 179, 180, 183
Poidebard, Père Antoine, 13, 54, 61, 94–110, 112, 149, 208, 257, 259, 268
Poland, 258, 268, 283
Poverty Point, Louisiana, 244–6
Pueblo, culture and ruins, 186, 188, 189, 190, 217, 279
Punjab, 36, 99
pyramids: Maya, 187, 195, 196, 202–3, 212; Peru, 219, 229, 230; *see also* mounds

Quintana Roo, 188, 199, 201, 211

radar, 261, 276
rainfall, 101, 104, 107, 121
ramparts, 59, 62, 73
Ravenna, 169, 171, 172, 182, 183, 272
Reeves, Major Dache M., 216, 246
Regolini-Galassi tomb, Cerveteri, 145
Reiche, Dr Maria, 235–7, 238
Reifenberg, A., 268
religion and worship, 24, 46–8, 167, 168, 233, 235, 251
resistivity probes, electrical, 159, 160, 254
Rey, Léon, 13, 34, 100, 268
Rhineland, 67, 114, 117, 270
Ricketson, Oliver H., 193–7, 199
Riley, D. N., 71
river terraces, 82, 253
roads, ancient, 28, 44, 97, 102, 104, 105, 108, 154, 206, 207, 229, 230, 255, 272, 278
Roman Britain, 78–80, 86–90, 93–4
Roman camps, 67, 86, 87, 88, 94, 97, 111, 167, 254, 267, 269, 270
Roman cities and town-sites, 28, 33, 56, 70, 78–80, 88, 89, 94, 97, 105, 124, 138
Roman fortifications, 88, 93, 107, 115; *see also* limes
Roman roads, 41, 70, 86, 94, 102, 104, 106, 109, 117, 118, 139, 213, 215, 268, 270
Roman 'villae', 29, 71, 83, 84, 88, 206, 267, 270
Romanelli, M., 165
Rowe, John Howland, 279
Royal Air Force, 38, 41, 42, 43, 46, 52, 53, 57, 59, 74, 77, 78, 80, 85, 86, 87, 111, 122, 124, 147, 148, 150, 154, 165, 262, 268, 271
Rumania, 34, 106
rye, 67

Sahara, 58, 93, 116, 118, 120
St Albans (Verulamium), 79–80, 88
St Joseph, Dr J. K. S., 13, 18, 54, 62, 69, 71, 83–8, 223, 267, 268, 270, 281

Salisbury Plain, Wiltshire, 32, 60
Salt River, Arizona, 217, 218
salvage archaeology, 281–3
Samarra, Old, 35, 111
San Jorge river and valley, Colombia, 246–7, 248, 249, 250
sand drawings: *see* desert sand drawings
Santa river and valley, Peru, 222, 223, 224, 225–6, 228
Saumagne, Charles, 112
Schaedel, R. P., 228
Schmidt, Erich F., 54, 109–110
Schmiedt, Guido, 272
Schuchhardt, Carl, 37, 47
Scollar, Irwin, 13, 54, 67, 263, 270
Scotland, 61, 73, 75, 85, 86, 87, 88, 93, 114, 118, 262
seasons, in aerial archaeology, 33, 60, 69, 70–71, 83, 100, 127, 135, 254; *see also* spring; summer
Servicio Aerofotografico Nacional, Lima, 128, 230, 236
Setzler, Frank M., 243–4
shadow-marks, 29, 40, 60–62, 63, 65, 68, 73, 82, 100, 102, 218, 263
shelters, Stone Age, 253
Shippee, Robert, 220–28
shipwrecks, 276–7
shorelines, ancient, 62, 253, 261
Siam, 130, 273
Sicily, 129, 130, 272
Sidon, 109, 274
Silchester (Calleva Atrebatum), 56, 79, 80, 88
snow-marks, 40, 62
soil, 54, 123; acidity of, 67; composition of, 254; dampness of, 100; differences of, 71; disturbance of, 57, 58, 63, 64, 67, 69; influence of vegetation, 69, 100; latosolic, 215; transformed by human occupation, 203; variety of English, 72–3; volcanic, 149; *see also* chalk; lime and limestone; soil-marks; subsoil; topsoil
soil chemistry, modified by human occupation, 214, 215, 220, 254
soil-marks, 56, 62, 63, 64, 73, 83, 156

solstice lines, Nazca, 234–7
Somme Valley, 63, 267
sonar, 261, 276, 277
South America, 126, 224, 273
South-East Asia, 214, 279
South-West US, 56, 186, 188, 189, 190, 208, 217
Soviet Russia, 268
Spain, 158, 167, 273, 283
Spina, 169–85
sport pilots and planes, 264–5
spring, air photography in, 63, 64, 100
Stanton Harcourt, Oxfordshire, 82
Steer, Kenneth, 262
Stein, Sir Aurel, 111–12, 274
steppes, 61, 98, 100, 108, 116, 273–4
stereoscopy and stereoscopic photographs, 28, 30, 124, 257, 259, 262
Stone Age, 105, 254; *see also* Neolithic; Palaeolithic
Stonehenge, 32, 39, 46–51, 52, 75, 77, 271
Stonehenge Avenue: *see* Avenue, The
street grids, of levelled towns, 78, 79, 80, 89, 111; *see also* town plans
strip air photographs, continuous, 218, 258; *see also* stereoscopy
Stubbs, Stanley A., 279
subsoil, 63, 65, 68, 160
Sudan, 33, 41, 55, 158, 258, 282–3
summer, air photography in, 63, 64–5
sunken cities, 25, 269
sunken ships, 25, 277
sunlight, in air photography, 59, 60, 61, 63, 83, 97
surveying and mapping, 28, 30, 41, 42, 98, 102–3, 110, 111–12, 124, 126, 148, 175–6, 218–19, 228, 256, 262, 266–7, 279–80, 282–3
Switzerland, 268
Sybaris, 158, 255
Syria, 17, 43, 54, 61, 94–109, 111, 116, 167, 185, 257, 265, 274

Tarquinia (Tarquinii), 141, 142, 146, 147, 148, 153, 163-4, 165, 179, 273
Tavoliere, Italy, 121-4, 126, 127-8, 130, 132, 134, 138, 147
tells, 23, 96, 97
Thames, river and valley, 68, 77, 82, 122, 264, 267
Thompson, Eric, 205
Tigris river and valley, 36, 94, 97, 106, 111
tomb robbers, 141, 145, 146-7, 155, 157, 177
tombs: *see* barrows; burial mounds; tumuli
topography, 39, 70, 115, 139, 175, 182, 189, 194, 201, 208, 219, 254, 272
topsoil, 43, 49, 63, 69, 73, 152
town plans, 35-6, 111, 167, 169, 181, 182-3, 184-5, 272; *see also* centuriation
Transvaal, 253
Troy, 34, 85
tumuli, 39, 267; *see also* barrows; burial mounds
Tunisia, 112, 113
Turkey, 16, 34, 35, 158, 273, 277
Tuscany, 142, 143
Tyre, 109, 274

underwater archaeology, 18, 25-6, 34, 109, 275-7
underwater features, air photographs of, 109, 275-7
United States, 58, 188-93, 216-19, 238, 240-46
University of Pennsylvania, Philadelphia, 25, 158, 210, 211, 213, 276
Upjohn Light, Richard and Mary, 279

Valvassori, Vitale, 180-82, 183, 184
Van Dusen, William I., 194, 197, 199, 201, 205, 206, 207
von Riet Lowe, Clarence, 253
vegetation, growth differentials, of, 56, 64-5, 69-70, 100, 152, 203, 214, 215, 218; *see also* crop-marks; vegetation-marks

vegetation, unresponsive, 68
vegetation-marks, 56, 73, 104, 110, 122, 150, 151, 182, 202, 217, 263; early reports of, 56; *see also* crop-marks; grass-marks
Vercoutter, Jean, 282
vertical air view and photographs, 29, 30-31, 32, 41, 69, 101, 110, 112, 124, 125, 126, 207, 212, 218, 249, 259, 262, 266
Verulamium (by St Albans), 79-80, 88
Virú Valley, Peru, 228, 244
Vogt, Evon, 279
von Hagen, Victor W., 213, 227
Vulci, Etruria, 147, 154, 165, 166, 168, 273

Wales, 41, 73, 75, 85, 88
Ward Perkins, J. B., 165
water bodies, and aerial reconnaissance, 260, 275-7
Wattenmeer, Holstein, 269
weeds and wildflowers, 58, 68, 100, 121, 135, 152
Wellcome, Sir Henry, 33, 41, 258
Wessex, 52, 65, 69, 73, 74, 77, 81, 82
West Germany, 68, 106, 270
Western Europe, 18, 37, 39, 73, 75, 132, 137
Weyer, Edward Moffat, Jr, 190, 191, 192
wheat, 56, 121
Wheeler, (Sir) R. E. M., 78, 79, 82, 134
Wiegand, Theodor, 13, 34
Williams-Freeman, J. P., 13, 40, 42, 46
Williams-Hunt, Peter, 122, 124, 126, 128, 129, 274, 279
Wiltshire, 52, 77, 126
winter rains, and air photography, 63
Woodhenge, Arminghall, Norfolk, 75, 78
Woodhenge, Wiltshire, 75-7, 78, 111
Woodward, Arthur, 240, 241, 243-4
Woolley, (Sir) Leonard, 34, 55, 56, 57

World War I, 13, 32, 33–7, 52,
  95, 99, 111, 115, 275
World War II, 13, 32, 38, 62, 85,
  86, 91, 117, 119, 122, 124, 147,
  158, 180, 259, 267, 268, 270,
  271, 275

Wroxeter, Shropshire, 79, 88

Yadin Yigael, 268
Yucatán, state and peninsula,
  187, 188, 192, 193, 195, 196,
  197, 198, 199, 201, 202, 204, 211